RICHARD ROLLE

COLLECTION

2 BOOKS

A E T E R N A   P R E S S

PUBLISHED BY AETERNA PRESS.
COVER DESIGN BY AETERNA PRESS.

ISBN-13: 978-1-78647-061-4

AVAILABLE AS AN E-BOOK:
WWW.AETERNAPRESS.COM

CONTENTS

OF THE EXCELLENCE OF GHOSTLY SONG: AND THAT IT NEITHER CAN BE SAID NOR WRITTEN, NOR RECEIVES ANY FELLOWSHIP: AND OF THE CHARITY OF SPIRITUAL SINGERS: AND THE PRIDE OF THEM THAT HAVE GOTTEN KNOWLEDGE

RICHARD ROLLE COLLECTION

Richard Rolle was an English hermit, mystic, and religious writer. He is also known as Richard Rolle of Hampole or de Hampole, since at the end of his life he lived near a Cistercian nunnery in Hampole, Yorkshire. In the words of Nicholas Watson, scholarly research has shown that "during the fifteenth century he was one of the most widely read of English writers, whose works survive in nearly four hundred English...and at least seventy Continental manuscripts, almost all written between 1390 and 1500."

THE FIRE
OF LOVE

RICHARD ROLLE

AVAILABLE IN PAPERBACK.

TRANSLATED BY RICHARD MISYN FROM THE "INCENDIUM AMORIS" AND THE "DE EMENDA-TIONE

VITAE" OF RICHARD ROLLE, HERMIT OF HAMPOLE

METHUEN & CO. LTD. 36 ESSEX STREET W.C. LONDON

SECOND EDITION

FIRST PUBLISHED . . . . . APRIL 2, 1914

SECOND EDITION 1920

THE FIRE
OF LOVE

INTRODUCTION

THE MYSTICISM OF RICHARD ROLLE

BY EVELYN UNDERHILL

The four great English mystics of the fourteenth century—Richard Rolle, Walter Hilton, Julian of Norwich and the anonymous author of "The Cloud of Unknowing"—though in doctrine as in time they are closely related to one another, yet exhibit in their surviving works strongly marked and deeply interesting diversities of temperament. Rolle, the romantic and impassioned hermit; his great successor, that nameless contemplative, acute psychologist, and humorous critic of manners, who wrote "The Cloud of Unknowing" and its companion works; Hilton, the gentle and spiritual Canon of Throgmorton; and Julian, the exquisitely human yet profoundly meditative anchoress, whose "Revelations of Divine Love" are perhaps the finest flower of English religious literature—these form a singularly picturesque group in the history of European mysticism.

Richard Rolle of Hampole, the first of them in time, and often called with justice "The father of English Mysticism," is in some aspects the most interesting and individual of the four. Possessed of great literary power, and the author of numerous poems and prose treatises, his strong influence may be felt in all the mystical and ascetic writers who succeeded him; and some knowledge of his works is essential to a proper understanding of the currents of religious thought in this country during the two centuries which preceded the Reformation. Sometimes known as the "English Bonaventura," he might have been named with far greater exactitude the "English Francis": for his life and temperament—though we dare not claim for him the unmatched gaiety, sweetness, and spiritual beauty of his Italian predecessor—yet present many parallels with those of the "little poor man" of Assisi. Both Francesco Bernadone and Richard Rolle were born romantics. Each represents the revolt of the unsatisfied heart and intuitive mind of the natural mystic from the comfortable, the prudent, and the commonplace: its tendency to seek in the spiritual world the ultimate beauty and the ultimate love. Both saw in poverty, simplicity, self-stripping, the only real freedom; in "carnal use and wont" the only real servitude. Moreover, both were natural artists, who found in music and poetry the fittest means of expression for their impassioned and all-dominating love of God. Francis held that the servants of the Lord were nothing else than His minstrels. He taught his friars to imitate the humility and gladness of that holy little bird the lark; and when sweet melody of spirit boiled up within him, would sing troubadour-like in French to the Lord Jesus Christ. For Rolle, too, the glad and eager life of birds was a school of Christian virtue. At the beginning of his conversion, he took as his model the nightingale, which to song and melody all night is given, that she may please him to whom she is joined. For him the life of contemplation was essentially a musical state, and song, rightly understood, embraced every aspect of the soul's communion with Reality. Sudden outbursts of lyrical speech and direct appeals to musical imagery abound in his writings, as in those of no other mystic; and perhaps constitute their outstanding literary characteristic.

Further, both these impassioned minnesingers of the Holy Ghost made the transition from the comfortable life of normal men to the ardours and deprivations of the mystic way at the same age, and with the same startling and dramatic thoroughness. They share the same horror of property and possessions, "the I, the me, the mine." In each, personal religion finds its focus in an intense and beautiful devotion to the Name of Jesus. Francis was "drunken with the love and compassion of Christ." "The mind of Jesu" was to Rolle "as melody of music at a feast." For each, love, joy, and humility govern the attitude of the self to God. Each, too, adopted substantially the same career: that of a roving lay-missionary, going, as Rolle tells us in "The Fire of Love," from place to place, dependent upon charity for food and lodging, and trying in the teeth of all obstacles to win other men to a clearer view of Divine Reality a life surrendered to the will of God. Each knew the support of a woman's friendship and sympathy. What St. Clare was to St. Francis, that Margaret Kirkby the recluse of Anderby was to Rolle. Seeking only spiritual things, both these mystics have yet left their mark upon the history of literature. Rolle was a prolific writer in Latin and Middle English, in prose and in verse, and his vernacular works occupy an important place in the evolution of English as a literary tongue: whilst the Canticles of St. Francis are amongst the earliest of Italian poems.

True, Francis had the gayer, sunnier and more social nature. Once the first, essential act of renunciation was accomplished, he quickly gathered about him a group of disciples and lived in their company by choice. Rolle, temperamentally more intense and ascetic, loved solitude; and only in the lonely hermitage "from worldly business in mind and body departed," does he seem to have achieved that detachment and singleness of mind through which he entered into the fullness of his spiritual heritage. To him Divine Love was "as it were a shameful lover, that his leman before men embraces not": but "in the wilderness more clearly they meet," where "true lovers accord, and merry solace of lovely touching is, unable to be told." Yet the enormous influence which he exercised upon the religious life of the fourteenth century, the definitely missionary character of many of his writings, is a sufficient answer to those who would condemn him on these grounds as a "selfish recluse." Francis upon La Verna, Rolle in his hermit's cell, were caught up to the ultimate encounter of love: but each felt that such heavenly communion was no end in itself, that it entailed obligations towards the race. For both, contemplation and action, love and work, went ever hand in hand. "Love," says Rolle, "cannot be lazy": and his life is there to endorse the truth of those golden words. True contemplatives, he says again—and we cannot doubt that he here describes the ideal at which he aimed—are like the topaz "in which two colours are," one "pure as gold" and "t'other clear as heaven when it is bright." "To gold they are like a passing heat of charity, and to heaven for clearness of heavenly conversation": exhibiting, in fact, that balanced character of active love to man and fruitive love to God—the double movement of the perfect soul—which is the peculiar hallmark of true Christian mysticism.

As with St. Francis, so with Rolle, the craving for reality, the passionate longing for fullness of life, did not at first turn to the religious channel. The life of chivalry, the troubadour-spirit, first attracted Francis; the life of intellect first attracted Rolle. Already noticed as a boy of unusual ability, he had been sent to Oxford by the help of the Archdeacon of Durham. But the achievement of manhood found him unsatisfied. He was already conscious of some instinct within him which demanded as its objective a deeper Reality: of a spiritual vocation which theological study alone could never fulfill. At the crucial age of eighteen, when the genius for God so often asserts itself, St. Francis definitely abjured all that he had seemed to love, and embraced Poverty with a dramatic thoroughness; abandoning home, family, prospects, and stripping off his very clothes in the public square of Assisi. At the same age Richard Rolle, sacrificing his scholastic career—and the high literary merit of his writings shows us what that career might have been—suddenly returned from Oxford to the North, his soul "lifted from low things," his mind set on fire with love for the austere and solitary life of contemplation. There, with that impulse towards concrete heroic sacrifice, decisive symbolic action, which so often appears in the childhood and youth of the mystical saints, he begged from his sister two gowns, one white, one grey, together with his father's old rain-hood; retired into the forest; and with these manufactured as best he might a hermit's dress in which to "flee from the world." His family thought him mad: the inevitable conclusion of the domestic mind in all ages, when confronted with the violent other-worldliness of the emerging mystical consciousness. But Rolle knew already that he obeyed a primal necessity of his nature: that singular living, solitude, some escape from the torrent of use and wont, was imperative for him if he were to fulfill his destiny and order his disordered loves. "No marvel if I fled that that me confused . . . well I knew of Whom I look." The way in which he realized this need may seem to us, like the self-stripping of St. Francis, crude and naive: yet as an index of character, an augury of future greatness, it must surely take precedence of that milder and more prudent change of heart which involves no bodily discomforts. There is in both these stories the same engaging mixture of singleminded response to an interior vocation, boyish romanticism, and personal courage. Francis and Richard ran away to God, as other lads have run away to sea: sure that their only happiness lay in total self-giving to the one great adventure of life.

It was primarily the life of solitude which Rolle needed and sought, that his latent powers might have room to grow. "Great liking I had in wilderness to sit, that I far from noise sweetlier might sing, and with quickness of heart likingest praising I might feel; the which doubtless of His gift I have taken, Whom above all thing wonderfully I have loved." Yet the first result of his quest of loneliness was the discovery of a friend. Going one evening to a church—probably that of Topcliffe near Thirsk—and sitting down in the seat of Lady Dalton, he was recognized by her sons, who had been his fellow-students at Oxford: with the immediate result that their father, Sir John Dalton, impressed by his saintly enthusiasm, gave him a hermit's cell and dress, and provided for his daily needs, in order that he might devote himself without hindrance to the contemplative life.

Rolle has described in "The Fire of Love"—which is, with the possible exception of the Melum, the most autobiographical of his writings—something at least of the interior stages through which he now passed, in the course of the purification and enlightenment of his soul. One of the most subjective of the mystics, he is intensely interested in his own spiritual adventures; and a strong personal element may be detected even in his most didactic works. As with all who deliberately give themselves to the spiritual life, his first period of growth was predominantly ascetic. With his fellow mystics he underwent the trials and disciplines of the "purgative way": and for this, complete separation from the world was essential. "The process truly if I will show, solitary life behooves me preach." The essence of this purification, as he describes it in the "Mending of Life," lies not so much in the endurance of bodily austerities—as in "Contrition of thought, and pulling out of desires that belong not to loving or worship of God":—self-simplification in fact. The object of such a process is always the same: the purging of the will, and unification of the whole life about the higher centres of humility and love; the cutting out, as St. Catherine of Siena has it, of "the rooting of self-love with the knife of self-hatred." In the old old language of Christian mysticism, Rolle speaks of the action of Divine Love as a refiner's fire, "fiery making our souls, and purging them from all degrees of sin, making them light and burning." We gather from various references in the Incendium that the trials of this purgation included in his own case not only interior contrition for past sin and bodily penance. It also involved the contempt, if not the actual persecution of other men, and the inimical attitude with "with wordys of bakbyttingis" of old friends, who viewed his eccentric conduct with a natural and prudent disgust: a form of suffering, intensely painful to his sensitive nature, which he recognizes as specially valuable in its power of killing self-esteem, and encouraging the mystical type of character, governed by true mortification and total dependence on God. "This have I known, that the more men have tried with words of backbiting against me, so muckle the more in ghostly profit I have grown.". . . ."After the tempest, God sheds in brightness of holy desires."

The period of pain and struggle—the difficult remaking of character—lasted from his conversion for about two years and eight months. It was brought to an end, as with so many of the greater mystics, by an abrupt shifting of consciousness to levels of peace and joy: a sudden and overwhelming revelation of Spiritual Reality—"the opening of the heavenly door, that Thy face showed." Rolle than passed to that affirmative state of high illumination and adoring love which he extols in the "Fire": the state which includes the three degrees, or spiritual moods of Calor, Dulcor, Canor—"Heat, Sweetness and Song." At the end of a year, "the door biding open," he experienced the first of these special graces: the Heat of Love Everlasting, or "Fire" which gave its name to the Incendium Amoris. "I sat forsooth in a chapel and whilst with sweetness of prayer or meditation muckle I was delighted, suddenly in me I felt a merry heat and unknown."

Now, when we ask ourselves what Rolle really meant by this image of heat or fire, we stand at the beginning of a long quest. This is one of those phrases, half metaphors, yet metaphors so apt that we might also call them descriptions of experience, which are natural to mystical literature. Immemorially old, yet eternally fresh, they appear again and again; nor need we always attribute such reappearances to conscious borrowing. The fire of love is a term which goes back at least to the fourth century of our era; it is used by St. Macarius of Egypt to describe the action of the Divine Energy upon the soul which it is leading to perfection. Its literary origins are of course scriptural—the fusion of the Johannine "God is love" with the fire imagery of the Hebrew prophets. "Behold! the Lord will come with fire!" "His word was in my heart as a burning fire." "He is like a refiner's fire."

But, examining the passages in which Rolle speaks of that "Heat" which the "Fire of Love" induced in his purified and heavenward turning heart, we see that this denotes a sensual as well as a spiritual experience. Those interior states or moods to which, by the natural method of comparison that governs all descriptive speech, the self gives such sense-names as these of "Heat, Sweetness, and Song," react in many mystics upon the bodily state. Psycho-sensorial parallelisms are set up. The well-known phenomenon of stigmatization, occurring in certain hypersensitive temperaments as the result of deep meditation upon the Passion of Christ, is perhaps the best clue by which we can come to understand how such a term as "the fire of love" has attained a double significance for mystical psychology. It is first a poetic metaphor of singular aptness; describing a spiritual state which is, as Rolle says himself in "The Form of Perfect Living," "So burning and gladdening, that he or she who is in this degree can as well feel the fire of love burning in their soul as thou canst feel thy finger burn if thou puttest it in the fire." Secondly, it represents, or may represent in certain temperaments, an induced sense-automatism, which may vary from the slightest of suggestions to an intense hallucination: as the equivalent automatic process which issues in "visions" or "voices" may vary from that "sense of a presence" or consciousness of a message received, which is the purest form in which our surface consciousness objectivizes communion with God, to the vivid picture seen, the voice clearly heard, by many visionaries and auditives.

The "first state" of burning love to which Rolle attained when his purification was at an end, does seem to have produced in him such a psycho-physical hallucination. He makes it plain in the prologue of the Incendium that he felt, in a physical sense, the spiritual fire, truly, not imaginingly; as St. Teresa—to take a well-known historical example—felt the transverberation of the seraph's spear which pierced her heart. This form of automatism, though not perhaps very common, is well known in the history of religious experience; and many ascetic writers discuss it. Thus in that classic of spiritual common sense, "The Cloud of Unknowing," we find amongst the many delusions which may beset "young presumptuous contemplatives," "Many quaint heats and burnings in their bodily breasts"—which may sometimes indeed be the work of good angels (i.e., the physical reflection of true spiritual ardour) yet should ever be had suspect, as possible devices of the devil. Again, Walter Hilton includes in his list of mystical automatisms, and views with the same suspicion, "sensible heat, as it were fire, glowing and warming the breast." In the seventeenth century Augustine Baker, in his authoritative work on the prayer of contemplation mentions "warmth about the heart" as one of the "sensible graces," or physical sensations of religious origin, known to those who aspire to union with God. In our own day, the Carmelite nun Soeur Therese de l'Enfant-Jesus describes an experience in which she "felt herself suddenly pierced by a dart of fire." "I cannot," she says, "explain this transport, nor can any comparison express the intensity of this flame. It seemed to me that an invisible force immersed me completely in fire." Allowing for the strong probability that the form of Soeur Therese's transport was influenced by her knowledge of the life of her great namesake, we have no grounds for doubting the honesty of her report; the fact that she felt in a literal sense, though in a way hard for less ardent temperaments to understand, the burning of the divine fire. Her simple account—glossing, as it were, the declarations of the historian and the psychologist—surely gives us a hint as to the way in which we ought to read the statements of other mystics, concerning their knowledge of the "fire of love."

Rolle's second stage, to which he gives the name of "sweetness", is easier of comprehension than the first. It represents the natural movement of consciousness from passion to peace, from initiation to possession, as the contemplative learns to live and move in this new atmosphere of Reality: the exquisite joy which characterizes one phase of the soul's communion with God. He calls it a "heavenly savour"; a "sweet mystery"; a "marvellous honey." "With great labor it is got; but with joy untold it is possessed." It is of such sweetness that the author of "The Cloud of Unknowing"—that stern critic of all those so called mystical experiences which come in by the windows of the wits—writes in terms which almost seem to be inspired by a personal experience.

"Sometimes He will inflame the body of devout servants of His here in this life: not once or twice, but peradventure right oft and as Him liketh, with full wonderful sweetness and comforts. Of the which, some be not coming from without into the body by the windows of our wits, but from within; rising and springing of abundance of ghostly gladness, and of true devotion in the spirit. Such a comfort and such a sweetness shall not be had suspect: and shortly to say, I trow that he that feeleth it may not have it suspect."

That intimate and joyful apprehension of the supersensuous which Rolle calls "sweetness" is not rigidly separated either from the burning ardour which preceded it, or the "third" state of exultant harmony, of adoring contempla-tion—prayer pouring itself forth in wild yet measured loveliness—which he calls "song"; and which is the most characteristic form of his communion with the Divine Love. All three, in fact, as we see in the beautiful eighth chapter of "The Form of Perfect Living," are fluctuating expressions of the "Third Degree of Love, highest and most wondrous to win." They co-exist in the soul which has attained to it: now one and now the other taking command. "The soul that is in the third degree is all burning fire, and like the nightingale that loves song and melody, and fails for great love: so that the soul is only comforted in praising and loving God . . . and this manner of song have none unless they be in the third degree of love: to the which degree it is impossible to come, but in a great multitude of love."

This true lover, he says again in the Incendium, "has sweetness, heat and ghostly song, of which before I have oft touched, and by this he serves God, and Him loving without parting to Him draws . . . Sometime certain more he feels of heat and sweetness, and with difficulty he sings, sometime truly with great sweetness and busyness he is ravished, when heat is felt the less; oft also into ghostly song with great mirth he flees and passes, and also he knows the heat and sweetness of love with him are. Nevertheless heat is never without sweetness, although sometime it be without ghostly song."

Rolle's own first experience of this state of song, like the oncoming of the "Fire," seems to have had a marked psycho-sensorial character. His passion of love and praise translated itself into the "Song of Angels"; and the celestial melody was first heard by him with the outward as well as with the inward ear. "In the night before supper, as I mine Salves I sung, as it were the noise of readers or rather singers about me I beheld. Whilst also praying to heaven with all desire I took heed, on what manner I wot not suddenly in me noise of song I felt; and likingest heavenly melody I took, with me dwelling in mind."

We gather from the writings of other mystics of the medieval period that such an experience was a well understood accompaniment of the contemplative life. Like the "burning of the fire" it was one amongst those "sensible com-forts"—or, as we should now say, automatisms—which were never accepted at their face value as certain marks of divine favour, but were studied and ana-lyzed with the robust common sense that characterizes true spirituality. Walter Hilton, in a tract on the "Song of Angels" which is certainly inspired by, and was long attributed to Rolle himself, says of it: "When the soul is lifted and ravished out of the sensuality, and out of mind of any earthly things, then in great fervour of love and light (if our Lord vouchsafe) the soul may hear and feel heavenly sound, made by the presence of angels in loving of God . . .

Methinketh that there may no soul feel verily angel's song nor heavenly sound, but he be in perfect charity; though all that are in perfect charity have not felt it, but only that soul that is so purified in the fire of love that all earthly savour is brent out of it, and all mean letting between the soul and the cleanness of angels is broken and put away from it. Then soothly may he sing a new song, and soothly he may hear a blest heavenly sound, and angel's song without deceit or feigning."

Such "Song"—where it really represents the soul's consciousness of supernal harmonies, and is not merely the hallucination of one who "by indiscreet travailing turneth the brains in his head" so that "for feebleness of the brain, him thinketh that he heareth wonderful sounds and songs"—does for the temperament which inclines to translate its intuitions into music, that which the experience of vision does for those whose apprehensions of reality more easily crystallize into a pictorial form. One seems to see, another seems to hear, that Perfect Beauty which is the source and inspiration of all our fragmentary arts. For Rolle, by nature a poet and a musician, the language of music possessed a special attraction and appropriateness: and not only its language but its practice too. Like Francis of Assisi, Catherine of Genoa, Teresa, Rose of Lima, and many other saints, he was driven to lyrical and musical expression by his own rapture of love and joy. "Oh Good Jesu! my heart Thou hast bound in thought of Thy Name, and now I cannot but sing it."

All mystics are potential poets. Rolle was an actual poet too. Hence by the Canor, which was the third form by which his rapture of love was expressed, we must understand not only the "Celestial Melody" in which he participated in ecstatic moments, not only those exultant moods of "great plenty of inward joy" when the spiritual song "swelled to his mouth" and he sang his prayers "with a ghostly symphony," as St. Catherine of Genoa "sang all day for joy"; but also the genuine poetic inspiration to which his writings give ample testimony. All these are varying expressions of one life and one love: for the great mystic, living in contact with Eternity, is seldom careful to note the exact boundary which marks off "inward" from "outward" or earth from heaven. To Rolle, contemplation was the song of the soul: song was contemplation expressed. Some, he observes in "The Mending of Life," think that contemplation is the knowledge of deep mysteries: others that it is the state of total concentration on spiritual things: others again that it is an elevation of mind which makes the self dead to all fleshy desires. All these no doubt are true in their measure: but "to me it seems that contemplation is joyful song of God's love." It is love and joy "with great voice out-breaking" as the ascending spirit stretches towards the Only Fair. Rolle's mysticism is fundamentally of the "outgoing" type. He seldom uses the language of introversion, or speaks of God as found within the heart; but pictures the soul's quest of Reality as a journey, a flight from self, an encounter "in the wilderness" with Love. "Love truly suffers not a loving soul to bide in itself, but ravishes it out to the lover, that the soul is more there where it loves, than where the body is that lives and feels it." When the Canor seizes him, his spirit seems to rush forth on the wings of its own music, that "music that to me is come by burning love, in which I sing before Jesu": for indeed his "song", whether silent melody or articulate, is love in action; the glad and humble passion of adoration taking poetic form.

We see then at last that Heat, Sweetness, and Song are each and all names for, and psycho-physical expressions of, one thing—that many-coloured, many-graded miracle of Love which is the substance of all mysticism, and alone has power to catch man into the divine atmosphere, initiate him into the friendship of God. "O dear Charity . . . Thou enterest boldly the bedchamber of the King Everlasting: thou only art not ashamed Christ to take. He it is that thou hast sought and loved. Christ is thine: hold Him, for He may not but take thee, to whom thou only desirest to obey."

Here we find, fused together, the highest flights of mystical passion for the Ineffable God, and the intense devotion to the Person of Christ: the special quality which marked all that was best in English religion of the medieval period. In such passages—and his works abound in them—Rolle sets the pattern to which all the great English mystics who followed him conformed. Were we asked, indeed, to state their peculiar characteristic, I think that we must find it here: in the combination of loftiest transcendentalism with the loving and intimate worship of the Holy Name. Thus it is that they solve the eternal mystic paradox of an unconditioned yet a personal God. "The Scale of Perfection," "The Cloud of Unknowing," "The Revelations of Divine Love," all turn on this point: and those who discount their strongly Christian and personal quality, gravely misunderstand the nature of the vision by which their writers were inspired.

Of the two works of Richard Rolle which Miss Comper here presents in a modernized form, "The Fire of Love" represents his subjective manner—"The Mending of Life" an attempt towards the orderly presentation of his ascetic doctrine. The whole system of his teaching, in so far as a system was possible to so poetic and "inspired" a temperament, aims at the induction of other men to that state in which they can fulfill the supreme vocation of humanity: take part in "angels' song," the music of adoration which all created spirits sing to God. He knows that the "ghostly song" of highest contemplation is a special gift, a grace shed into the soul, and does not hesitate to proclaim his own peculiar possession of it: yet he is sure that the heavenly melodies may be evoked, in a certain measure, in all who are surrendered to divine love. The method by which he would educate the soul to the point at which it can participate in the life of Reality, is that method of asceticism—profound contrition, mortification and prayer—which he has followed himself: here conforming to the doctrine of the three great masters of the spiritual life whose writings had influenced him most, St. Bernard, Richard of St. Victor, and St. Bonaventura. Though he often seems in his more didactic works to echo the teaching of these doctors, and in some passages repeats their very words—as for instance in his description of the Three Degrees of Love, and in his doctrine of Ecstasy—yet all that he says has been actualized by him in his own personal experience. His most "dogmatic" utterances burn with passion: he uses the maps of his great predecessors because he has tested them and found them true. It is commonly said that the Incendium Amoris—that most personal and unconventional of works—is an imitation of St. Bonaventura's Stimulus Amoris. Apart from the fact that the Stimulus Amoris is no longer accepted as an authentic work of St. Bonaventura, but was probably composed by James of Milan, the two books—as any may see who take the trouble to compare them—have hardly a character in common. True, both are largely concerned with the Love of God; but so are all the works of Christian mysticism. The subjective element which occupies so large a place in the Incendium is wholly absent from the Stimulus. There we find no autobiography, rather an orderly didactic treatise, miles asunder from the Yorkshire hermit's fervid rhapsodies. The Incendium is not an artificial composition, but a work of original genius. It is the rhapsody and confession of a "God-intoxicated" poet, who longed to tell his love, yet knew that all his powers of expression could not communicate one little point of the vision and the ecstasy to which he had been raised: "Would God of that melody a man I might find author, the which though not in word, yet in writing my joy he should sing."

Passionate feeling taking artistic form: this perhaps is the ruling character of all Rolle's mystical writings. He has been accused of laying undue emphasis upon emotional experience. Yet a stern system of ethics—as we may see from his life as well as from his works—underlies this exultant participation in the music of the spheres. Though some may be repelled by his love of that solitude in which heart speaks to heart, or amused by his quaint praise of the virtues of "sitting"—the attitude which he found most conductive to contemplation— surely none can fail to be impressed by the heroic self-denials, the devoted missionary labours, which ran side by side with this intense interior life. His love was essentially dynamic; it invaded and transmuted all departments of his nature, and impelled him as well to acts of service as to songs of joy. He was no spiritual egotist, no mere seeker for transcendental satisfaction; but one of those for whom the divine goodness and beauty are coupled together in insoluble union, even as "the souls of the lover and the loved."

> NOTE: My quotations from "The Fire of Love" and "The Mending of Life" are made direct from Richard Misyn's fifteenth century English translation, as printed by the Early English Text Society: save only for modernization of the spelling. They may not therefore agree in all particulars with Miss Comper's version. I have used Miss Geraldine Hodgson's edition of "The Form of Perfect Living" (1910); my own of "The Cloud of Unknowing" (1912), and the text of "The Song of Angels" which is printed from Pepwell by Mr. Edmund Gardner in "The Cell of Self-knowledge" (New Medieval Library, 1910).

EDITOR'S PREFACE

Of mysticism, as of all the greatest things in life, the characteristic notes are sincerity and simplicity. Its nature and birth are better felt by the heart than uttered by the tongue. Therefore the increasing interest in mysticism, evidenced by the multiplication of books, essays, criticism, and correspondence on the subject, is rather to be dreaded than welcomed by the mystic. For mysticism like love is shy as the wild bird. Criticism destroys it; discussion frightens it away. Doubtless it can live in the heart of every man; only that heart must be pure, and free from anxiety and worldly love; since to the Christian mysticism is nothing else that that love which is the sole definition of God that man can comprehend.

He that has found the secret of this love, which possesses alike the world of nature and of man, has found the secret of the mystic. For it is not a respecter of persons, nor reserved for the few. The old woman sitting over her peat fire, the shepherd upon the lonely hills, the workman breaking stones by the roadside, even the "great divine lapped in infinite questions" or the anchoress in her cell; all indeed who are "more busy to know God than many things," have glimpses of this secret. And it was for those who would rather know God's love than know about it that this book was written so long ago.

For six centuries the dust of oblivion has hidden Richard Rolle from our knowledge. True, his name was known as the author of a long Northern poem called the Prick of Conscience, but it has lately been proved that, whatever else he may have written, this most certainly he did not write. Of him and of the other English mystics of his time, we knew but little. As we may have stood by and watched a statue, modeled by some sculptor dead these many hundred years, being slowly and carefully unearthed in a villa garden near Rome, so now we look on with interest as scholars, mostly of other nations than our own, are laboriously restoring to us the mystical writings of these Englishmen, long ago dead, and now for the most part nameless.

Yet Richard Rolle, the first of these great mystics, had revealed himself to us in his writings. Race counts for much in character, and in reading his books we can never forget that he comes of the sturdy stock of Yorkshiremen. Honest, somewhat blunt and plainspoken, especially in regard to women, and full of common sense, it is the more remarkable that he should in so many ways recall to us the sweet singer of Assisi. And yet, as Miss Underhill has shown us, he joins hands across the century with the poet of love and poverty who preached to the birds under the ilex-tree at the Carceri; while from another point of view he has kinship with the monk of Windesheim, the words of whose Ecclesiastical Music are constantly recalled to our minds by this other Melody of Love. As we read it we find that the problems which confronted Richard in his hermit's cell at Hampole are the same as confront the thoughtful man today. He is distressed by the friendlessness, rather than the poverty, of the poor; the oppression and worldliness of the rich; the wrong and selfish acquisition of land; the utter destructiveness of sin; the hypocrisy and backbiting of those who "fill the kirks." Then, as now, men desired to escape from the transient to the eternal; from the overwhelming power of the material to the spiritual; from the turmoil and confusion of strange ideas and social upheaval and crying injustice, to the rest and peace to be found in humility and brotherly love. As in the old emblem of the two crossed pieces of wood bearing the wayfarer safely over the stormy sea, the love of God laid athwart the love of man bears the soul safely over the waves of this life.

And this love is the sum and substance of Rolle's mysticism. We find in his writings few definitions or classifications, which are so frequent in many mystical works; for it was as impossible for him as for Saint Francis—who in his life was the greatest exponent of mysticism that the world has ever seen—to lay down rules regarding love. The love of child and parent, of young man and maid, with all the deeds of heroism and sacrifice which such love has engendered, are but as pale symbols of the love which has given birth to the ancient literature of mysticism. This love is as a fire or a raging flame. "It verily inflames the mind," says Richard; "Love sets my heart on fire," sings Francis.

To most this love comes only as the reward of long search and striving. It is a quest on which a man may start out in company, but he must end alone—with God: and in proportion as we attain to it we find the solution of many problems, the secret of life, and the key to the "mysteries of the Kingdom."

METHOD AND AIM OF THIS MODERNIZATION

This book is not meant for the scholar. For him Rolle's own versions are accessible in numerous MSS.; and Misyn's Middle English translation has been printed by the Early English Text Society. But there are many who find in Misyn's curious spellings and constructions a serious obstacle to the sense, and it is for such that this edition has been prepared. My aim has been to make Rolle's meaning clear to the modern reader with as little alteration of Misyn's text as possible. I have modernized the spelling, have simplified long and involved constructions, and have tried to elucidate the meaning by careful punctuation. But I have dealt very sparingly with the vocabulary, keeping as many of the old words as seemed likely to be understood, and especially those which still linger in Scottish dialect, as being a reminder to the reader of the Northern origin of the book. Where the text appears to be corrupt and emendation has been necessary, I have used for this purpose, for The Fire of Love the Cambridge MS. Dd. 5.64 (which I call L), and for The Mending of Life the printed editions; comparing them with the MSS. referred to in the notes at the end of this book, where I have given the Latin and Middle English originals. A short passage has been omitted as unsuited for modern readers; and, on the other hand, where obvious omissions occur in Misyn's text, they have been supplied from the MSS. mentioned. When I have altered an obsolete word I give such, the first time it occurs, in a foot note. Any words of difficult meaning will be found in the Glossary, and I have in this case also added a footnote on their first occurrence in the text. Other points I have gone more fully into under the section Treatment of Words.

It has been, and very probably may again be contended, that a better result would have been obtained by translating straight from the original. This would in many ways have been easier, but the insuperable objection to such a course lies in the fact that the Latin MSS. of these works of Rolle have not yet been collated; and no satisfactory translation can be made until we have discovered which is Rolle's autograph. Moreover there is a certain charm in this early translation of Misyn's which no modern one, however excellent, could reproduce. Rolle died in 1349, but the Office for his canonization was not prepared until 1381, and still later the Miracula were collected. His memory must have remained fresh in men's minds; indeed this is born out by the fact that so many extant copies of his works date from the fourteenth and fifteenth centuries. The influence of his spirit was still a living one; and this translation has embodied and preserved for us the simple faith and enthusiastic love of the generation for which it was written. Read and meditated upon by English men and women of long ago although it has been lost to sight nearly five hundred years it deals with a theme that is ever fresh. It will be an interesting experiment to see whether it can yet appeal to us—whether a genuine English book of piety can hold its own with those of other nations.

In my modernization I am aware that I have laid myself open to criticism in many directions. I have not striven after consistency, but have tried solely to retain as far as possible the simplicity and charm of the original translation. Misyn has been called a slavish translator; certainly he has not avoided the faults of his master. Repetitions, especially of words and phrases, are even more constant in this version than in the original, while some of the forms and spelling he employs make the modernizer's task by no means an easy one. Dr. Horstman, in his interesting preface to the collection of the English writings of Richard Rolle, after laying stress upon his originality and lyric gift, thus sums up his defects: "His defects lie on the side of method and discrimination; he is weak in argumentation, in developing and arranging his ideas. His sense of beauty is natural rather than acquired, and his mind is too restless to perfect his writings properly. His form is not sufficiently refined, and full of irregularities; his taste not unquestionable; his style frequently difficult, rambling, full of veiled allusions—much depends on the punctuation to make it intelligible; his Latin incorrect and not at all classic— . . . But all this cannot detract from his great qualities as a writer, the originality and depth of his thought, the truth and tenderness of his feeling, the vigour and eloquence of his prose, the grace and beauty of his verse; and everywhere we detect the marks of a great personality, a personality at once powerful, tender and strange, the like of which was perhaps never seen again."

This criticism is perhaps a little severe for a part of Rolle's charm lies in his restlessness of thought. His mind moved rapidly, and he loved to play with a word. His writings are full of antitheses and balance and rhythm—in this respect anticipating Lily —which Misyn's translation well reproduces. If to us his repetitions appear wearisome and monotonous, we must at least remember that they were written not to be read as a continuous whole, but aloud, in chapter or refectory; for one copy had probably to do service for the community.

I have therefore aimed at reproducing Misyn's translation with all its irregularities, only endeavouring to make his meaning clear. My method of doing so will be more fully explained in the following section.

SOURCES

The Fire of Love and The Mending of Life were first printed by the Early English Text Society, in 1896 from the Corpus Christi College MS. 236, at Oxford. At that time it was the only MS. known of Misyn's translation, but four years ago, at Lord Amherst's sale, the British Museum bought an English MS. of the fifteenth century, known as Add. MS. 37790, containing several very important mystical treatises, and among them these two translations by Misyn. This I have collated with the Corpus MS. (which I call C), and have noted any important differences in the text as they occur. They are very few and are mostly confined to spelling; the Amherst MS. showing the influence of a Southern scribe. From the doubling of vowels and consonants in such words as bee, wee, off, nott, ffor, etc., and the writing of th for þ, one would infer that the Amherst is probably of rather later date than the Corpus MS. In this latter The Fire of Love precedes The Mending of Life, although the explicits give 1434 as the date of the translation of The Mending of Life, and 1435 for The Fire of Love; but in the Amherst MS. they are given in their correct chronological order. I have, however, kept to the order of the Corpus MS., since The Fire of Love is by far the longer and more important of the two works.

The editor of the Corpus MS. for the Early English Text Society draws attention to the fact that the explicit to the second book of The Fire of Love contains the statement that it was translated by Richard Misyn, with the addition of these words, "per dictum fratrem Richardum Misyn scriptum et correctum." This was by some too easily considered a proof that we have here Misyn's autograph; but judging from the wrong chronological order Mr. Harvey concludes that this is not the case. It is therefore worth noting that the explicit in the Amherst MS. is word for word the same as in the Corpus MS., which fact, added to the probability of its later date, makes it unlikely that here either we have Misyn's autograph. It is more probable that both were copies of the autograph—the Corpus being the work of a more Northern scribe than the Amherst—and that neither copyist exercised sufficient discretion to omit Misyn's personal note.

At present the question of the Rolle canon is most confused and uncertain. Scholars are working at it, and it is to be hoped the autograph of both Rolle and Misyn will soon be discovered. In the meantime the only possible course open to me was to choose the best available Latin MS. with which to compare Misyn's translation whenever difficulties arose. For the Incendium I have taken a Cambridge MS. (Dd. 5.64, referred to as L). For the De Emendatione it has been less simple, because several printed versions exist of this work, all differing considerably. Misyn sometimes seems to follow one and sometimes another, showing clearly that he is translating from neither of these versions; and in the MSS. to which I have had access the variants are as numerous. For this reason I have been very chary of suggesting any emendations in my version of this work. Obvious omissions I have supplied from another early translation in the Bodleian (Douce MS. 322, which I call D). It seems to be of much the same date as Misyn's, if anything rather later. It is not Northern, and is on the whole a freer translation and has more attempt after style; whereas Misyn's rendering is rather bald, being often very little more than a gloss on the Latin. I have, however, followed Misyn, since we owe to him the longer and more important work of Rolle which this volume contains.

I owe some apology to the reader for the notes, which may seem too numerous for a popular edition; but the difficulties and obscurities in the text have called for emendations and explanations which have necessitated rather full notes. I have been careful to place these at the end, so that they who use this book as it was intended by the author to be used need not be distracted by them.

The portrait of Rolle in the frontispiece is taken from a Cotton MS. (Faust. B. VI. 2.) in the British Museum of a Northern poem called the Desert of Religion. The authorship of this poem is unknown, although it has usually been ascribed to Walter Hilton. It describes the trees which grow in the wilderness, or desert, of religion. These symbolical trees are drawn on the first side of each page; the reverse side is divided into two columns, the one containing the poem itself, while on the other some saint of the desert is depicted.

On the first side of the page containing this picture of Richard the Hermit there is a rude drawing of a tree, with six leaves on either side, representing the twelve abuses that grow among religions. They are as follows:

A prelate negligent: A discipil inobediente. A youngman idill: Ane alde mane obstinate. A mownke cowrtioure: A mounke pletoure. Ane habite preciouse: Mete daintinouse. New tithandes in clostere: Strivynge in the chapitour. Dissolucioun in the qwere: Irreverence aboute the auter.

In the picture the hermit is represented seated on the grass in a white habit, with the sacred monogram in gold on his breast, and holding a book in his left hand. On either side is a stiffly drawn tree. Above, resting on clouds, are three angels bearing a scroll with the words: Sanctus, sanctus, sanctus; Dominus Deus Sabaoth; pleni sunt celi et terra gloria tua. Round the picture the following verse is written:

A solitari here: hermite life i lede, For ihesu loue so dere: all flescli lufe i flede; Pat gastli comforthe clere; that in my breast brede, Might me a thowsande yeere: in heuenly strengthe haue stedd

There is no evidence that this picture is a genuine portrait. It recalls some early portraits of Saint Francis. The hair is light in colour, and cut evenly round the head, and the beard divided into two small points. The saint's face is not emaciated, but of a clear complexion with a touch of red upon the cheeks. Both the other manuscripts of The Desert of Religion contain pictures of Richard Hermit, but since none are known to be authentic, I have chosen this which seems the most interesting.

TREATMENT OF WORDS

Personally I should have preferred to retain all the words which Misyn employs, in the hope that some would find their way back into our too much latinized English; but I feared to outweary the patience of the reader. The following is a list of those which I have altered in the text, with their nearest modern equivalents.

addling to earning aseth satisfaction bolnes puffs up chinche miser fagiar, faged flatterer, flattered fliting reproof forthink repent foyd pledge groching grumbling groundly from the root inhiry inward or inner lat behave large generous leman beloved loving, lufing praise menged, melled mingled ugg abhor undirlowt overcome unneth scarcely sam together scrithe glide sparples scatter tityst soonest wode, wodeness mad, madness well to wither

I have kept words which are of common occurrence in the Bible and Prayer Book, and those still in use in Scotland. There are, however, some words which remain in modern English but which have altered or restricted their meaning. Such are very apt to mislead the modern reader. I have, therefore, treated them freely, retaining them when in a modern sense or when their meaning is quite apparent, but changing them if the meaning is at all ambiguous. I append here a full list of these, to avoid the multiplication of footnotes.

Misyn often uses "withouten" for "without," for the sake of rhythm, and in this I have followed him; nor have I taken upon myself to suppress his constant repetition of "truly," "forsooth," "doubtless," "certain," "sickerly." Sometimes these translate the Latin vero, valde, certe, etc., but more often than not stand for an ordinary conjunction, such as enim, namque, autem. O.E.D. against a word in the footnote signifies that the actual word or phrase found in Misyn is quoted in the Oxford English Dictionary.

Where the meaning is obscure I have altered:

against to towards avoid make void barely utterly beholding contemplating, or considering busily continually charge care, consider cherish allure deadly, deadliness mortal, mortality drawn to cleave (L. adhaerere) emonge in the meantime herefore hence honily honeyed, honey-sweet ill evil kind nature, essence lasts perseveres liking delight, pleasure lovely lovable longs languishes lust pleasure manner measure mind memory namely especially plainly entirely, altogether (L. penitus) rots, unable to rot corrupts, incorruptible softly little by little, slowly soundly with sweet sound, songful stands continues swells inflates show declare taken received taught imbued thinking meditating, or meditation use enjoy, exercise wanting lacking wherefore whence withhold hold to, retain worship honour wretchedness wickedness

BIOGRAPHICAL

(i) RICHARD ROLLE

It is interesting to remember that B. Richard H. of Hampole was among the names included in the prospectus which Newman drew up for The Lives of the English Saints. He tells us in a note to the Apologia , that "He has included in the series a few eminent or holy persons, who, though not in the Sacred Catalogue, are recommended to our religious memory by their fame, learning, or the benefits they have conferred on posterity." Unfortunately Rolle shared the fate of the hundred and eighty-three whose lives were never written.

Various short biographies of Richard Rolle have appeared recently appended to editions of his works, the most complete of which are those of Dr. Horstman and the Rev. H. R. Bramley. These are drawn from the Legenda or Lections, given in the special Office, which the nuns of Hampole prepared in the hope of his canonization. This did not take place because of the unsettled state of the church, due to the rise of Lollardry, although, from the note prefixed to it, the Office seems to have been used privately. The Miracula were included in it, and were arranged to be read as Lections during the octave of the Feast.

Since the Legenda are the source of our knowledge of Rolle's life, and are largely drawn from his own writings, and more especially from the Incendium Amoris, it has seemed well to give them in full. I have translated them from the collation of the three MSS. published by the Surtees Society. They form the nine lections, to be read at Matins on the Feast Day of the saint.

The nuns, to whom Richard ministered and with whom he died, belonged to a well-known Cistercian House at Hampole. Nothing now remains of the convent, but the Rev. R. H. Benson gives the following interesting description of the place. "Hampole is still a tiny hamlet, about seven miles distant from Doncaster. There has never been a parish church there, and in Richard's time the spiritual needs of the people would no doubt be met by the convent chapel. Of the nunnery there are now no certain traces, except where a few mounds in the meadows by the stream below the hamlet mark its foundations, and beyond a few of its stones built into the school house. The few grey stone houses nestle together on the steep slope in a shallow nook in the hill, round an open space where the old village spring still runs. There is no trace of Richard's cell; but, in spit of the railway line in the valley, the place has a curious detached air, lying, as it does, a complete and self-contained whole, below the Doncaster road, fringed and shadowed by trees, and bordered with low-lying meadows rich, in early summer, with daisies and buttercups, and dotted with numerous may trees; the farthest horizon from the hamlet is not more than a mile or two away."

RICHARD MISYN

The only fact we are certain of in regard to Richard Misyn is that he was the translator of the two treatises of Rolle which this volume contains. In the explicit to Book II of The Fire of Love we are told that he was then Prior of Lincoln and belonged to the Order of the Carmelites, 'per fratrem Ricardum Misyn, sacre theologie bachalaureum, tunc Priorem Lyncolniensem, ordinis carmelitarum'; but in the previous explicit to Book I he is mentioned only as a hermit belonging to the order, 'per fratrem Ricardum Misyn heremitam and ordinis carmelitarum Ac sacre theologie bachalaureum.'

Rolle had died eighty-six years before, in 1349, but two of his miracles are dated and are as late as 1381 and 1383, so there is little reason to doubt that his name was very familiar to this other Richard, who also styled himself a hermit, and who, as far as we can gather, was of the same country.

There are scanty records of a Richard Mysyn, a Carmelite and Suffragan, who is thought to be identical with Bishop Mesin or Musin of Dromore; for at that time to have a see in Ireland did not necessarily mean to reside there. This Frater Ric. Mysyn, Suffragenus, ordinis Fratrum Carmelitarium, is put first in the Register of the Corpus Christi Guild of York, under the date 1461-1462, and was admitted to the Guild by Dom. J. Burton, Rector of the Church of S. Martin in the Mickelgate, York. Bishop Musun's name also occurs in the legend round the famous cup preserved in the vestry of York Minister, and known as the Scrope Indulgence Cup. This inscription runs: Recharde arche beschope Scrope grantes on to all tho that drinkis of this cope xl dayis to pardun. Robert Gubsun. Beschope Musin grantes in same forme afore saide xl dayis to pardun. Robert Strensall.'

In the Carmelite records preserved in a manuscript in the British Museum, the death is noted of a Richard Mesin, Bishop of Dromore, under the year 1462, who was buried with the other Fathers of the order in their monastery at York, i.e., in the same year as Richard Mysyn was admitted a member of the Corpus Christi Guild. But at present it must remain a matter merely of conjecture if these references relate to the Richard Misyn to whom we owe our translation.

It now only remains for me to thank all those who have helped me by their kind advice and interest. I should like here to record my especial gratitude to Miss Evelyn Underhill, who read a part of my MS., and to whose kindly aid and suggestions I am much indebted; to Father Cuthbert, O.S.F.C., who helped me over many difficulties in the Latin text; to Father Congreve, S.S.J.E., for his unfailing sympathy and help; and to Miss Corrie Prior who read the proofs with me. I also owe a very especial debt of gratitude to Professor H. J. C. Grierson, not only for his kindness in overlooking my preface, but also because anything I may have learnt of the beauty and inspiration of literature is due to his teaching. And there are many others I am not allowed to name, but for whose assistance I am none the less grateful.

By a curious coincidence I find that I am writing the last words of my preface on the eve of the day set apart in the English Martyrology for the commemoration of Blessed Richard, Confessor and Eremite. May we not take it for a sign that he is still present with us in spirit, and as desirous of helping us today by his spiritual books and treatises, and—may we not add—by his prayers, as when he ministered to the nuns at Hampole, or repaired to his cell to sing psalms and hymns in honour of God.

A TRANSLATION OF THE LEGENDA IN THE OFFICE PREPARED FOR THE BLESSED HERMIT RICHARD

The office of Saint Richard, hermit, after he shall be canonized by the Church, because in the meantime it is not allowed to sing the canonical hours for him in public, nor to solemnize his feast. Nevertheless, having evidence of the extreme sanctity of his life, we may venerate him and in our private devotions seeks his intercessions, and commend ourselves to his prayers.

LECTION I

The saint of God, the hermit Richard, was born in the village of Thornton, near Pickering, in the diocese of York, and in due time, by the efforts of his parents, he was sent to be educated. When he was of adult age Master Thomas Neville, at one time Archdeacon of Durham, honourable maintained him in the University of Oxford, where he made great progress in study. He desired rather to be more fully and perfectly instructed in the theological doctrine of Holy Scripture than in physics or the study of secular knowledge. At length, in his nineteenth year, considering that the time of mortal life is uncertain and its end greatly to be dreaded (especially by those who either give themselves to fleshly lusts or only labour that they may acquire riches, and who, for these things, devote themselves to guile and deceit, yet they deceive themselves most of all), by God's inspiration he took thought betimes for himself, being mindful of his latter end, lest he should be caught in the snares of sinners.

Hence, after he had returned from Oxford to his father's house, he said one day to his sister, who loved him with tender affection: My beloved sister, thou hast two tunics which I greatly covert, one white and the other grey. Therefore I ask thee if thou wilt kindly give them to me, and bring them me tomorrow to the wood near by, together with my father's rain hood.' She agreed willingly, and the next day, according to her promise, carried them to the said wood, being quite ignorant of what was in her brother's mind. And when he had received them he straightway cut off the sleeves from the grey tunic and the buttons from the white, and as best he could he fitted the sleeves to the white tunic, so that they might in some manner be suited to his purpose. Then he took off his own clothes with which he was clad and put on his sister's white tunic next his skin, but the grey, with the sleeves cut out, he put on over it, and put his arms through the holes which had been cut; and he covered his head with the rain hood aforesaid, so that thus in some measure, as far as was then in his power, he might present a certain likeness to a hermit. But when his sister saw this she was astounded and cried: My brother is mad! My brother is mad!' Whereupon he drove her from him with threats, and fled himself at once without delay, lest he should be seized by his friends and acquaintances.

LECTION II

After having thus put on the habit of a hermit and left his parents, he went to a certain church on the vigil of the Assumption of the most Blessed Virgin, Mother of God, and therein he set himself to pray, in the place where the wife of a certain worthy squire, named John de Dalton, was wont to pray. And when she entered the church to hear vespers, the servants of the squire's house wished to remove him from their lady's place. But she from humility would not permit them, lest he should be disturbed in his devotions. But when vespers were over, the sons of the said squire, who were scholars and had studied in the University of Oxford, noticed him as he rose from prayer, and said that he was the son of William Rolle, whom they had known at Oxford.

Then, on the day of the aforesaid feast of the Assumption he again entered the same church; and without bidding from any one, he put on a surplice and sang matins and the office of mass with the others. And when the gospel had been read in the mass, having first besought the blessing of the priest, he went into the preacher's pulpit and gave the people a sermon of wonderful edification, insomuch that the multitude which heard it was so moved by his preaching that they could not refrain from tears; and they all said that they had never before heard a sermon of such virtue and power. And small wonder, since he was a special instrument of the Holy Spirit, and spoke with the very breath of Him whose it is, as saith the apostle to the Romans, to divide to every man severally as He will, and to make intercession for us with groanings which cannot be uttered.

LECTION III

Therefore, after mass, the aforesaid squire invited him to dinner, but when he entered his manor he betook himself to a certain mean and old room; for he would not enter the hall, but sought rather to fulfill the teaching of the gospel, which says, When thou art invited to a wedding, sit down in the lowest room; that when he that bade thee cometh, he may say unto thee, Friend, go up higher;' and this too was fulfilled in him. For when the squire had sought for him diligently, and at last found him in the aforesaid room, he set him above his own sons at the table. But he kept such perfect silence at dinner that not a word proceeded from his mouth. And when he had eaten enough he rose, before the table was removed, and prepared to depart. But the squire who had invited him said that this was not customary, and so prevailed upon him to sit down again. When the meal was over he again wished to depart, but the squire, seeking to have some private talk with him, detained him until all who were in the room had gone, when he asked him if he were the son of William Rolle. Then he rather unwillingly and with reluctance answered: Perchance I am'; since he feared that if he were recognized the plan on which his mind was set would be hindered. For this squire loved his father as a friend with warm affection. But Richard—newly made a hermit without his father's knowledge and against his wish—had taken this estate upon him because he loved God more than his earthly father.

LECTION IV

And when the aforesaid squire had examined him in private, and convinced himself by perfect evidence of the sanctity of his purpose, he, at his own expense, clad him according to his wish, with clothing suitable for a hermit; and kept him for a long time in his own house, giving him a place for his solitary abode and providing him with food and all the necessities of life. Then he began with all diligence, by day and night, to seek how to perfect his life, and to take every opportunity he could to advance in contemplative life and to be fervent in divine love. And to what excellent perfection he at length attained in this art of fervent love for God he himself records, not for boastfulness nor to seek vainglory, but rather after the example of the glorious and humble apostle Paul, who, narrating his rapture to the third heaven, where he heard secrets which are not lawful for a man to utter, also avows the greatness of the revelations made to him by God, and openly exalts his own labours above the labours of all the other apostles. All which things he wrote in his epistles for the profit and edification of others, and left them for others to read. So too this holy hermit, Richard, in chapter one of his first book of The Fire of Love, tells to what high and sweet delights he attained by contemplation, so that others may obtain hope of advancing likewise in acts of contemplation and of love for God, if only watchfully, constantly, and perseveringly they persist in those works which are ordained for the attainment of this most desirable state of perfection, and hate and cut off as poison all impediments to contemplation.

LECTION V

For in the aforesaid book he thus speaks: I marvelled more than I can say when I first felt my heart grow warm and burn, truly, not in imagination but as it were with sensible fire. I was indeed amazed at that flame which burst forth within me; and at this unwonted comfort—because of my inexperience of this abundance—I have often felt my breast to see if perchance this heat was due to some outward cause. But when I knew that this fire of love had blazed forth only from within, and was not of the flesh but a gift of my Maker, I was full of joy and dissolved in a desire for yet greater love; and chiefly because of the inflowing of this most sweet delight and internal sweetness which, with this spiritual burning, bedewed my mind to the core. For I had not thought before that such sweet heat and comfort might come to pass in this exile.

See then by these words how far he had advanced in attaining the most sweet love of God; but, because there are many steps preparatory to the kindling of this love—as, for example, those things which diminish and remove the loves opposed to it—therefore this saint wore down the lusts of the flesh; to the love of which many are borne off by a mad and bestial impulse. He spurned the world too with its riches, being content with only the bare necessaries of life, that he might more freely enjoy the delights of true love. For these reasons, therefore, he mortified his flesh with many fasts, with frequent vigils, and repeated sobs and sighings, quitting all soft bedding, and having a hard bench for a bed, and for a house a small cell; fixing his mind always on heaven, and desiring to depart and be with Christ, his most sweet Beloved.

LECTION VI

Yet wonderful and beyond measure useful was the work of this saintly man in holy exhortations, whereby he converted many to God, and in his sweet writings, both treatises and little books composed for the edification of his neighbours, which all sound like sweetest music in the hearts of the devout. And amongst other things it seems worthy of great wonder that once, when he was seated in his cell (one day, after dinner) the lady of the house came to him, and many other persons with her, and found him writing very quickly. And they besought him to leave off writing and speak a word of edification to them, which he immediately did, exhorting them most eloquently to virtue and to renounce worldly vanities and stablish the love of God in their hearts. Yet in no way on account of this did he cease from writing for two hours without interruption, but continued to write as quickly as before, which could in no wise have been possible unless the Holy Spirit had at that time directed both his hand and tongue; especially as the occupations were discrepant one from another, and the spoken words differed utterly in meaning from those which he wrote. The saint also was sometimes so absorbed in spirit while he prayed that once, when his cloak with which he was clad was taken from him, he did not feel it; and when, after patching and stitching it, they replaced it on him he did not notice it.

LECTION VII

But the more laboriously and effectively this blessed hermit, Richard, studied to acquire perfect holiness of life, so much the more cunningly the devil—the enemy of the human race—sought to entangle him by deceitful snares. So, as appears from a writing in the saint's own hand found after his death in a small volume of his works, the devil, in the form of a certain woman, tried to subvert him with the cords of illicit desire. Thus in the aforesaid book he says: When I had perceived my especial vocation, and laying aside my worldly dress had determined to serve God rather than man, it befell that on a certain night in the beginning of my conversion there appeared to me, while resting on my bed, a very beautiful young woman, whom I had seen before and who loved me—in honourable love—not a little. And when I looked on her and was marvelling why she had come to me in solitude and at night, suddenly, without delay or speech, she placed herself beside me. When I felt this, fearing lest she should entice me to evil, I said I would arise and, with the sign of the cross, invoke the blessing of the Holy Trinity upon us. But she held me so strongly that I could neither speak nor move my hand. Whereupon I perceived that not a woman, but the devil in the form of a woman, was tempting me. So I turned me to God, and when I had said in my mind: "O Jesu, how precious is Thy blood!" and made the sign of the cross on my breast with my finger, which had now begun in some measure to be capable of movement, behold, suddenly all disappeared, and I gave thanks to God who had delivered me. From that time therefore I sought to love Jesus, and the more I advanced in His love the sweeter and more pleasant did the Name of Jesus savour to me; and even to this day it has not left me. Therefore blessed by the Name of Jesus for ever and ever. Amen.

LECTION VIII

Also this holy hermit, Richard, out of the abundance of his charity used to show himself very friendly to recluses and to those who were in need of spiritual consolation, and who suffered disquiet and vexation in soul or body through the malignant work of evil spirits. God granted him singular grace in helping those who were troubled in that way. And thus it once happened that when a certain lady was drawing nigh to death—in whose manor Richard had a cell (but a long way off from the family), where he was wont to live alone, and give himself to contemplation—a great multitude of horrible demons came to the room where the lady lay. It was little wonder, therefore, that when she saw them visibly she fell into great fear and trembling. Her attendants sprinkled holy water in the room and made devout prayers; nevertheless, the demons departed not, but still continued to vex her greatly. At length, by the wise and discreet advice of her friends, the blessed Richard was called to the room, so that, if possible, he might bring the said lady the aid of comfort and peace. And when he had come to her consolation, and had admonished her holily, and had urged her to place all her hope in the superabundant mercy of God and in His overflowing grace, he then set himself to pray God with a fervent heart that He would take from her the fearsome sight of the demons. And the Lord heard him instantly, and at the prayer of His beloved Richard was pleased to put all that terrible troop to flight. Yet as they fled they left behind them astounding traces of their passage; for all the bystanders saw that in that rush-strewn floor of the room where the demons had passed the rushes seemed to be burned and reduced to black ashes, and in these ashes there were marks impressed like the hoof prints of oxen.

But when the demons had lost the prey which they had sought in that place, they tried to take vengeance on Richard, who had put them to flight. Accordingly, they went forthwith to his cell and disturbed him so much that for the time they made the place unfitted for his contemplation. But the saint of God, being stedfast in his faith, fled repeatedly for refuge to the sanctuary of prayer, and by his entreaties once more prevailed with the Lord to put them to flight. And, to the comfort of the aforesaid lady's friends, he told them that she was saved, and that after quitting this life she would be a joint-heir in the kingdom of heaven.

After this the saint of God, Richard, betook himself to other parts, doubtless through the providence of God so that dwelling in many places he might benefit many unto salvation, and sometimes also that he might escape impediment to contemplation, as we read in the book of the Lives of the Fathers that many of the most holy fathers in the desert used to do. For frequent change of place does not always come from inconstancy; as in the accusation of certain who are given to quick and perverse judgment of their neighbours, but whose crooked interpretations and habits of detraction ought not to make a sensible person neglect those things which he has found by experience to be good and conducive to virtue. For in the canon and decrees of the Church many causes sometimes are assigned for which change of place may be made; of which the first is when pressure of persecution makes a place dangerous; secondly, when some local difficulties exist; and thirdly, when the saints are harassed by the society of evil men.

When, therefore, this holy man, for urgent and most practical reasons had betaken himself to dwell in Richmondshire, it befell the Lady Margaret, who had once been a recluse at Auderby in the diocese of York, on the very day of the Lord's Supper was so overcome by a grave attack of illness that for thirteen days continuously she was utterly deprived of the power of speech. Moreover, it caused her such pains and prickings in her body that she could not rest in any position. Now a certain goodman of that town, knowing that the holy hermit Richard loved her with a perfect affection of charity—since he was wont to instruct her in the art of loving God, and to direct her, by his holy teaching, how to order her life—quickly hastened on horseback to the hermit, who was then living twelve miles from the dwelling of the recluse, and besought him to come to her with all speed and bring her consolation in her great need. And when he came to the recluse he found her unable to speak and troubled with very grievous pains. And as he sat by the window of her dwelling and they were eating together, it befell at the end of the meal that the recluse desired to sleep; and so, oppressed by sleep, she drooped her head at the window where Richard, the saint of God, reclined; and after she had slept thus for a short time, leaning slightly upon Richard, suddenly a violent convulsion seized her in her sleep with fearful vehemence, so that it seems as if she wished to break the window of her house. And being still in this most terrible convulsion, she awoke from sleep, and the power of speech being granted her, with great devotion she burst forth with these words: Gloria tibi Domine,' and blessed Richard finished the verse which she had begun, saying: Qui natus es de Virgine,' with the rest which follows in the compline hymn. Then he said to her: Now thy speech is restored to thee, use it as a woman whose speech is for good.'

A little while after, when she was again eating at the aforesaid window, in exactly the same way as before, after dinner she fell asleep, and leaning upon the saint aforesaid, the same convulsions returned, and she became, as it were, mad, and was shaken by extraordinary and violent movements. But when the holy Richard was trying to hold her with his hands, lest she should rend herself or strive in any way to injure the house, she suddenly slipped from them, and in her fall was shaken out of sleep and thoroughly wakened. Then Richard said to her: Truly I thought that even if thou hadst been the devil I should still have held thee; nevertheless, I give thee this word of comfort, that as long as I shall remain in this mortal life thou shalt never again suffer the torment of this illness.'

None the less, when the courses of several years had passed, the same illness—except that she had her tongue free for speech—returned to her. Therefore the recluse sent for the goodman aforesaid, and asked him to hasten quickly on horseback to the house of the nuns at Hampole—which place was far distant from her own dwelling—where the said Richard at that time led a solitary life, and to see what had befallen him. For she doubted not that he had passed from this world, because she knew that he was faithful to his promise; and he had promised her that as long as he lived in the flesh she should never again suffer such torment. So the said man came to Hampole, and he learnt that the saint was dead to this world; and after diligently inquiring the hour of his passing, he found that the aforesaid illness had returned to the recluse shortly after the hour of Richard's departure. But afterwards the recluse betook herself to Hampole where the holy body of the said hermit was given burial; and never afterwards was she afflicted with the suffering of this horrible illness.

LECTION IX

But yet, lest it should lie hidden from men—especially from those who by devout and diligent study are instant towards the attainment of the perfect life—how and by what means that blessed zealot of God, the hermit Richard, reached the stage of perfect love and charity, as far as is allowed in mortal life, so that all other love became mean and worthless for him and begat a dreadful horror: be it known, therefore, that he himself, in his first book concerning the Fire of Love, chapter thirteen, speaks thus: In process of time,' he says, great increase of spiritual joys was given me. For there passed three years—all but three or four months—from the beginning of the change of my life and mind to the opening of the heavenly door, so that, with unveiled face, through the eyes of the heart, the soul might contemplate the heavenly beings, and see by what way to seek her Beloved and pant after Him. Then, the door remaining open, nearly a year passed before the heat of eternal love was verily felt in my heart. I was sitting, forsooth, in a certain chapel, and, while I was finding great delight in the sweetness of prayer or meditation, suddenly I felt within me an unwonted and pleasant heat. And though at first I wavered, doubting for a long time whence it might be, I became convinced that it was not from the creature but from the Creator, because I found it grow more warm and pleasant. But when half a year, three months and some weeks had passed by—during which that warmth of surpassing sweetness continued with me—there was borne in on my perception a heavenly spiritual sound, which pertains to the song of everlasting praise and the sweetness of the invisible melody. Invisible I call it because it can be neither known nor heard except by him to whom it is vouchsafed; and he must first be purified and separated from the world. For while I was sitting in the same chapel, and chanting psalms at night before supper, as I could, I heard as it were the tinkling music of stringed instruments, or rather of singers, over my head. And while my whole heart and all my desires were engrossed in prayer and heavenly things, suddenly, I know not how, I felt within a symphony of song, and I overheard a most delightful heavenly harmony, which remained in my mind. For straightway, while I meditated, my thought was turned into melody of song, and for meditation I, as it were, sang songs. And that music voiced itself even in my prayers and psalmody; and by reason of the interior sweetness which was outpoured upon me, I was impelled to sing what before I had only said. Not publicly, forsooth, for I did it only before God the Creator. Those who saw me knew it not, lest if they had known they might have honoured me above measure; and thus I might have lost part of that most fair flower, and might have fallen into desolation.

Meanwhile wonder seized me that I had been chosen for such great joy while I was in exile, because God had then given me gifts which I knew not to ask, nor thought that even the most holy could receive such in this life. Therefore I trow that these are not given for merit, but freely, to whomsoever Christ will. Nevertheless I think no man shall receive them, unless he especially love the Name of Jesus and honour it so greatly that he never lets It from his mind except in sleep. He to whom it is given to do this may, I think, attain that also.

Whence, from the beginning of my conversion even to the highest degree of the love of Christ to which, by the gift of God, I was able to reach—and in which state I proclaimed the praise of God with joyous songs—I remained for four years and about three months. For this state, when once the previous states are conformed to it, remains unto the end; nay, it will be more perfect after death, because here the joy of love and charity begins and in the heavenly kingdom shall receive its glorious consummation.'

The following prayers are from the Mass for the Saint.

SECRET

O Lord, we beseech thee that these our oblations may, through the holy intercession of the blessed hermit, Richard, be accepted by Thee; that by their virtue we may be protected from all dangers, and may be strengthened in the love of Thy Name ever more and more. Through our Lord.

POSTCOMMUNION

We beseech Thee, Almighty God, that by the prayers of the blessed hermit, Richard, we, Thy servants, refreshed by the sacrifice of the Body and Blood of Thy Son Jesu Christ, may ever receive that most precious food to our salvation; and so be inwardly nourished by the most sweet charity and peace which that sacrifice represents. Through the same our Lord.

HERE BEGIN THE MIRACLES OF THE BLESSED HERMIT RICHARD

To be read during the Octave of the Feast

(The following extracts are from the Sunday Lesson.)

LECTION I

But after the passing of this saint, Richard, so dearly beloved by God, God did not desist from showing forth to men his sanctity and glory by wonderful miracles. For example, in a town near to the dwelling of the nuns of Hampole there was a certain householder called Roger, who on the night of the Feast of the Assumption of the Virgin Mary, Mother of God, and on the two following nights, in his dreams saw the blessed hermit Richard come to him, and he conversed with him about many things. Afterwards, for six nights together, he appeared to him when he was wide awake, and taught him plainly about many secret things, and inflamed him with the love of God and with a spirit of holy devotion. Therefore he made up his mind that he would at once honour the saint with grateful acts of reverence; and he believed that he could please him especially by bringing stones, with his own labour and that of his beasts, to build his tomb in the church of the nuns of Hampole, where now his body is buried.

LECTION II

One day, therefore, while he was occupied with the aforesaid work of piety, and had got ready twelve oxen for drawing, it happened that when he had reached the gate of the churchyard at Hampole carrying great stones, his poor beasts by an unhappy accident turned aside from the path, and the cart collided with the side-post of the gate and cast the said stones with great force upon Roger himself. Yet he was in no wise hurt by this, nor felt any shaking or pain of body; and though his foot was very tightly jammed by the stones, he was able to get it out without injury to foot or leg. And, indeed, that this miracle should not be forgotten, one of those stones was set up at the gate of the churchyard, so that those coming that way might see it; and another is placed on the tomb of the saint.

Thus, as long as he lived, this saintly man was wholly on fire with divine love, seeking nothing except that he might please Jesus Christ, his most sweet Beloved; and any who would offer him faithful service, and by devout prayers make him his mediator and intercessor with the same Jesus Christ, has a most powerful argument from this history. And if he be not in himself an obstacle, he will obtain his wholesome purpose.

LECTION IV

A certain woman called Joan being vexed with demons lost the use of speech, and her bodily strength was so reduced and exhausted that every one that saw her thought she must die. But one day the blessed Virgin Mary, Mother of God, appeared to her in most beautiful white garments, drawing near to her and leading the blessed hermit Richard by the hand. And he, seeing the demons cruelly vexing the woman, placed himself between them and her and made them depart. Then the blessed Richard put a ring on the woman's finger as a token of the miracle and his saving help. When he had done this, at once the woman ceased to feel the vexation of the demons; and recovered the use of her speech and was healed of all her infirmities.

ALL THE MIRACLES OF RICHARD:

Preserved Roger from accident while engaged in building the saint's tomb

John: wounded by an enemy, is raised from apparent death by prayer and the placing of money on his body, as an offering to the saint.

Joan: Demoniac: cured by intervention of B.V.M. and the saint, who places a ring on her finger.

Woman: the saint appears to a paralyzed woman and restores her, bidding her tell her neighbours.

Thomas: bedridden: hearing in the night a voice bidding him to send a candle of 1 1/2 lbs. to be burnt before the image of the B.V.M. at Hampole, Thomas does so by his wife and family; and being alone in the house the saint appears to him and, asking where the pain is, touches the spot and heals him.

Son of Isabella: boy drowned by falling into a well. A passing pilgrim tells them to visit the hermit's tomb at Hampole. They do so, and pay a denarius at the tomb and the child is restored to life.

Hugh: falls into a well; is revived by his mother's vow to offer a candle of the length of her dead son at the saint's tomb.

William: bitten by a snake and thought to be dead; but restored by a vow to make a pilgrimage to the saint's tomb. This miracle is confirmed on oath.

John: Crippled in arms and legs: restored by promise of yearly pilgrimage to the saint's tomb.

Isabella: deaf for seven years: cured by praying at the saint's tomb.

Beatrice: dumb for six days: cured by praying at the tomb.

Julia: demoniac and dumb for twelve days: falls asleep at the saint's tomb, and Richard and the B.V.M. appear in a vision and tell her to ask the priest to whom she will confess her sins, and she will be healed in mind and body. She narrates that the brightness of the vision nearly blinded her.

John: deaf for ten years; cured by praying at the saint's tomb.

Woman: also deaf; cured at the saint's tomb.

Alice: dumb from S. Katherine's Day to Easter: cured by praying at the saint's tomb.

John: insane: led to the tomb by his friends and there cured.

Agnes: insane for three months. Her friends offer a wax candle, measured to her height, at the saint's tomb, and she is immediately restored to her senses.

Isabella: blind of one eye for twenty years: makes a pilgrimage to the tomb and is cured.

Agnes: deaf for three years: restored at the tomb.

Robert: totally blind for three years: hears a voice bidding him go to the hermit's tomb, and, obeying, is cured.

Boy of 5: choked by an apple for three days and thought to be dead: revived by a denarius placed on his head as an offering to the saint.

Boy of 4: bad ulcer in the child's mouth prevented his feeding. By wise counsel a denarius is laid upon his head, and the ulcer vanishes and the child can suck.

Joan: fell into a mill pool: rescued after an hour, and revived by prayer and being measured for a candle.

Woman: deaf for two years: makes a pilgrimage to the saint's tomb and is cured on the spot.

John: deaf for a long time: is cured by the merits and prayers of the saint.

Woman: her child is still-born and she is thought to be dead: restored by being measured for a candle to the saint.

Isabella: the child falls asleep upon a heap of straw and is smothered by it. When found is thought to be dead, but restored to life on being measured for a candle.

THE FIRE OF LOVE OR MELODY OF LOVE, AS TRANSLATED BY RICHARD MISYN IN 1435 A.D. FROM THE INCENDIUM AMORIS' BY RICHARD ROLLE OF HAMPOLE: AND NOW DONE INTO MODERN ENGLISH

PROLOGUE OF RICHARD MISYN

For the honour of our Lord Jesu Christ, at the asking of thy desire, Sister Margaret, coveting to make satisfaction, and for increase also of ghostly comfort, to thee and more, that understand not curiosity of Latin, I, among lettered men simplest and in living unthriftiest, have taken this work to translate from Latin into English for the edification of many souls. And since it is so that all good pleasure and ghostly life of man's soul stands in perfect love, therefore this holy man, Richard Hampole, has named his book Incendium Amoris, that is to say "The Fire of Love." The which book I think to change neither in meaning nor substance, but truly to write it in good exposition after mine understanding.

Therefore I pray all readers hereof, if your discretion find aught thankworthy, to God give the praise thereof and to this holy man; and if any thing be mis-said, to my ignorance ascribe it. Nevertheless I make protestation to reform, with intent to write or say nothing against the faith or determination of holy kirk, God being witness.

Furthermore, sister, have in mind the mortality of this life, and always in thy hand some holy lesson keep. For if thou keepest holiness thou shalt not love fleshly sins; and holiness, wherein it stands, I said before, in perfect love.

But perfect love, what may that be? Certain, when thy God, as thou ought-est, for Himself thou lovest; thy friend in God; and thine enemy thou lovest for God. For neither God without thy neighbour, nor thy neighbour without God, is truly loved. Perfect love therefore stands in love of God and of thy neighbour; and love of God in keeping of His commandments.

Keep, therefore, His commandments, and when thou enterest thy prayers or contemplation, all worldly things altogether forsake; forget the care of all outward things, and to God only take heed. If thou find any doubts call to thee sad counsel, for dread thou arrest; especially in such things as touch the twelve articles of thy faith; also of the Holy Trinity, and divers others as in this holy book following is wisely written to our learning.

PROLOGUE OF RICHARD ROLLE

More have I marvelled than I showed when, forsooth, I first felt my heart wax warm, truly, and not in imagination, but as if it were burned with sensible fire. I was forsooth amazed as the burning in my soul burst up, and of an unwont solace; ofttimes, because of my ignorance of such healthful abundance, I have groped my breast seeking whether this burning were from any bodily cause outwardly. But when I knew that it was only kindled inwardly from a ghostly cause, and that this burning was nought of fleshly love or concupiscence, in this I conceived it was the gift of my Maker. Gladly therefore I am molten into the desire of greater delight and ghostly sweetness; the which, with that ghostly flame, has pithily comforted my mind.

First truly before this comfortable heat, and sweetest in all devotion, was shed in me, I plainly trowed such heat could happen to no man in this exile: for truly so it enflames the soul as if the element of fire were burning there. Nevertheless, as some say, there are some, burning in the love of Christ, because they see them despising this world, and with busyness given only to the service of God. But as it were if thy finger were put into the fire it should be clad with sensible burning, so, as beforesaid, the soul set afire with love, truly feels most very heat; but sometimes more and more intense, and sometimes less, as the frailty of the flesh suffers.

O who is there in mortal body that all this life may suffer this great heat in its high degree, or may bear for long its continual existence? Truly it behoves him fail for sweetness and greatness of desire after so high an outward love; and no marvel though many, passing out of this world, full greedily would catch it and yearn after it with full hot desire; so that unto this honey-sweet flame with wonderful gifts of mind he might yield his soul, and so be taken, and forthwith enter the companies of them that sing praises to their Creator withouten end.

But some things happen contrary to charity; for filth of the flesh creeps up tempting restful minds; bodily need also and the frail affections of man, imprinted with the anguish of this wretched exile, sometimes lessen this heat, and the flame which under a figure I called fire, because it burns and lightens, they hinder and heavy. And yet truly they take not fully away that which may not be taken away, for it has umbelapped all my heart. But this most happy heat, sometimes absent on account of such things, appears again; and I, as it were abiding grievously cold, think myself desolate until the time it come again, whiles I have not, as I was wont, that feeling of ghostly fire which applies itself gladly to all parts of the body and soul, and in the which they know themselves secure.

And, moreover, sleep gainstands me as an enemy; for no time heavies me to lose save that in which, constrained, I yield to sleeping. Waking truly I am busy to warm my soul, thirled as it were with cold, the which, when settled in devotion, I know well is set on fire, and with full great desire is lifted above all earthly things.

Truly affluence of this everlasting love comes not to me in idleness, nor might I feel this ghostly heat while I was weary bodily for travel, or truly unmannerly occupied with worldly mirth, or else given without measure to disputation; but I have felt myself truly in such things wax cold, until, putting aback all things in which I might outwardly be occupied, I have striven to be only in the sight of my Saviour and to dwell in full inward burning.

Wherefore I offer this book to be seen: not to philosophers nor wise men of this world, nor to great divines lapped in infinite questions, but unto the boisterous and untaught, more busy to learn to love God than to know many things; for truly not disputing but working is to be known and loved. For I trow these things here contained may not be understood of these questionaries; in all science most high in wisdom but in the love of God most low.

Therefore to them I have not written, except, all things forgetting and putting aback that are longing to this world, they love to be given only to the desires of our Maker. First truly they must flee all earthly dignity, and hate all pride of knowledge and vainglory, and at the last, conforming themselves to highest poverty, meditating and praying, they be constantly given to the love of God.

Thus no marvel the fire within of unwrought charity shall appear to them; and dressing their hearts to receive the heat with which all darkness is consumed, it will lift them up into that most lovely and merry burning, so that they shall pass temporal things and hold for themselves the seat of endless rest. The more knowledge they have, truly the more they are able to love rightly, if they be glad to be despised of others, and gladly despise themselves.

And since I here stir all manner of folk to love, and am busy to show the hottest and supernatural desire of love, this book shall bear the name: "Burning of Love."

THE FIRE
OF LOVE

BOOK I

CHAPTER I

OF MAN'S TURNING TO GOD; AND WHAT HELPS AND WHAT LETS HIS TURN-
ING

Be it known to all manner of people in this wretched dwelling place of exile
abiding, that no man may be imbued with love of endless life, nor be anointed
with heavenly sweetness, unless he truly be turned to God. It behoves truly he
be turned to Him, and from all earthly things be altogether turned in mind,
before he may be expert in the sweetness of God's love, even in little things.
Soothly by ordinate love is this turning done; so that he loves that that is
worthy to be loved, and loves not that that is not worthy to be loved; and that
he burn more in love of those things that are most worthy, and less in them
that are less worthy.

Most is God for to be loved: mickle are heavenly things for to be loved: little, or nought but for need, are earthly things to be loved. Withouten doubt
thus every man is turned to Christ whiles nought is desired by him but only
Christ.

Truly turning from these goods that in this world deceive their lovers and
defend them nought, stands in want of fleshly desire, and hatred of all wickedness; so that they savour not earthly things, nor desire to hold to worldly things
beyond their strait need. For they truly that heap riches and know not for
whom they gather, having their solace in them, are not worthy to be sometimes gladdened in the mirth of heavenly love; although they seem by devotion, not holy but simulated, to feel in their dis-eases something of that felicity
which is to come. For truly for their foul presumption they have fallen from
that sweetness with which God's lovers are softened and made sweet because
they have unmannerly loved worldly money. All love truly that ends not in
God is sinful and makes the havers evil. Wherefore, loving worldly excellence,
they are set on fire with sinful love, and they are further from heavenly heat
than is the space betwixt the highest heaven and the lowest place of the earth.

They sicker are made like to that love because they are conformed to wanton concupiscence; and holding to old manners of wickedness, they love the
vanity of this life before holy love. Wherefore they change the joy of incor-

ruptible clearness to wantoned beauty that shall not last. This soothly would they not do unless they were blinded with the fire of froward love, the which wastes the burgeoning of virtue and nourishes the plants of all vice. Forsooth many are not set on womanly beauty nor like lechery, wherefore they trust themselves saved, as it were with sickerness; and because of chastity only, which they bear outwardly, they ween they surpass all others as saints. But wickedly they thus suppose and all in vain, when covetousness, the root of sins, is not drawn out. And truly, as it is written, nothing is worse than to love money. For whiles the love of temporal things occupies the heart of any man, it altogether suffers him to have no devotion. Truly the love of God and of this world may never be together in one soul, but whichever love is stronger puts out the other that thus it may openly be known who is this world's lover and who Christ's follower. (For the heat of love breaks out in works which are seen.) Certainly as Christ's lovers behave themselves towards the world, and the flesh, so lovers of the world behave themselves towards God and their own souls.

They truly that are chosen, eat and drink but ever with all their mind to God they take entent, and in all earthly things not lust, but need they only seek. Of earthly things they speak with anguish and nought but passingly, nor in them making tarrying; and then in mind they are yet with God; and the remainder of time they yield to God's service; not standing in idleness nor running to plays nor wonders—that is the token of the rejected—but rather behaving themselves honestly, they irk not either to speak or do or think those things that long to God.

The rejected truly alway behave themselves idly towards God; they hear God's word with hardness, they pray without affection, they think of God without sweetness. They enter the kirk and fill the walls; they knock their breast and yield sighs, but plainly but feigned, for why they come to the eyes of men, not to the ears of God. For when they are in kirk in body, in mind they are distracted to worldly goods, which they have or else desire to have, where-fore their heart is far from God. They eat and drink not to their need but to their lust, for but in lecherous food find they savour or sweetness. They give moreover bread to the poor, clothing peradventure to the cold; but whiles their alms is done in deadly sin, or for vainglory, or sickerly of things untruly gotten, no marvel if they please not our Gainbuyer, but unto vengeance provoke our Judge.

Wherefore, as the chosen, whiles they take heed to the world or the flesh, alway have their mind busily to God; so the rejected, whiles they seem to do God service are busy with the world, and to those things that pertain to the world and the flesh they are greatly ravished in busyness of heart. And as the chosen displease God nought when they relieve their need, so the rejected please not God in the good deeds they are seen to do; for their full few good deeds are mingled with many ill deeds.

The fiend has many also which we trow be good. He has forsooth alms givers, the chaste, and meek—that is to say sinners calling themselves so—clad with hair and punished by penance. Truly under weening of health ofttimes deadly wounds are hid.

The fiend has also not a few hasty to work and busy to preach; but doubtless all those want to him that are warmed in charity (and who are always eager to love God) and slow to all vanity. The wicked truly are alway greedy after vile delectations, and as dead unto ghostly exercises; or else cast down with full great feebleness: whose love is ever inordinate; for they love temporal goods more than eternal, and their bodies more than their souls.

CHAPTER II

THAT NO MAN MAY SUDDENLY COME TO HIGH DEVOTION, NOR BE WET WITH THE SWEETNESS OF CONTEMPLATION

Truly it is shown to lovers that, in the first years of their turning, no man may attain to high devotion, nor be fully moistened with sweetness of contemplation. Scarcely truly and seldom, and as it were in the twinkling of an eye, are they granted to feel somewhat of heavenly things; and profiting little by little at the last they are made strong in spirit. Then afterward they have received sadness of manners, and so far as this present changeableness suffers, have attained to stability of mind; for with great travails is some perfection gotten, that they may feel some joy in godly love.

Nevertheless it is not seen that all, though they be great in virtue, anon feel verily the actual warmth of uncreate or unwrought charity, nor melting in the unmeasured flame of love, may sing within themselves the song of God's praise. This mystery from many truly is hidden, and to a most special few it is shown; for the higher this degree is, the fewer finders has it in this world.

No marvel that we seldom find any saint, nor one so perfect in this life and rapt with so high love, that in contemplation he might be lift up to sweetness of melody; that is to say, that he might receive into himself the heavenly sound shed into him, and as it were with melody he should yield it again in praise to

God, making many notes in ghostly praising; and that he might feel in himself the heat of God's love. And nevertheless it is marvellous that any contemplative man should be trowed otherwise; for the psalmist, transformed into the person of contemplative man, says: 'Transibo in domum Dei in voce exultationis et confessionis,' that is to say: I shall go into God's house in the voice of gladness and shrift'; which praise is the sound of him that feasts, that is to say, of him that is glad with heavenly sweetness.

The perfect, forsooth, that are taken up into this surpassing plenty of endless friendship, and imbued with sweetness that shall not waste, live anew in the clear chalice of full sweet charity; and in the holy counsel of mirth they draw into their souls happy heat, by the which greatly gladdened, they have greater comfort of ghostly lectuary than may be trowed. This refreshment is the height of endless heritage in them who truly love, and to whom, in this exile forsooth, diseases happen and in the meanwhile it shall not appear unprofitable to them that they be punished for some years, the which shall be lift up to sit, without parting, in heavenly seats. Of all flesh also are they chosen to be most dear in the sight of our Maker, and to be clearly crowned. As the seraphim in high heaven truly are they burnt, who sit in solitude of body, yet their minds walk among the angels to Christ their Beloved, whom they have desired: the which also most sweetly have sung this prayer of endless love, in Jesu joying.

O honey sweet heat, than all delight sweeter, than all riches more delectable.

O my God! O my Love! into me glide; with Thy charity thirled; with Thy beauty wounded:

Slide down and comfort me, heavy; give medicine to me, wretched; show Thyself to Thy lover.

Behold in Thee is all my desire, and all my heart seeks.

After Thee my heart desires; after Thee my flesh thirsts.

And Thou openest not to me but turnest Thy Face.

Thou sparrest Thy door, and hidest Thyself; and at the pains of the innocent Thou laughest.

In the meantime nevertheless Thou ravishest Thy lovers from all earthly things; above all desire of worldly things Thou takest them, and makest them takers of Thy love and full great workers in loving. Wherefore in ghostly song, of burning up bursting, to Thee they offer praises, and with sweetness they feel the dart of love.

Hail therefore O lovely Everlasting Love, that raisest us from these low things and presentest us with so frequent ravishings to the sight of God's

Majesty. Come into me, my Beloved! All that I had I gave for Thee, and that I should have, for Thee I have forsaken, that Thou in my soul mightest have a mansion for to comfort it. Never forsake Thou him that Thou feelest so sweetly glow with desire for Thee; so that with most burning desire I desire, to be ever within Thy halsing. So grant me grace to love Thee, and in Thee to rest, that in Thy kingdom I may be worthy for to see Thee withouten end.

CHAPTER III

THAT ILK MAN CHOSEN OF GOD HAS HIS STATE ORDAINED

Contemplative men that are highly burnt with the love of everlasting life are forsooth highest in this most lovely burning, and most beloved of the Lover Everlasting; so that they seldom or never go out to worldly business, nor yet receive the dignity of prelacy nor honours; but rather, certainly, withholding themselves within themselves, with joy and in song of praise they alway in mind ascend to Christ. Truly in this the kirk follows the hierarchy of angels, in the which the highest angels are not sent outward, being evermore near to God. They that are high in Christ's love and contemplation are so busy in the sight of God alone, that they take not sovereignty among men; but it is kept for others, that are more occupied with the business of man, and enjoy less of inward delight.

Therefore irk one chosen has his degree ordained before of God; so that whiles this one is chosen to prelacy, this other is busy to take heed to God within, and God within uplifts him thereto, so that he leaves all outward occupations. Soothly such are most holy and yet of men are held lowest, because they only dwell in mind for they seldom go outward to do miracles.

Others truly both submit themselves to God's service and discreetly govern their subjects.

Others also that live in fleshly penance, unseen in the sight of men, are oft-times in their lives granted or shown tokens; or else after their death, although they be full sharply punished some while in purgatory.

Truly all saints have not done miracles, either in their life or after their death; nor all damned have lacked miracles, either in their life or after their death. The doom truly of God is privy, lest, by seen tokens of sinners, evil should be made worse, and they that are good, despising those things that may be had in common by good and ill, should be more quick in the love of their Maker.

Some forsooth have wrought good deeds, but not God's but man's honour have they sought; and this perishes after their death, only having what they have desired in this world. Truly ofttimes it happens that the meanly good and less perfect, have done miracles; also full many of those high in devotion are placed in heavenly seats, and altogether rest before the Majesty of God, having their meed among the high companies of heaven. For the feast of Saint Michael is specially honoured, and yet he is not trowed of the highest order of angels.

Some also, turned to God and doing penance, and forsaking worldly errands, joy in mind if, after death, their name may be honoured among the living; to the which Christ's true servant should take no heed, as peradventure he may lose all that he works for.

Those things truly that are common to good and ill, are not to be desired by saints; but charity and ghostly virtues should be fastened without ceasing in their hearts; the which not only keep the soul from filth of sins, but in the doom shall raise the body also to endless memory.

All things that are done here soon cease and flee. There truly, either in honour or confession, they shall last withouten end. The active therefore and prelates, eminent in cunning and virtue, should set contemplative men before themselves, and hold them their betters before God; not trowing themselves worthy to be given to contemplation, unless peradventure God's grace to that should inspire them.

CHAPTER IV

THE DIFFERENCE BETWIXT GOD'S LOVERS AND THE WORLD'S: AND THEIR MEEDS

The soul of man feels nothing of the burning of endless love the which has not first perfectly forsaken all worldly vanity, studying busily to be given to heavenly things, and to desire God's love without ceasing, and mannerly to love all creatures to be loved. Truly if all things that we love, we love for God, rather God in them, than them we love; and so not in them but in God we delight, whom to enjoy withouten end we shall be glad.

The wicked truly love this world, setting therein the lust of their delectation; and those things only that belong to this world's joy, withouten ceasing they covet. And how may a man do more fondly, more wretchedly, or damnably than fully to love, for themselves only, transitory and failing things.

The Trinite God truly is to be loved for Himself only. Put we therefore our mind fully into it, and be we busy to bear all our thoughts unto that end, that withouten end we may be gladdened by it; so that ourselves and all things that we love, we love for that alone.

But that sinner lies that says he loves God and yet dreads not to serve sin. Ilk man truly that loves God is free, nor binds himself to bondage of sin, but steadfastly continues in the service of righteousness. Whiles we love earthly things or comfort for themselves, withouten doubt we love not God, serving Him not forsooth; but if we be delighted in creatures, so that we set our Maker behind, and care not to follow those things that are eternal, we shall be deemed as hating God. Full froward truly is it to the soul, and the token of damnation and of endless death, when a man gives himself wholly unto this world; and in divers desires and errors of the flesh, he goes as him lists. Thus no marvel a wretch is destroyed; and, while he seems to flow in pleasure, he hies to the aylasting penance of hell.

Therefore no man should dare presume, nor rise himself up by pride when he is despised to his reproach, or when insults are cast him; nor defend himself, nor for ill words give ill again; but all things, praise as well as reproof, bear evenly. Truly, doing in this wise, we shall withouten end with Christ be glad, if in this life we love Him without ceasing. Whose love, rooted in our hearts and made sicker, makes us like unto His likeness; and other joy, that is to say godly, He puts into us; mirthing our minds wholly with burning love. His love truly is fire, making our souls fiery and purging them from all degrees of sin, making them light and burning; which fire, burning in them that are chosen, ever makes them look up in mind, and continually to hold to the desire for death.

Wherefore, whiles we can sin, let us charge ourselves to flee this world's prosperity, and to bear adversity gladly. Forsooth an evil mind while it joys is lost, and while it seeks gladness in creatures it, as it were with a flattering venom, kills the self; whose contagion let us be well aware to eschew, beholding the ghostly food that is ordained in heaven for burning lovers.

And so, Christ granting, be we comforted by sweet songs of charity and be we delighted in so sweet devotion; while the wicked sleep in horrible darkness, and full of sins, go down to pains.

Full great marvel it seems that mortal man may be taken up into such high love for God that he feels nothing but heavenly solace in his most privy substance; and so as, in the noise of an organ, he ascends on high to contemplate high desire. That which is done by others to sorrow then turns to joy, so that they seem unable to suffer pain in soul; also they can not be troubled with the dread of death, nor in any way be moved from restfulness to unease.

Truly he who is stirred with busy love, and is continually with Jesu in thought, full soon perceives his own faults, the which correcting, henceforward he is ware of them; and so he brings righteousness busily to birth, until he is led to God and may sit with heavenly citizens in everlasting seats. Therefore he stands clear in conscience and is steadfast in all good ways the which is never noyed with worldly heaviness nor gladdened with vainglory.

Truly those obstinate in unclean works know not the love of Christ, for they are burned with fleshly likings; and they yield no devotion to God because of the burden of riches by the which they are thrust to the earth. They are not, forsooth, ordained to have the delights of paradise, but go on in their frowardness unto their death; and therefore, worthily, their heaviness shall not be lessened, nor shall the sorrow of their damnation be put aback; because they wilfully walk in lusts and sin, and have frowardly, for false love, lost the love of the Endless Lover. Wherefore in perpetual pains they shall plainly repent that they have sinned; and yet they shall never be cleansed from sin, but be burned endlessly by continued fires withouten any comforter.

CHAPTER V

WHEREFORE IT IS BETTER TO TAKE ENTENT TO THE LOVE OF GOD THAN TO KNOWLEDGE OR DISPUTATION

In all things that we work or think be we more taking heed to the love of God than to knowledge or disputation. Love truly delights the soul and makes conscience sweet, drawing it from love of lusty things here beneath, and from desire of man's own excellence. Knowledge without charity builds not to endless health but puffs up to most wretched undoing.

Be our souls therefore strong in the taking of hard labours for God; and be they wise with heavenly, not worldly, savour. May they desire to be lightened with endless wisdom, and to be inflamed by that fire with which some are stirred to love and desire our Maker only, and mightily are made strong to the despising of all transitory things. Not counting their greatest solace in these things that abide not, for they here have no dwelling, but without ceasing they seek the heavenly place not made with hands, and cry: Mihi vivere Christus est, et mori lucrum. Christ to me is life, and great winning to die.'

He forsooth truly loves God that consents to no wicked likings. Certainly man is far from Christ's love in as mickle as he delights himself in worldly things. Wherefore if thou love God thy work shows that; for he is never proved to love God whiles he is made to consent to wicked desires.

Therefore to all that are in this exile this I dare show: that all they that will not love the Maker of all things shall be cast into endless darkness; and there shall they that would not here be lightened with the love of their Gainbuyer feel the burning withouten end of the fire of hell. They shall be sundered from the company of singers, in charity with their Maker; and busily shall they sorrow cast out from the mirth of those singing in Jesu, wanting in the clearness and the joy of them that shall be crowned. For liever had they tarry a little while in worldly softness than suffer penance that their sins might be cleansed, and they might come full of piety before the Defender of all good.

Truly, in this vale of weeping, they have been delighted in the slippery way and the broad; where is no place of gladness but of labour, wherefore in torments withouten release they shall sorrow: when the poor, which were arrayed with virtues, shall be born to everlasting peace and be made glad in the delight of full truly seeing the Life-giving Godhead. And in ghostly heat they have happily flourished, although they have taken no solace in the worthy height of this world, nor have sown pride among foolish wise men; but they have borne griefs from wicked men, and have excluded temptations from the soul that they might be holden in peace at the throne of the Trinity. And they have truly voided old unthriftiness of venomous life, clearly and most gladly praising ghostly beauty; and plays of softness, which youth accepts and unwise worldly men desire, they have deems worthy reproof, thinking with continuance of the song full of charity ascending to our Maker.

For which thing the receivers of the joy of love, conceiving heat that may not be consumed, join together in song of clear chorus; and in lovely harmony and friendly mirth have they set a heavenly shadow against all heat of lechery and filth. Wherefore in this burning of sweetest love they are taken up to the beholding of their Beloved, and by means of this most happy flame they are flourishing in virtue, and freely enjoy their Maker: and their mind, changed, now passes into the melody that lasts. And from henceforth their thoughts become song, and heaviness being cast out, the hall of their soul is fulfilled with wonderful music, so that it has entirely lost the former pricking and evermore abides whole in high sweetness, full marvellously singing in heavenly sweet meditation.

Furthermore when they go from this hardness and from the diseases that happen here, then the time comes that they shall be taken, and withouten doubt be born withouten sorrow to God, and have their seats among the seraphim; for they are altogether set on fire with the most high fire of love, burning within their souls. So sweetly and devoutly have they loved God that whatsoever they have felt in themselves was ghostly heat, heavenly song and godly sweetness. Herefore it is truly that they die without heaviness, soothly passing with joy; and are lift up unto so great a degree in endless worship, and are crowned in the contemplation of the great plenteousness of their Maker, singing with clearest choirs; the which also more burningly desire after that Godhead that rules all things.

And forsooth though now they clearly behold the chere of truth, and are moistened with the most delectable sweetness of the Godhead, yet no marvel if after a little while they shall be made more marvellous: when the bodies of the saints, that are at this time holden in earth, shall be raised from their graves, and their souls shall be knitted to them in the last examination. Then forsooth shall they take principality among the peoples, and the unrighteous shall they deem to be damned; and they shall show that the meanly good were blessed to come to Blissfulness. The general doom thus done, soothly they shall be borne into everlasting song, and go up with Christ to the height of truth, enjoying the Face of God in love withouten end.

By this it is shown that everlasting sweetness moistens their minds, the which binds the bands of true charity, unable to be loosed. Wherefore let us seek rather that the love of Christ burn within us than that we take heed to unprofitable disputation. Whiles truly we take heed to unmannerly seeking, we feel not the sweetness of the eternal savour. Wherefore many now so mickle savour in the burning of knowledge and not of love, that plainly they know not what love is, or of what savour; although the labour of all their study ought to spread unto this end, that they might burn in the love of God. Alas, for shame! An old wife is more expert in God's love, and less in worldly pleasure, than the great divine, whose study is vain. For why, for vanity he studies, that he may appear glorious and so be known, and may get rents and dignities: the which is worthy to be held a fool, and not wise.

CHAPTER VI

CONCERNING HERETICS: AND FAITH IN THE TRINITY

The plenteousness and the whole of holy truth shows itself to them that seek it; and to the children of unity hidden mysteries are open. Wherefore, soothly, springs the frowardness of heretics but from an untaught and inordinate mind, which is blinded by desire of its own excellence? For truly they cease not to resist God within themselves by vain desires; and it is also by their earning that with open arguments they gainstand the truth outwardly.

When the Christian religion wills to cut away all that is contrary, and fully accord in unity of love, the manner of heretics and the proud is to get new opinions, and to make known questions, unwont and from the saying of holy kirk; and so those thing that true Christian men hold holy they joy to scatter with their vanities.

Whose errors casting away we say: Truly the Son of God, even to the Father, and without beginning, is evermore to be trowed and understood; for except the Father had begotten Him without beginning, truly the full Godhead should not have been in Him. Soothly if God had been at sometime the Father when He had no Son, then no marvel He was less than afterward, when He had gotten a Son; that shall no man of good mind say.

Therefore God unchangeable begets God unchangeable; and whom He has begotten from eternity He ceases not this day also to beget. For neither might the substance of the Son be called at any time unbegotten, nor the being of the Getter ever be conscious of Himself without any only begotten Son of Himself. Truly even as the beginning of the Godhead may not be found of reason or wit because it has not beginning, so the generation of the Son with the eternal Godhead unchangingly abides.

When truly the marvel and worship of God almighty shows itself clearly in infinity, without beginning, to what end shall man's folly raise itself in striving to make known to the ears of mortal men a sacrament unable to be spoken? He truly knows God perfectly that feels Him incomprehensible and unable to be known. Nothing, soothly, is perfectly known unless the cause thereof, how and in what wise it is, be perfectly known. In this present life we know in part and we understand in part; in the life to come, truly, we shall know perfectly and fully, as is lawful or speedful to creatures. Forsooth he that desires to know of our Everlasting Maker above that that is profitable, without doubt falls fonder from perfect knowledge of Him.

Thou askest what God is? I answer shortly to thee: such a one and so great is He that none other is or ever may be of like kind or so mickle. If thou wilt know properly to speak what God is, I say thou shalt never find an answer to this question. I have not known; angels know not; archangels have not heard. Wherefore how wouldest thou know what is unknown and also unteachable? Truly God that is almighty may not teach thee what He Himself is. For if thou knew what God is thou shouldest be as wise as God is: that neither thou nor any other creature may be.

Stand therefore in thy degree, and desire not high things. For if thou desirest to know what God is, thou desirest to be God; the which becomes thee not. Wot thou well God alone knows Himself, and may know. Truly it is not of God's unpower that He may not teach thee Himself as He is in Himself, but for His inestimable worthiness; for such a one as He is, none other may be. Soothly if He might be truly known, then were He not incomprehensible. It is enough for thee therefore to know that God is; and it were against thee if thou would know what God is.

Also it is to be praised to know God perfectly; that is to say, He being unable to be fully conceived: knowing Him to love Him; loving Him to sing in Him; singing to rest in Him, and by inward rest to come to endless rest. Let it not move thee that I have said to know God perfectly, and I have denied that He may be known: since the prophet in the psalm has said: Praetende misericordiam tuam scientibus te, that is to say: Thy mercy show to them knowing Thee.' But thus understand this authority if thou wilt not err: To them knowing Thee,' that is to say: God is to be loved, to be praised, to be worshipped and glorified, the only Maker of all things; above all things; through all things; and in all things; that is blessed in the world of worlds. Amen.

CHAPTER VII

THAT IN THE GODHEAD WE OUGHT NOT TO SAY THREE GODS OR THREE ESSENCES, AS WE SAY THREE PERSONS: AND THAT ILK MAN SHALL BE CALLED GREAT OR SMALL AFTER THE QUANTITY OF HIS LOVE

If any, erring, would say in the Trinity are three Essences because they say three Persons, why should they not also say three Gods; since to God it is all one to be God and to be His Essence? We say truly, the Father is God; the Son is God; the Holy Ghost is God; the Father also is His Essence; the Son is His

Essence; the Holy Ghost is His Essence: and yet not three Gods nor three Essences we say; but one God and three Persons to be of one Essence, with strong faith we grant.

One Godhead truly there is, of three Persons, full and perfect; and ilk Person in the self contains the whole Godhead; evenhood and onehood, forsooth, having after the Substance of the Godhead; not lacking distinction of diversity after the property of the Name.

They are also three Persons and one god; one Essence; one Substance; one Godhead: and, though ilk Person betokens the Essence, although there be three Persons yet three Essences shall not therefore be understood. And as our God, the Father the Son and the Holy Ghost we call one Essence and not three, so we shall say the High Trinity to be three Persons, not one alone.

The Father is so called, because of Himself He gat a Son; the Son is so called, because of the Father He is gotten; the Holy Ghost, because of both the Holy Father and the Holy Son He is inspired. The Father, Life, getting the Son, Life, has given to Him His whole Substance: so that the Father should be as mickle in His Son as in Himself (and the Son is not less in the Father than in Himself). But the Father has taken His Essence of none; the Son truly of His Father alone has taken in His birth that He is; the Holy Ghost forsooth of the Father and the Son forth passing, and with Them and in Them endlessly being, is no more in Himself than in Either: for truly He is even and everlasting with Them of whom He is; since He is of the same Substance, of the same Kind, and of the same Godhead; and the third Person in the Trinity.

Truly the everlasting Son of the Father is become Man in time, born of a maiden, that He might gainbuy man from the fiend's power. This is our Lord Jesus Christ: the which only be fastened in our minds the which for us only was tied on the cross.

Nothing truly is so sweet as to love Christ. And therefore ransack we not too mickle those things that we in this life may not conceive. Truly in heaven they shall be clearer than light, if we give all our hearts to love God. For we shall be able to be taught of God; and we shall joy in full marvellous melody, and in high mirth praise our Maker, in full sweet easiness without grief and irksomeness and withouten end.

He forsooth that loves mickle is great, and he that loves least is least: for after the greatness of the charity we have in us, shall we be praised before God. So is it not before men, but he that has most riches or goods is most considered and especially dreaded; when they ought not so to do, but most honour and dread them that they suppose be best in knowledge.

Truly the mighty men of this world can do nothing but for their bodies or their goods. Holy men truly have more worthiness; for they shall have power to spar heaven to them that disease them and would not therefore do penance: and also to open heaven to them that have honoured them in God, and maintained them in this exile: whiles they were arrayed with charity and have not received vainglory. Wherefore they should travail to get, to have, and to hold to charity with all their might and all their strength, that in the day of temptation they may manfully stand against the enemy; and when they shall be proved they may receive the crown of life. Charity truly makes men perfect; and only those loving perfectly are granted to come to the height of contemplative life.

And truly the poor, although they be clad with heaviness and uncleanness, yet they should not be despised; for they are friends of God and breathren of Christ, if they bear the burden of poverty with deeds of praise. Then sickerly the persons ye despised without, ye honour within as heavenly citizens; and in so mickle as ye grow to honour them for God, in so mickle He privily works in His Godhead; the which, comforting them, says: Beati pauperes quoniam vestrum est regnum Dei, that is to say: Blessed be ye poor, for yours is the kingdom of God.'

For the great tribulation and need that they suffer in this life they are purged of their sins. For whiles the poor man is noyed in body with hunger, thirst, cold, nakedness and other griefs of this world, he is purged in soul from uncleanness and worldly filth. And truly in the time to come poor men shall feel the sweeter rest of the everlasting, in as mickle as in this life they have borne most grievous labours. It shall belong to them truly to say: Laetati sumus pro diebus quibus nos humiliasti, annis quibus vidimus mala; that is to say: Gladdened are we for the days in which Thou hast meeded us, for the years in which we have seen grief.'

Wherefore halse the burden of poverty with joy, and have mind to bear goodly other wretchedness; that by the sufferance of tribulation thou mayest be worthy to come to the joy of everlasting peace!

CHAPTER VIII

THAT THE PERFECT LOVER OF GOD HAD LIEVER RUN INTO GREAT PAIN THAN BY SIN ONCE GRIEVE GOD: AND WHY GOD TORMENTS THE RIGHTEOUS BY THE WICKED

From the great fire of love so great beauty of virtue grows in souls that a righteous man would rather choose to suffer all pain than once grieve God; although he knew he might rise by penance and afterward please God more and be holier. For ilk one perfect understands this: that nothing is more dear to God than innocence, nothing more pleasing than good will. For truly if we love God rightly we would sooner lose great meed in heaven than once sin venially; for most righteous is it to ask no meed of righteousness but the friendship of God, that is Himself. Therefore it is better ever to suffer tormentry than once, wilfully and knowingly, to be led from righteousness to wickedness.

Wherefore it follows that they who so burningly love Christ that they will in no wise sin, not only shall be free from pain, but shall joy endlessly with angels. They truly that serve wicked deeds, and ween that worldly and fleshly solace is to be greatly loved, loving those things they desire, forsooth they lose both the joy that they love, and run into the wickedness that they eschewed not.

But it is wont to be asked by some why God almighty chastises the wicked and the righteous together. Thou seest under the flail both corn and chaff at once; but in the winnowing the chaff is cast out and the corn is busily gathered to man's use. If all men lived truly, without doubt we should dwell in peace and tranquillity, withouten debate and battle; but since among the few good are many evil, many diseases comes that evil may be chastised: and thus evil things happen to good men because they are mingled with the evil unto their death. The righteous also, because they are ready to sin, so that their readiness be not brought to deed are taught to take a light scouring here, that they may escape the bitter scouring that is to come.

Therefore if thou suffer persecution, wretchedness, and other diseases, thou hast that which accords to the place in the which thou dwellest. Is not this the vale of tears and tribulations in which thou art? How wouldest thou therefore be glad in prison, and live in all prosperity in thine exile, or go thy long pilgrimage withouten diseases? Have mind that Christ and His apostles have suffered tormentry, and thou by bliss seekest to come to joy! But thou shalt not. Forsooth either, in this life, the fire of God's love shall waste the rust of our sins and cleanse our souls to make them able to flee to bliss, or else, after this life, the fire of purgatory shall punish our souls, if it happen we escape the fire of hell. Or else, if the strength of love be not so mickle in us that it can altogther burn us, it behoves us to be cleansed with tribulation, sickness and dis-eases.

This also we have withouten doubt: that no young man can be made holy among flatterings, and sweet words of fair women, and plenteousness of liking things, unless it be by the untrowed greatness of God's grace; where so many and so great things stir many to fall, so that holy men have also ofttimes been lost. Wherefore I trow it is a great miracle when man by the grace of God and the love of Christ perfectly despises these cherishings and manfully goes up betwixt these enemies to the soul—although they seem soft to the flesh—to the high holiness of heavenly contemplation. And, withouten fail, the holier he is and the more plenteously filled within with the solace of God's love, alt-hough he be set in the fire, he knows not how to burn; and the foul lusts of an unclean life offering themselves, he has perfectly slakened them.

It is no marvel (that sometimes), though it be seldom, Christ works in some beloved to Him, of whom it is said: Expandit nubem in protectionem eorum, et ignem ut luceret eis per noctem; that is to say: He has spread a cloud, the shadow of God's grace, for their defence against fleshly desires, and the fire of endless love to give them light within to mind, through the night of this life, that they be not taken by the unlawfulness of vain beauty. Truly Christ's love burns in them with so great sweetness, that all fleshly and unlaw-ful liking they think of as most foul, and therefore they despise it.

Therefore touch thou not lecherously that which is lawful neither to desire nor to have. Have in mind also to withhold thy hand, thy tongue, and thy body; and displease not they conscience concerning women. Truly the stirrings of lechery are the array of men and women. Also hot lectuaries, and other meats that with their heat too mickle enflame the flesh—which nourishers of bodies and killers of souls are busy to make—should be eschewed by the chaste.

CHAPTER IX

THAT GOD IS TO BE LOVED AND WORSHIPPED IN DISEASES: AND ALSO OF THE MIRTH AND MEEKNESS OF THE GOOD

If temporal honour be destroyed by shame, and worldly be ended by villainy, it is known without doubt that reproach is better than worship, shame than high degree, and heaviness than praise. For by these things a man ofttimes slides into vainglory; by the other always, if a man bear it patiently, he in this life shall be taught meekness, and in the time to come shall suffer no pain—for God will not punish the righteous twice—and he shall be crowned: for the patience of the poor will not perish in the end.

Truly to holiness these things belong: first, to think, speak and do in no manner what displeases God; and then, to think, speak, and work what may please God. Do this after thy knowledge, so that thou neither fall into slander nor feign too mickle holiness. For he is a fool that desires to appear holy before men; and cruel that shows himself evil when he is good.

Some things truly there are that, taken heed unto, in themselves are neither good nor evil, for in their pure nature they are neither meedful nor unmeedful; and if such things be done they displease not God; nor if they be left undone please not God. For here we may see, smell, touch, and yet earn no meed or unmeed. All sin truly is done either to God's displeasing, or our neighbour's noying, or to our own harm. But many things may be found among men that are none of these. Truly to be despised, or lost, in the sight of men, makes man ascend to the joy of angels.

O good Jesu here chastise, here cut, here smite, here burn; yea, and whatsoever please Thy goodiness do to me, so that in the time to come I have none ill, but may feel Thy love here and everlastingly. To be despised by all men in confusion and shame for Thee, is sweeter to me than to be called brother by an earthly king, and to be honoured among all men and of all men. May wretchedness fall on me on ilka side in this life, so that Thou God spare me in the other. I will to be chastised and corrected here; and Christ that grant to me, if otherwise I may not escape pain to come.

The proud truly and those full of wrath seem to themselves so worthy that they can suffer nothing. Ofttimes at a light word and without cause they are moved. Therefore they are to be fled more than to be overcome, for they are froward. And that they have taken up they alway defend, though it be false or untrue; and neither with authority nor reason will they be overcome, that they should not be seen to have said what were unaccording. And when they are untaught—and that they wot well—yet they will behave as if they were inspired in all things that belong to God, so that they may speak in every place without the gainsaying of any man; and they had liever dwell still in error than be openly reproved for it.

Brethren, leave this proud madness and mad pride, and let us greatly meek ourselves whiles we are in this way: for it is better, lovely, and good that after our death Christ say to us, Friend, come uppermore,' than that He say Carl, go downermore': so truly shall it be of the meek and the proud.

Wherefore no tribulation, no disease, no wretchedness, no shame, no reproach is to dreaded by the righteous man as long as he sins not and always profits in contemplative life and the love of God. Truly before we may come to that kingly hall, in which, filled with sweetness, we shall be glad with the angels of God and all His saints, it befalls us here to be reproved by flatterers and wrong sayers; by fawners and backbiters; by praisers and blamers; so that, when we shall be examined, we may be found alway given to Christ's precepts and His counsel, in all patience and meekness and charity; as it is written: Tanquam aurum in fornace probavit eos; that is to say: As gold he has proved them in the furnace,' that has fire on ilka side, and has found them worthy to have Himself. Thus let us go through adversity and prosperity, through fire and water, unto the time we come to the refreshing of the heavenly life.

Have mind also that in all diseases and need and poverty thou never grumble, nor speak fondly nor frowardly—but in all things give thanks to God. Thereby truly shalt thou be lifted up more joyfully to the kingdom of the saints, if in this world thou suffer gladly the things beforesaid.

O my soul, among all things that happen praise thy Lord with liking devotion; praising, feel with sweetness; and singing, taste with honeysweet devotion, saying: Laudabo Dominum in vita mea, that is to say, I shall worship my Lord in my life,' whether I be diseased or eased: whether I receive honour or shame. As long as I am, I shall sing to my God. If I rest, I sing in Jesu; and if I suffer persecution, I forget not the love of God. Truly it is enough for me to love my God, and to come to Him; since I can do no other or feel myself disposed to the work of no other things but to love Christ.

And yet, I come not to as great love of God as mine elder fathers, the which have also done many other profitable things; whereof I am full greatly ashamed in myself, and confused. Therefore, O Lord, make broad my heart that it may be more able to perceive Thy love. Truly the more able man is to receive, so mickle the more of charity he takes and savours, and the less he cares for the flesh; but with discretion, so that it be with him after the sentence of the wise:

Modicum mihi laboravi et inveni mihi multam requiem; that is to say: A little have I travailed with myself, and I have found great rest to myself.' For after a few years of this life the righteous have found rest for everlasting.

The holy lover of God shows himself neither too merry nor full heavy in this habitation of exile, but he has cheerfulness with ripeness. Forsooth some reprove laughter and some praise it. Laughter therefore which is from lightness and vanity of mind is to be reproved, but that truly that is of gladness of conscience and ghostly mirth is to be praised; the which is only in the right-eous, and it is called mirth in the love of God. Wherefore if we be glad and merry, the wicked call us wanton; and if we be heavy, hypocrites.

Seldom, soothly, can any man trow in another good that he finds not in himself; and he weens another has the sin into which he stumbles. And the deed of the wicked is this: that if any follow not their life, they trust that he goes wrong and is deceived; and this is because he has forsaken meekness. The degrees also of meekness are: to hold the eyes low, not high; to have a measure in speech, and not to pass it; to hear gladly their betters and those more wise; and to will wisdom should be heard from others, rather than from themselves. Not to take the time of speaking too soon. Not to go from common life. To set others before thyself; to know thy frailties and to deem thyself worse than all others. If truly I wished to come among men, I have desired that I might sit last in number, and be held least in opinion, and so all my joy should be in Christ Jesu; and thus I should take no heed to man's praising or blaming, but with busy devotion I should desire after God.

Forsooth many that have spoken with me were like to scorpions; for they have fawned with their flattering head, and with their backbiting tail have smitten; from whose wicked lips and sorrowful tongue God shall deliver my soul, setting it in the joy of rest.

But whence is come so great madness into man's mind that none will be blamed, none will be reproved, but all truly seek to be praised; they joy in honour, and laugh in favour. They also bear the name of a holier life; but to me such seem either above measure holy, or else mad, although they be called wise and taught. For who of good mind is there who leaves himself, not taking heed to himself, and gladdens himself in the void words of vain men? Truly if he beholds himself busily, and cares to know of what kind he is in thought and deed, he may soon understand himself, and may find whether he be worthy of praise or reproof.

When therefore he sees himself in many things worthy of blame and in few things to be praised, he should not take with gladness the honour or favour of which he is not worthy; unless he be mad and has erred in mind. Truly, if carefully considering himself, he finds he waxes marvellously warm in the heat and sweetness of God's love, and rises highly in contemplative life, and also in this continually stands; and has also in mind that either he has not done great sins, or if he have done any he trows they be cleansed by true penance: then truly it behoves him not to sorrow for the honour of men, because clearly he was more worthy of the fellowship of angels.

Whosoever is thus disposed should no more joy to sit with a king than with a poor man; for he takes no heed to riches and honours from men, but unto the life and meeds of ilka man. He holds it not great to shine in gold, nor to be umbelapped with a great menge, nor to go in purple and be glad in the array of bishops: but truly he sets a holy and sweet conscience before all pleasures and riches.

CHAPTER X

THAT GOD'S LOVER FORSAKES THE WORLD, IDLENESS AND IRKSOMENESS: AND OF HYPOCRITES AND COVETOUS MEN

It is said in the Canticles: Love is strong as death and love is hard as hell.' Death truly kills the quick; hell soothly spares not the dead. So, certainly, the love of God not only utterly kills the love of this world in the man that it perfectly ravishes, but also, being slain to the world and quickened to heaven, it stirs him to suffer full mickle tribulation and worldly wretchedness for God.

Wherefore whosoever thou mayest be that hopest that thou lovest Christ to this take heed; for if thou yet behold earthly things with delight, and also find thy soul high to suffer wrongs or else death, thou showest forsooth that thou art not God's true lover. Soothly a true lover neither dresses his eyes to the world, nor dreads to suffer all that seems heavy or hard to the body for God; and whosoever happen to him yet he is not let from the thought of Jesu his Beloved.

Thou also that either art God's lover, or with thy whole mind desirest to be, study alway, as mickle as thou canst by Christ's grace, not to be noyed by irksomeness, nor to be taken with idleness. And if it sometimes happen that sweet easiness be not to thee in praying or in good thinking, and that thou be not made high in mind by the song of holy contemplation, and thou canst not sing as thou wast wont; yet cease not to read or pray, or else do some other good deed, inward or outward, that thou slide not into idleness or sloth.

Irksomeness, soothly, has drawn many to idleness; and idleness, to negligence and wickedness.

Wherefore be thou alway fervent in as mickle as in thee is; and have not thy desire bowed to anything of this world that may be had or desired. No man truly is perfectly knit to God, whiles he is bound in desire to any worldly creature.

There are some also that seem outwardly oned to God, and within they are given to fiends. These are simulators and false men, that challenge the wrath of God. Feigners forsooth they are, that despise the world with their words, and with their deeds are known to love it too mickle. They will be seen speaking of God, and are so mickle taken up within with love of money that they also strive sometimes for the weight of two halfpence. The which, opening their mouth to desire God, are utterly wanting in charity; and whiles they have no heat of faith and charity they show themselves most holy in gait, clothing, and speech. These also, moreover, boast themselves steadfast in light diseases, but when they come thereto where they should gainstand, there they are soonest broken, and there they fall. And then what before was hid is openly shown. Yet when they abound in riches and are fed with riches, they say they eat full little, and that they have so great thought that all this world is but vanity, that, as they say, they can scarcely last for feebleness. Deceitful also are they, because they have worldly wisdom; and they beguile by that, so that they are not perceived by others lying in wait, in as mickle as they are aware; and hiding covetousness under the title of ghostly rest, they eschew loss of worldly goods, in despite of things everlasting.

But such, although they lurk for a time, withouten doubt it shall appear of what kind they have been long before the end, or at least in the end. The which do alms, or any other deed they do, in the sight of men; that it may be seen of all men. And such worthily provoke the wrath of God for they desire, not to be, but to be seen holy; and within, where God sees, wanting in true charity, they challenge their own joy not God's.

Full hard it truly is [to have riches, and not to love them, and not less difficult is it] to have a winning craft or office, and not to be covetous. Wherefore ofttimes are priests defamed among the people: that though they be chaste they are found covetous, if they be generous they are made lechers. And ofttimes it happens that having taken the order of priesthood, they fall as mickle deep into sin as the degree which they unworthily have taken is high. Truly not a few, set on fire with noisome covetousness, under colour of sickness or poverty that may come say they gather their goods that they may eschew sudden wretchedness. But they are beguiled by fiends, for they both lose worldly goods, and run into the darkness that they dread, because they heed not God that delivers His servants in His sight: and that is worst of all, whiles within they are fulfilled with worldly covetousness, without they seem to themselves to shine with tokens of holiness.

But he that is our Lord's servant trusts in our Lord; and distributes the goods which he has over his need, to them that need. The servant of the world truly studies to keep evilly all that he has, because of his covetousness which is unable to be fulfilled: so great a niggard is he that he dare not eat, save foully and scarcely, so that, being sparing, he may gather mickle money. And these are they that the psalmist shames saying: Inimici ejus terram lingent; that is to say: His enemies shall lick the earth.'

CHAPTER XI

THAT LOVERS OF GOD SHALL DEEM WITH HIM: AND OF THE LOVE OF KNOWLEDGE GOTTEN BY LABOUR, AND OF GOD: AND THAT A TRUE LOVER ERRS NOT, NOR IS BEGUILED NEITHER WITH FASTING NOR ABSTINENCE, COUNSEL NOR PRESUMPTION

Man's soul is the taker of God only; anything less than God cannot fulfill it: wherefore earthly lovers never are fulfilled. The rest therefore of Christ's lovers is when their hearts are fastened by desire and thought in the love of God; and loving, burning and singing, contemplate Him.

Sweetest forsooth is the rest which the spirit takes whiles sweet godly sound comes down, in which it is delighted, and in most sweet and playful songs the mind is ravished to sing the delights of everlasting love. Now forsooth the praise of God sounds again in the mouth, and of the blest Maiden, in whom it joys more than may be trowed. And no marvel that this happens, whiles the heart of the singer is utterly burnt with heavenly fire and is figured into His likeness, in the which is all sweet and merry song, moistening our affections with heavenly savour. And therefore he abounds with inward delights, and in song and thought joys in the burning of love.

This truly is untrowable to all mortals; and he that has this trows not that anything so sweet and full of sweetness can be perceived by man, being yet in body that will rot, and being grieved with the fetters of mortality. The haver marvels also, but is gladdened, because of the goodness, unable to be told, of

God, that gives His goods plenteously and upbraids not; of whom he receives all that he feels.

Forsooth when that great thing wants—and truly it is called great formerly to mortals it is nearly unknown—he never trows himself to be in prosperity, but alway languishes in love; whiles he wakes he continually sings, or thinks, of love and of his lover: and if he be alone the more sweetly he sings.

Truly from the time that any man has received this, never afterwards shall he fully go from it; but evermore shall heat, sweetness, or singing—if all these be not near—bide. But all these truly bide together, unless they be repressed by full great sickness of the head, or of the breast, or of the side; or by great hunger or thirst by the which the flesh is broken; or with too mickle cold or heat or with travel, they be let.

Therefore it behoves him that will sing in God's love, and in singing will rejoice and burn, to be in the wilderness, and not to live in too mickle abstinence; nor to be given in any wise to superfluity or waste. Nevertheless it were better for him in little things to pass measure unknowingly, whiles he does it with good intent to sustain nature, than if for too mickle fasting he began to fail, and for feebleness of body he could not sing. But withouten doubt he that is chosen to this neither in eating nor in abstinence is overcome by falsehood of the fiend. Truly the true lover of Christ, and taught of Christ, with no less study is ware of too mickle than of too little. Withouten comparison truly shall he be worthy of more meed, that with songful joy, praying, contemplating, reading and meditating, and eating well but discreetly; than if he, withouten this, should fast evermore, or should eat bread alone or herbs, and should continually pray and read.

Eaten have I and drunken of this that seemed best, not because I loved pleasantness, but because nature must be sustained in the service of God and in the praise of Jesu Christ; conforming myself in good manners to them with whom I dwelt for Christ; and that I should not feign holiness where none is, nor that men should praise me too mickle where I was full little to be praised. From divers, also, I have gone, not because they fed me commonly or in hard measure, but because we have not accorded in manners, or for some other reasonable cause. Nevertheless I dare say, with blessed Job: Fools have despised me; and when I have gone from them they have backbitten me; nevertheless they shall be ashamed when they see me that have said that I would not abide but where I might be delicately fed.' It is better truly to see what I may despise, than to desire what I may not see.

No marvel that fasting is full good to cast down the desires of the flesh, and to make tame wild wantonness of mind. Truly fleshly desires lie as it were slaked in him who goes to the height of contemplation by song and the burning of love. For the death of ill affections belongs to him that takes heed to contemplation; whose soul is also turned within into another joy and another form. He lives now not to himself, but Christ truly lives in him; wherefore he melts in His love, and languishes within himself, and nearly fails for sweetness: he scarcely lives for love. His soul is it that says: Nunciate dilecto quia amore langueo: that is to say: Show to my Beloved, that I languish for love.' I desire to die: I covet to be loosed: full greatly I yearn to go. Behold for love I die! Lord, come down! Come, my Beloved, lift me from heaviness. Behold I love: I sing: I am full hot: I burn within myself. Have mercy upon me, wretched; bidding me be brought before Thee.

He that has this joy, and in this life is thus gladdened, is inspired of the Holy Ghost: he cannot err, whatever he do it is lawful. No mortal man can give him counsel so good as that is that he has in himself of God Immortal. If others truly would give counsel to him, withouten doubt they shall err because they have not known him: and if he would give assent to their skills he shall not be suffered of God that constrains him to His will, that he pass it not. Wherefore of such is said: Spiritualis omnia judicat, et a nemine judicatur; that is to say: The ghostly man deems all things, and is deemed of no man.'

But no man may be of so great presumption that he suppose himself to be such a one; although he has perfectly forsaken all the world, and though he has led a solitary life, unable to be reproved, and though he has gone up to the contemplation of heavenly things. For this grace truly is not granted to all contemplatives, but seldom, and to most few: the which, taking great rest of body and of mind, are only chosen to the work by the strength of God's love. Full hard soothly it is to find such a man; and because they are few, full dear are they held, desirable, and beloved before God and man; and angels also joy in their passing from this world, whom angels company becomes.

Many forsooth there are that oft, in great devotion and sweetness, offer their prayers to God, and praying and meditating they can feel sweetness of contemplation; the which also run not about but bide in rest.

CHAPTER XII

THAT NO MAN SHALL DEEM ANOTHER, BUT GIVE GOD PRAISE: AND OF EIGHT AFFECTIONS OF THE LOVE OF GOD: AND THAT WOMEN'S COMPANY BE ESCHEWED

If any man live holily and righteously, he also despises not the worst sinners. Truly they, being tempted, fall because they have no grace of gainstanding, although by their own malice they turn themselves from good to ill. No man can work well, and love God, and be chaste, except God give it to him. Also thou that swellest in pride because thou hast done well, for thou hast restrained thyself from fleshly lusts and thou hast suffered sharp penance, wherefore thou hast taken praise from the mouth of man: have mind that, except the goodliness of Christ had overcovered thee, thou shouldest have fallen into as many ills, or into worse, than he that is fallen. Truly of thyself thou hadst no grace of gainstanding, but of Him, to Whom is said: Diligam te Domine, fortitudo mea. 'Thee, Lord my strength, I shall love.' Wherefore, if thou have nought but that thou hast received, why pridest thou thyself as if thou hadst not received it?

I forsooth do thanks to my God; the which, without my merit, has so chastened His child—for my good and His honour—has so made His servant fear, that it seems full sweet to me to flee worldly pleasures, that are both few and soon slipping; in no mickle that I might be worthy to escape the pains of hell, that are both many and shall never end. And yet again He has so taught me, and given me virtuous teaching, that I should gladly bear this present penance and tribulation; in so mickle that I might come full lightly to everlasting delectation and most full prosperity. For if we will, in this life lightly and without great sharpness, we can perfectly repent and cleanse ourselves; as long as we, as mickle as we can, destroy vice. If we be not cleansed here, truly in the time to come, we shall find that the Apostle is true, saying these words: Horrendum est incidere in manus Dei viventis. 'Horrible is it to fall into the hands of the living God.'

Lord God, have mercy on me! My youth was fond; my childhood vain; my young age unclean. But now Lord Jesu my heart is enflamed with Thy holy love and my reins are changed; and my soul also will not now touch for bitterness what before was my food: and my affections now are such that I hate nothing but sin. Nought dread I but to grieve God: I joy not but in God: I sorrow not but for my sins: I love nothing but God: nothing I trust but Him: nothing heavies me but sin: nothing gladdens me but Christ.

Nevertheless now, lately, of three worthy women I worthily received reproof . . . Forsooth coming to myself I do praise to God, because by their words He taught me good, and has shown to me a sweeter way than I knew before; that Christ's grace so mickle working in me, I shall not be found worthy reproof in this way before women.

The fourth woman, to whom I was in part familiar, not reproving but as it were despising me, said: Nought hast thou but fair looks and fair words, deeds hast thou none.'

And therefore I trow it is better to want their speciality than to fall into their hands, that know not, either in love nor in despite, to keep measure. This truly has happened to me because I have sought their health; not that I have unlawfully desired anything of them with whom I have for some while taken my bodily sustenance.

CHAPTER XIII

THAT SOLITARY OR HERMIT'S LIFE PASSES COMMON AND MIXED LIFE. AND HOW IT COMES TO FIRE OF LOVE: AND OF SWEETNESS OF SONG

Some have been and peradventure are yet alive that alway set common life before solitary life; saying we ought to run to gatherings if we desire to come to high perfection. Against whom there is not mickle to dispute, because that life only they bear up with praise, the which they either covet to keep, or at the least know full little. Truly they praise not solitary life, for they know it not.

Truly there is a life which no man living in flesh can know, but he to whom it is given of God to have; and soothly no man deems truly of this thing, of which he is yet unsicker what, and in what manner, it works. Withouten doubt, I wot if they knew it more than another they would praise it.

Others err worse that cease not to reprove and slander solitary life, saying: Vae soli; that is to say: Woe be to a man alone'; not expounding alone' as without God', but without a fellow.' He truly is alone with whom God is not; for when he falls into death he is taken alive to tormentry, and is sparred from the joyful sight of God and of His saints.

Forsooth he that chooses solitary life for God, and leads it in good manner, is not near woe but fair virtue; and the name of Jesu shall continually delight his mind; and the more they dread not to take that life without man's solace, the more shall it be given them to be gladdened with God's comforting.

Ghostly visitations forsooth ofttimes they receive; the which, set in company, they know not at all. Therefore it is said to a beloved soul: Ducam cam in solitudinem, et ibi loquar ad car ejus. That is to say: I shall lead her into the wilderness, and there shall I speak unto her heart.'

Some truly are taught by God to desire the wilderness for Christ, and to hold a single purpose; the which forthwith, that they may more freely and devoutly serve God, forsaking the common clothing of the world, despise all transitory things, and cast away temporal things; and excelling in height of mind they desire only everlasting joy, and are only given to devotion and contemplation, and every effort of their life they cease not to give to the love of Christ. Of whom full many, although from men they dwell full far, yet they stumble not from heavenly desires, because their minds are full far from wicked conversation.

The righteous hermits have also a single purpose. They live in the charity of God and of their neighbour; they despise worldly praise; as mickle as they can they flee man's sight; they hold ilk man more worthy than themselves; they continually give their minds to devotion; they hate idleness; they manly gainstand fleshly lusts; they savour and burningly seek heavenly; earthly they covet not, but forsake; in sweetness of prayer they are delighted. Truly some of them feel the sweetness of eternal refreshment; and with chaste heart and body, with the undefiled eye of the mind, truly behold God and the citizens of heaven. Because by the bitter drink of penance they have loved great labour, they are now set afire with the love of high contemplation, and alone are worthy to take heed to God, and to bide the kingdom of Christ.

Therefore great is the hermit's life if it be greatly done. And truly the blessed Maglorius was full of miracles, and from his childhood gladdened by the sight of angels. When according to the prophecy of his former father, Saint Sampson, he was made archbishop, and had a long worthily governed God's kirk, being warned by the visit of an angel, he left his archbishopric and chose a hermit's life. And at the end of his life his passing was betokened to him. Saint Cuthbert also went from his bishopric to an anchorite's life.

Therefore if such men have done thus for to have more meed, who of good mind will be hardy to set any state in holy kirk before solitary life? Truly in this they occupy themselves with no outward things, but only take heed to heavenly contemplation; and that they be continually warm in the love of Christ, and set worldly business perfectly behind.

Wherefore a heavenly noise sounds within them, and full sweet melody makes the solitary man merry; for clatterings distract them who are set among many, and but seldom suffer them to think or pray. Of which solitary the psalmist speaks in the Song of Love, saying: I will go into the place of the marvellous tabernacle, into the house of God.' And he describes the manner of going, in rejoicing and songs of praise, saying: In voce exultationis et confesionis; that is to say: In voice of gladness and shrift.' And that loneliness withouten noise and bodily song is needful to that—that man may receive that songful joy, and hold it in joying and singing—he openly shows in another place: Elongavi, inquit, fugiens; et mansi in solitudine. That is to say: Fleeing by myself, I have withdrawn, and in the wilderness I have dwelt.'

In this life truly he is busy to burn in the fire of the Holy Ghost; and into the joy of love to be taken and, comforted by God, to be glad. For the perfect lonely man hugely burns in God's love; and whiles in surpassing of mind he is rapt above himself by contemplation, he is lift up joying unto that sweet sound and heavenly noise. And such a one, forsooth, is likened to the seraphim, burning within himself anchorite without comparison and most steadfast, whose heart is figured to godly fire; and in full light and burning he is borne up into his love. And forsooth after this life he shall be suddenly taken up to the high seats of the heavenly citizens, that in the place of Lucifer he may full brightly be. For so great is the burning of love and more than can be shown to him that has sought only the glory of his Maker, and who, going meekly, has not raised himself above sinners.

CHAPTER XIV

OF THE PRAISE OF SOLITARY LIFE AND OF THE FIRST LOVERS THEREOF: AND THAT LOVE OF GOD STANDS IN HEAT, SONG, AND SWEETNESS: AND THAT REST IS NEEDFUL: AND THAT SUCH ARE SAVED FROM DECEITS, AND ARE NOT SET IN PRELACY

Saint Job in tormentry was taught by the Holy Ghost the commendation of many manner of holy hermits knit into one, saying: Quis dimisit onagrum liberum, etc. that is to say: Who left the wild ass free, and loosed her bands?' etc.

First, therefore, he commends the freeness of grace, when he says: who let the wild ass loose?' Second, the putting away of fleshly desires; when he says:

and his bands loosed.' Third, solitary conversation, when he adds: to her he gave a house in the wilderness.' Fourth, the desire of endless bliss, when he says: and his tabernacle in the land of saltness,' for salt truly slakes not, but increases thirst; and so the more they have received anything of the sweetness of everlasting life, the more they desire to have, and the more to taste.

Forsooth John Baptist, after Christ the prince of hermits, tarrying in no desire, chose a solitary life; and others have also chosen it, like to a gadfly, the which, says Solomon, has no leader or commander, and goes forth by companies of gifts and virtues. Truly there are bands of nature and of sin, which our Lord has loosed in them, and has confirmed the bands of charity.

The house of the wilderness may also be said to be the rest of a sinner; for holy hermits are sundered from worldly strifes and sins; and, Christ, giving it, they receive the sweetness of a clear conscience, and singing the joys of everlasting love, they rest, refreshed by the most merry heat: and although with sharpness and frowardness they be pricked in body, nevertheless they resolutely hold within their soul praise and burning.

There is another ill wilderness of pride: when any man either prefers himself before all others, or what he has he ascribes to the might of his freewill; of whom it is said: Vae soli: 'Woe to the man alone'; if he fall he has no helper up. In the beginning truly of a hermit's turning—I speak not of runners about that are the slander of hermits—they are made weary with many and divers temptations; but after the tempest of ill movings God insheds the brightness of holy desires, that if they use themselves manly in weeping, meditating, and praying, and seeking only the love of Christ, after a little while they shall seem to themselves to live more in delight, than in weeping, or straitness of labour. They shall have Him whom they loved; whom they sought; and whom they desired: and then shall they joy and not be heavy.

What is it truly to joy but to have the good desired; of it to think; and in it to rest? No marvel that mirth is sweet where true lovers accord, and where the merry solace is of the touching of love; truly unable to be told is the desire of burning lovers, and the sight and speech of each to the other is sweet to them, above honey and the honey-comb.

Jeremy truly commends solitary life saying: Good it is to be a man when he has borne the yoke of God from his young age; he shall sit solitary and be in peace; for by the desire and contemplation of things everlasting he has raised himself above himself.' Whence it is written in scripture: Natus non est in terra quasi Enoch; that is to say: None is born on earth as Enoch,' because forsooth he was taken from the earth. For contemplative men are higher than others both in excellence of work and heartiness of love.

Love forsooth dwells in the heart of the solitary if he seek nothing from vain lordship. Here he utterly burns and longs for light whiles he thus clearly savours things heavenly; and sings with honey-sweetness and without heaviness; as the seraphim—to whom he is like in loving mind—cries and says to his noble Lover; Behold, loving, I burn; greedily desiring.'

Thus with fire untrowed and thirling flame the soul of a lover is burned. It gladdens all things and heavenlike sparkles. Nor happily desiring do I make an end but alway going to that I love death to me is sweet and sicker.

Forsooth the holy solitary, because he suffered to sit in the wilderness for his Saviour, shall receive a golden seat in heaven, and excellence amongst the orders of angels. And because for the love of his Lord he was clad with vile clothes, he shall do on a kirtle to his heels, everlasting, and wrought with the clearness of his Maker. And because, taming his flesh, he shamed not to have a pale and lean face, he shall receive a full marvellous shining of face; and shall bear a most fair mantle, inwoven with precious stones, for his despised clothes, among the mighty of Paradise withouten end. And truly because he voided vice, and burgeoning not in jollity of this life, has entirely cast out the species of sin, the burning of the love of God Almighty he has received into himself most sweet heavenly sound; and the sound of singers of songs full of charity is worthily inshed sweetly into his mind. Therefore bodily and without dread he goes out from this exile hearing in his end angels songs; and he that loved most burningly, going into the Everlasting Hall, shall full worthily be taken up to a degree most joyful, so that with the seraphim he may be in a full high seat.

As I forsooth, seeking in scripture, might find and know, the high love of Christ soothly stands in three things: in heat; in song; in sweetness. And I am expert in mind that these three can not long remain without great rest. For if I would contemplate standing, walking, or lying, methought I lacked full mickle thereof in myself and me-seemed desolate; wherefore, constrained by need, that I might have and abide in high devotion, I chose to sit. The cause of this I know well; for if a man stands or walks for some time, his body waxes weary and so the soul is let, and in a manner irks for the charge, and he is not in high quiet and, it follows, not in perfectness; for, after the philosopher, the soul is made wise sitting or resting. He therefore that as yet is more delighted in God standing than sitting, may know that he is full far from the height of contemplation.

Whence truly in these three that are tokens of most perfect love, the highest perfection of Christian religion without all doubt is found; and I have now, Jesu granting, received these three after the littleness of my capacity. Nevertheless I dare not make myself even to the saints that have shone in them, for they peradventure have received them more perfectly. Yet shall I be busy in virtue that I may more burningly love, more sweetly sing, and more plenteously feel the sweetness of love. Ye err, brethren, if ye trow that none now are so holy as the prophets or apostles have been.

Soothly, heat I call it when the mind is truly kindled in love everlasting; and the heart in the same manner, not hopingly but verily, is felt to burn. For the heart turned into fire gives the feeling of burning love.

Song I call it when in a soul the sweetness of everlasting praise is received with plenteous burning, and thought is turned into song; and the mind is changed into full sweet sound.

These two are not gotten in idleness, but in high devotion; to the which the third is near, that is to say sweetness untrowed. For heat and song truly cause a marvellous sweetness in the soul; and also they may be caused by full great sweetness. Truly there is not any deceit in this plenteousness, but rather it is the most perfect ending of all deeds. Yet some ignorant of contemplative life are deceived by the fiend of the midday into a false and feigned sweetness, for they trow themselves full high when they are low.

But the soul in which the foresaid three things run together, bides altogether unable to be thirled with the arrows of our enemy, whiles she is continually thinking of the lover; for with mind unsmitten she raises herself to heaven and stirs herself to love.

And marvel not if melody be sent to the soul thus ordinate in love, and though she continually receives comfortable songs from the Beloved; for she lives not as if under vanity, but as it were clad with the heavenly, yea so that she may burn withouten end in unwrought heat and never fall. When she also loves unceasingly and burningly, and as it was before said, feels this most happy heat in her soul, and knows herself subtly burnt with the fire of endless love, plainly feeling her most beloved in desired sweetness, meditation is turned into songs of joy, and nature is renewed and umbelapped in heavenly mirth. Wherefore her Maker whom she has desired with all her heart, has granted her to pass without dread and heaviness from the corruptible body, that without heaviness of death she may forsake the world; the which being the friend of light and enemy of darkness has loved nothing but life.

This manner of man forsooth that is taken to so high love, ought to be chosen neither to office nor outward prelacy; nor to be called to any secular errand. Truly they are like the stone that is called topaz, the which is seldom found, and therefore it is held most precious and full dear, in which are two colours: one is most pure even as gold, and the other clear as heaven when it is bright. And it overcomes all the clearness of all stones; and nothing is fairer to behold. But if any would polish it, it is made dim, and truly if it be left to itself its clearness is withholden.

So holy contemplatives, of whom we spake before, are most rare and therefore most dear. They are like to gold for surpassing heat of charity, and to heaven for clearness of heavenly conversation; the which pass the lives of all saints, and therefore are clearer and brighter among the precious stones, that is to say the chosen, because loving and having this lonely life they are clearer than all other men that are, or else have been. But truly who will polish such, that is to say honour them with dignities, are busy to lessen their heat, and in a manner to make their fairness and their clearness dim; for truly if they get the honour of principality, they shall forsooth be made fouler and of less meed. Therefore they shall be left to take heed to their studies, that their clearness may increase.

CHAPTER XV

HOW AND IN WHAT TIME I CAME TO SOLITARY LIFE: AND OF THE SONG OF LOVE: AND OF CHANGING OF PLACE

When I was prospering unhappily, and to youth of wakeful age had now come, the grace of my Maker was near, the which restrained the lust for temporal shape and turned it into unbodily halsing to be desired; and lifting my soul from low things has borne it to heaven, so that I might truly burn in desire for the everlasting mirth, more than ever I was gladdened before by any fleshly company, or else by worldly softness.

If I will truly show this process it behoves me preach solitary life. The spirit forsooth has set my mind on fire to have and to love this, the which henceforth to lead according to the measure of my sickness I have taken care. Nevertheless I have dwelt among them that have flourished in the world, and have taken food from them. Flatterings also, that ofttimes might draw worthy fighters from high things to low, I have heard. But these out-casting for the sake of one, my soul was taken up to the love of my Maker; and desiring to be endlessly delighted with sweetness, I gave my soul up so that in devotion she should love Christ. The which she has forsooth received of her Beloved so that now loneliness appears most sweet to her, and all solace in which the error of man abounds she counts for nought.

I was wont forsooth to seek rest, although I went from place to place. For it is not ill for hermits to leave cells for a reasonable cause, and afterwards, if it accord, to turn again to the same. Truly some of the holy Fathers have done thus, although they have therefore suffered the murmuring of men; nevertheless not of the good. The evil truly speak ill; and if they had abode right there they would also have done that, for it is customary to them. If the covering of a privy is put by, nothing but stink flies out; and ill speaking is spoken out of the heart's plenty, in which the venom of adders lurks.

This have I known, that the more men have raved against me with words of backbiting, so mickle the more I have grown in ghostly profit. Forsooth the worst backbiters I have had are those which I trusted before as faithful friends. Yet I ceased not for their words from those things that were profitable to my soul; truly I used more study, and ever I found God favorable. I called to mind what is written: Maledicent illi, et tu benedices, that is to say: They shall curse him, and thou shalt bless.'

And in process of time great profit in ghostly joy was given me. Forsooth three years, except three or four months, were run from the beginning of the change in my life, and of my mind, to the opening of the heavenly door; so that, the Face being shown, the eyes of the heart might behold and see by what way they might seek my Love, and unto Him continually desire. The door forsooth yet biding open, nearly a year passed until the time in which the heat of everlasting love was verily felt in my heart.

I was sitting forsooth in a chapel, and whiles I was mickle delighted with sweetness of prayer or meditation, suddenly I felt within me a merry and unknown heat. But first I wavered, for a long time doubting what it could be. I was expert that it was not from a creature but from my Maker, because I found it grow hotter and more glad.

Truly in this unhoped for, sensible and sweet-smelling heat, half a year, three months and some weeks have out run, until the inshedding and receiving of this heavenly and ghostly sound; the which belongs to the songs of everlasting praise and the sweetness of unseen melody; because it may not be known or heard but of him that receives it, whom it behoves to be clean and departed from the earth.

Whiles truly I sat in this same chapel, and in the night before supper, as I could, I sang psalms, I beheld above me the noise as it were of readers, or rather singers. Whiles also I took heed praying to heaven with my whole desire, suddenly, I wot not in what manner, I felt in me the noise of song, and received the most liking heavenly melody which dwelt with me in my mind. For my thought was forsooth changed to continual song of mirth, and I had as it were praises in my meditation, and in my prayers and psalm saying I uttered the same sound, and henceforth, for plenteousness of inward sweetness, I burst out singing what before I said, but forsooth privily, because alone before my Maker. I was not known by them that saw me as, peradventure, if they had known me, they would have honoured me above measure, and so I should have lost part of the most fair flower, and should have fallen into desolation.

In the meanwhile wonder caught me that I should be taken up to so great mirth whiles I was in exile; and because God gave gifts to me that I knew not to ask, nor trowed I that any man, not the holiest, could have received any such thing in this life. Therefore I trow this is given to none meedfully, but freely to whom Christ will; nevertheless I trow no man receives it unless he specially love the Name of Jesu, and in so mickle honours It that he never lets it pass from his mind except in sleep. I trow that he to whom it is given to do that, may fulfill the same.

Wherefore from the beginning of my changed soul unto the high degree of Christ's love, the which, God granting, I was able to attain—in which degree I might sing God's praises with joyful song—I was four years and about three months. Here forsooth, with the first disposition of love gathered into this degree, she bides to the very end; and also after death she shall be more perfect: because here the joy of love or burning of charity is begun, and in the heavenly kingdom it shall receive its most glorious ending. And forsooth she profits not a little, set in these degrees in this life, but she ascends not into another degree; but, as it were confirmed in grace, as far as mortal man can, she rests.

Wherefore without ceasing I desire to give grace and praise to God, the which both in diseases, heaviness, and persecution gives me solace; and in prosperity and flatterings makes me with sickerness await an endless crown. Therefore, in Jesu joying, I continually yield praise; the which has vouchsafed me, least and wretched, to mingle with sweet ministers, from whom songs of melody, yet heavenly, spring forth through the Spirit.

Continually with joy shall I give thanks because He has made my soul in clearness of conscience like to singers clearly burning in endless love; and whiles she loves and seethes in burning, the changed mind, resting and being warmed by heat, and greatly enlarged by desire and the true beauty of lovely virtue, blossoms without vice or strife in the sight of our Maker; and thus beating praise within herself, gladdens the longer with merry song and refreshes labours.

Many and great are these marvellous gifts, but among the gifts of this way none are such as those which full dearly in figure confirm the shapeliness of the unseen life in the loving soul; or which so sweetly comfort the sitter, and being comforted, ravish him to the height of contemplation and the accord of the angels praise.

Behold, brethren, I have told you how I came to the burning of love, not that ye should praise me, but that ye should glorify my God, of whom I received ilk good deed that I had; and that ye, thinking that all things under the sun are vanity, may be stirred to follow, not to backbite.

CHAPTER XVI

THE PRAYER OF THE POOR, AND THE LOVING AND DESIRING TO DIE: AND OF THE PRAISING OF GOD'S CHARITY

When the devout poor man is noyed on account of his defaults, he can, if he will, pray and say:

Lord my God, Jesu Christ, have mercy on me and vouchsafe to behold the grievous yoke that is put upon my body, and therefore tarries not to cast down my soul. My flesh truly fails in the griefs of this life; wherefore also ghostly virtue is made weary. For all that I had in this world or of this world is ended, and nought is left but that Thou lead my soul to another world where my treasure is most precious and my substance richest, and unfailingly abides. Wherefore I shall live without default; I shall joy without sorrow; I shall love without irksomeness; and loving Thee, seeing Thee, and joying in Thee, I shall be endlessly fed. Thou truly art my Treasure, and all the Desire of my heart; and because of Thee I shall perfectly see Thee, for them I shall have Thee.

And I spake thus to death:

O Death, where dwellest thou? Why comest thou so late to me, living but yet mortal? Why halsest thou not him that desires thee?

Who is enough to think thy sweetness, that art the end of sighing, the beginning of desire, the gate of unfailing yearning? Thou art the end of heaviness, the mark of labours, the beginning of fruits, the gate of joys. Behold I grow hot and desire after thee: if thou come I shall forthwith be safe. Ravished, truly, because of love, I cannot fully love what I desire after, until I taste the joy that Thou shalt give to me. If it behoves me, mortal—because forsooth it so befalls—to pass through thee as all my fathers have gone, I pray thee tarry not mickle; from me abide not long! Behold, I truly languish for love; I desire to die; for thee I burn; and yet truly not for thee, but for my Saviour Jesu, whom, after I have had thee, I trow to see withouten end.

O Death, how good is thy doom to needy man, whose soul, nevertheless, is made sweet by love; to the man, forsooth, truly loving Christ and contemplating heavenly things, and sweetly burned with the fire of the Holy Ghost. After death he is taken soothly to songs of angels; because now being purged, and profiting, he dwells in the music of the spirit. And in melody full marvellous shall he die, the which when alive thought pithily upon that sweet Name; and with the companies meeting him, with heavenly hymns and honour, he shall be taken into the hall of the Eternal Emperor, being among heavenly dwellers in the seat of the blessed.

To this has charity truly brought him, that he should thus live in inward delight, and should gladly suffer all that happens, and should think on death, not with bitterness but with sweetness. Soothly then he trows himself truly to live, when it is given him to pass from this light.

O sweet Charity, thou art plainly the dearest sweetness; that catchest and takest the mind to thy love; and so clearly thou moistenest it that quickly thou makest it despise all passing things and vain joys, and only to marvellously yearn after thy desires. Thou hast come into me, and behold, all mine inward soul is fulfilled by the sweetness of heavenly mirth, and plenteous in the fervour of ghostly joy.

Therefore, truly I long after love, the fairest of flowers, and I am inwardly burned by the flame of fire. Would God I might go from the dwelling of this exile!

Thus it warms, man thinks not how, save that he feels solace in himself; the heart singing ditties and taken captive with the charge of charity. Soothly this that I thus receive is most merry, and I nearly die while it is thus made steadfast with burning love. Now grant my best Beloved that I may cease; for death, that many dread, shall be to me as heavenly music. Although I am sitting in the wilderness, yet I am now as it were set stable in Paradise, and there sweetly is sounding a loving song in the delights that my Love has given me.

CHAPTER XVII

HOW PERFECT LOVE IS GOTTEN BY CLEANNESS AND LOVE: AND OF IMPER-
FECT LOVE AND FAIRNESS, AND OF THREE MIGHTS OF GOD'S LOVE: AND OF
THE RICH AND POOR: AND OF ALMS

From cleanness of conscience and plenteousness of ghostly gladness and inward mirth, rises the song of joy and the burning of endless love in a mind
loving truly. No marvel that loving in this manner, love has been perfectly had,
great in desire, with a moving altogether dressed to God, and by no letting
removed from His love; withouten strife of vain thoughts, constantly cleaving
to Christ; in Jesu ever joying; from Him never distracted; with ill never moved;
whom dead flies never deceive or cast down from the sweetness of the ointment.

The world, the flesh, and the devil have none effect upon him, although
they prick him; but he treads them under his feet, setting their strength at
nought. Withouten seething he boils; he loves with great desire; he sings with
sweetness; he shines with heat; he is delighted in God without gainstanding; he
contemplates with unbroken upgoing. He vanquishes all things; he overcomes
all things; of all the things that he likes nothing seems to him impossible.
Truly whiles any man is busy to love Christ with all his strength he feels in
himself, forsooth, great sweetness of eternal life.

We are turned truly to Christ if we strive to love Him with our whole
mind. Certain, so marvellous a Thing is God and so liking to see, that I wonder that any man can be so mad and go out of the way that he should take no
heed to the sight of Him in his soul. Truly not he that does great and many
things is great; but he that loves God mickle is great, and loved of God.

Philosophers forsooth have travailed mickle, and yet without fruit they have
vanished. And many that seemed Christians have done great things and
showed forth marvels, and yet they were not worthy to be saved; for the plenteousness of the heavenly crown is not for the doers, but for the lovers of God.

Lord Jesu, I ask Thee, give unto me movement in Thy love withouten
measure; desire withouten limit; longing withouten order; burning without
discretion. Truly the better the love of Thee is, the greedier it is; for neither by
reason is it restrained, nor by dread distressed, nor by doom tempted. No man
shall ever be more blest than he that for greatness of love can die. No creature
truly can love too mickle. In all other things all that is too mickle turns to vice,
but the more the strength of love surpasses the more glorious it shall be. The

lover truly languishes if he has not by him the likeness of that he loves. Therefore it is said: Nunciate dilecto quia amore langueo, that is to say: Show to my
love that I languish for love.' As who should say: Because I see not that I love,
for love I wax slow also in body.'

Forsooth turned to Christ with all my heart, I am tied first by true penance,
and so forsaking all things that long to vanity, after the taste of ghostly sweetness, I shall be ravished to sing in songful and godly praise. Whereof I say: Ego
cantabo dilecto meo; and in the psalm: In te cantatio mea semper. That is to
say: To my love I shall sing'; and in the psalm: In thee is ever my song.' No
marvel that they therefore that thus have lived in God's love, and sweetly have
burned in inward flagrance withouten dread, in death shall pass from this light,
but truly with joy; and after death ascend to the heavenly kingdoms.

Therefore it is said of the flame of God's love that it takes the mind to
wound it. I am wounded by charity, and I am made to languish for my love';
whereof it is said, Amore langueo, for love I languish'; and to moisten it, that it
so goes out towards the Beloved that it forgets the self and other things besides
Christ. Therefore he says: Pone me ut signaculum super cor tuum; that is to
say: As a token set me on Thy heart.'

What is love but the transforming of desire into the thing loved? Or love is
great desire for the fair, the good, and lovely, with continuance of thought
going in to that thing that it loves, the which, when it has, then it joys; for joy
is not caused save by love. All those loving are truly made like to their love, and
love makes him that loves like to that that is loved.

Truly neither God nor other creature disdains or forsakes to be loved, but
gladly all things say they would be loved, and are gladdened by love. They are
not heavy truly in loving unless they have loved an unkind thing; or if they
trow they can not have that thing they have lovingly sought. This is never so in
the love of God, but ofttimes this happens in the love of the world or of woman.

I dare not say that all love is good, for that love that is more delighted in
creatures than in the Maker of all things, and sets the lust of earthly beauty
before ghostly fairness, is ill and to be hated; for it turns from eternal love and
turns to temporal that can not last. Yet peradventure it shall be the less punished; for it desires and joys more in love and be loved than to defile or be
defiled. The fairer a creature is, the more lovable it is in the sight of all. Therefore some were wont busily to get health from a shapely form rather than from
a despised, which has many occasions of bringing in ill. And nature teaches the
fairer the thing, the more sweetly to be loved. Nevertheless ordinate charity
says the greater the good, the more it is to be loved; for ilk fleshly beauty is as

hay, lightly vanishing, but godliness truly hides; and ofttimes God chooses the sick and despised of the world, and forsakes the strong and fair. Wherefore it is said in the psalm: Tradidit in captivitatem virtutem eorum, et pulcritudinem eorum in manus inimici; that is to say: Their strength has he given to bondage, and their fairness into the hands of their enemies.' And in another place: Habens fiduciam in pulcritudine tua, fornicata es; that is in English: Having trust in thy fairness, thou hast done fornication.'

It is of love also to melt the mind; as it is written: Anima mea liquefacta est, ut dilectus locutus est; that is to say: My soul was molten as my Love spake.' Truly sweet and devout love melts the heart in God's sweetness, so that the will of man is made one with the will of God in wonderful friendship. In which onehood such sweetness of liking heat and song is inshed into a loving soul, how great the feeler cannot tell.

Love forsooth has strength in spreading, in knitting, and turning. In spreading, truly: for it spreads the beams of its goodness not only to friends and neighbours, but also to enemies and strangers. In knitting truly: for it makes lovers one in deed and will; and Christ and every holy soul it makes one. He truly that draws to God is one spirit, not in nature but in grace, and in onehood of will. Love has also a turning strength, for it turns the loving into the loved, and ingrafts him. Wherefore the heart that truly receives the fire of the Holy Ghost is burned all wholly and turns as it were into fire; and it leads it into that form that is likest to God. Else had it not been said: Ego dixi dii estis et filii Excelsi omnes; that is to say: I have said ye are gods, and are all the children of the high God.'

Forsooth some men have so loved each other that they nearly trowed there were but one soul in them both. Truly the man poor in worldly goods, though he is rich in mind, is far from such love. It were marvel truly if he that behoves ever to take and seldom or never can give, had a friend in the which he might trust in all things. By others, therefore, trowed unworthy of true love, he has a steadfast friend, Christ; and of Him he can faithfully ask whatsoever he will. Truly where man's help fails, without doubt God's is near.

Nevertheless it were more profitable to the rich if he chose a holy poor man to his special friend, with whom he would share in common and gladly give him all that he had, yea more than the poor wills, and love him affectionately as his best and kindest friend. Therefore Christ said unto the rich, Make you friends,' meaning, forsooth, the holy poor who are God's friends; and gladly God gives to the true lovers of such poor, for their love, the joys of Paradise. Soothly I trow that such rich should be well pleased with their friendship! But the verse now is true that saith: Pontus erit siccus cum pauper habebit amicum; The sea shall be dry when a poor man has a friend.'

Some rich soothly I have found giving as they thought their meat to the holy poor, who would not give clothing or other necessaries, trowing it were enough if they gave but meat; and so they make themselves half friends, or in part; caring no more for the friendship of the good poor than of the evil poor. And all things of any price that might be given, they save for themselves and their children. And so the holy poor are holden no more to them but as they are to others of their good-doers, that give them clothes or other goods. And yet, what is worse, the poor seem a full great burden to the rich.

CHAPTER XVIII

OF THE PRAISE AND MIGHT OF CHARITY: AND OF FORSAKING THE WORLD: AND OF THE WAY OF PENANCE TO BE TAKEN

Charity is the queen of virtues; the fairest star; the beauty of the soul that does all these things in the soul: that is to say, it wounds her; makes her languish; moistens, melts and makes fair; it gladdens and enflames; whose ordinate deed is full fair habit. It behoves without doubt that all virtue, if it be truly called virtue, be rooted in charity. No virtue can be truly held that has not been set in God's love. Soothly he who multiplies virtues and good deeds without God's love, casts as it were precious stones into a bottomless privy. Shown it is and known that all deeds that men do help not in the end to get health, if they be not done in the charity of God and of their neighbour. Wherefore, since it is charity only that makes us blessed, we ought to desire rather to lose our life than in mind, or mouth, or deed, defile charity. In this the strivers with sin joy; in this the overcomers are crowned.

Truly ilk Christian is imperfect that cleaves with love to earthly riches, or is joined to any worldly solace; for he forsakes not all that he has, without which no man can come to perfection. When any man truly desires to love God perfectly, he studies to do away all things, inward as well as outward, that are contrary to God's love and let from His love. And that a man may do that truly he has great business, for he shall suffer great strifes in doing it; afterwards truly he shall find sweetest rest in that that he seeks.

We have heard truly that the way is strait that leads to life. This is the way of penance that few find, the which therefore is called strait; for by it, and it be right, the flesh is stripped from unlawful solace of the world, and the soul is restrained from shrewd pleasure and unclean thoughts, and is only dressed to the love of God. But this is seldom found in men, for nearly none savour that which belongs to God: but they seek earthly joy and in that they are delighted, wherefore following their bodily appetite, and despising their ghostly, they forsake all the ways that are healthful to their soul, and they abhor them as strait, sharp, and unable to be borne by their lust.

Nevertheless every mortal man ought to consider that he will never come to the heavenly kingdom by the way of riches and fleshly liking and lust, since, forsooth, it is written of Christ: Quod oportuit Christum pati, et ita intrare in gloriam suam; that is to say: that Christ behoved to suffer and so enter His joy.' If we be members of our Head, Jesu Christ, we shall follow Him; and if we love Christ, it behoves us go as He has gone; else are we not His members, for from the Head we are divided.

Truly if we be sundered from Him, it is greatly to be dreaded, for then are we joined to the fiend, and in the last doom Christ is to say: I have not known you.' He, truly, by a noyous gate and strait way entered to heaven; how should we, that are wretches and sinners, be made rich by the poor, and feed our lust with unlawful things and flatteries of this world, and all vanity and softness of flesh and desire for delight, and nevertheless reign with Christ in the life to come?

Christ when He was rich for us became poor; and when we are poor there is nothing that we so mickle covet as to be or seem plenteous. Christ when He was Lord of all is become the Servant of all: and we, whiles we are unprofitable and unworthy servants, yet would we be lords of all. He, when He was great God, is become a meek Man; and we, when we are sick and simple men, because of pride we raise ourselves in as mickle as if we were gods. He was conversant with men that He might raise us to the heavens; and we through all our life desire earthly things.

Therefore it is shown that we love Him not, for we will not meek our will to His; nor busy we to fulfill what ilk day we ask, saying: Fiat voluntas tua sicut in coelo et in terra; 'Thy will be done as in heaven and in earth.' In vain forsooth such men trow to receive the heritage with them that are chosen; for they are not partners of Christ's gainbuying, the which, by their wicked and unclean works, despise the blood by which we are gainbought, and freely yield themselves to the bondage of the fiend.

CHAPTER XIX

OF FAIRNESS OF MIND: VANITY OF THE WORLD: LOVE OF GOD: AND UNION
WITH OUR NEIGHBOUR: AND WHETHER PERFECT LOVE CAN BE LOST AND
GOTTEN IN THIS WAY

If thou be gladdened in fairness know it well, for the fairness of thy mind shall
make thee beloved of the highly Fair if for love of Him only thou keepest it
undefiled. Soothly the corruptible flesh with all its beauty is full feeble and to
be despised, because, soon passing, it beguiles all its lovers. Therefore the virtue
of our life stands in this: that vanity being despised and spurned, we cleave
unpartingly to truth.

All earthly things which are desired on earth are vain; true soothly are the
heavenly and eternal which can not be seen. Ilk Christian man in this shows
himself truly chosen of God, that he sets these earthly things at nought; his
desires are altogether spread in God, and he receives thereof a privy sound of
love that no man umbelapped with worldly desires knows, being wretchedly
withdrawn from the savour of heavenly joy. But no marvel that the shining
soul, utterly intent to the love of the everlasting and inwardly desiring Christ,
is wont to have his heart's capacity fulfilled with plenteousness of sweetness; so
that in this flesh made merry, as it were with angels' life, they are gladdened
with songful mirth.

Therefore if our love be pure and perfect, whatever our heart loves it is
God. Truly if we love ourself, and all other creatures that are to be loved, only
in God and for God, what other in us and in them love we but Him? For
when our God truly is loved by us with a whole heart and all virtue, then,
without doubt, our neighbour and all that is to be loved, is most rightly loved.
If therefore we shed forth our heart before God and in the love of God being
bound with Him, and holden with God, what more is there by which we can
love any other creature?

Truly in the love of God is the love of my neighbour. Therefore as he that
loves God knows not but to love man, so he that truly knows to love Christ is
proved to love nothing in himself but God. Also all that we are loved by and
love—all to God the Well of love we yield: because He commands that all the
heart of man be given to Himself. All desires also, and all movings of the mind,
He desires be fastened in Him. He forsooth that truly loves God feels nothing
in his heart but God, and if he feel none other thing nought else has he; but
whatso he has he loves for God, and he loves nought but that God wills he

should love; wherefore nothing but God he loves and so all his love is God. Forsooth the love of this man is true, for he conforms himself to his Maker, the which has wrought all things for Himself; and so he loves all things for God.

Soothly when the love of the everlasting is truly kindled in our souls, without doubt all vanity of this world and all fleshly love is held but as foulest filth; and whiles the soul is given to continual devotion, she desires nothing but the pleasance of the Maker. Marvellously she burns in herself with the fire of love, that, slowly profiting and growing in ghostly good, henceforth she falls not into the slippery way and the broad that leads to death, but rather, raised up by a heavenly fire, she goes and ascends into contemplative life.

Truly contemplative life is not perfectly gotten of any man in this vale of tears, even a little, unless first his heart is inflamed from its depths with the torches of eternal love so that he feels it burn with the fire of love, and his conscience he knows molten with heavenly sweetness. So no marvel a man is truly made contemplative whiles both tasting sweetness and feeling burning he nearly dies for the greatness of love. And therefore he is fastened in the halsing, as it were bodily, of endless love; for contemplating unceasingly with all his desire, he busies him to go up to see that undescried light. Forsooth such a man knows to grant no comfort in his soul but God's, in whose love now languishing to the end of his life he is made to desire, crying grievously with the psalmist: Quando veniam et apparebo ante faciem Dei? that is to say: When shall I come and appear before the face of my God?'

This is perfect love. But it may not incongrously be asked whether this standing in love, once had, may at any time be lost. Truly whiles man can sin he can lose charity; but not to be able to sin belongs not to the state of this way but to the country above: wherefore ilk man, howsoever holy he be in this life, yet he can sin and mortally; for the dregs of sin are fully slakened in no pilgrim of this life after common law. Truly if there were any such the which neither desire nor could be tempted, they should belong to the state of heaven rather than of this way; nor were it of meed to them not to default, whiles they can not sin. I wot not if any such be living anywhere in flesh for, I speak for myself, the flesh desires against the spirit, and the spirit against the flesh; and after the inward man I am glad in God's law, but I know not yet so mickle love that I could utterly slake all fleshly desire.

Nevertheless I trow that there is a degree of perfect love, the which whosoever attains he shall never afterwards lose. For truly it is one thing to be able to lose, and another alway to hold, what he will not leave although he can.

The perfect truly abstain themselves, as mickle as in them is, from ilk thing by which their perfection can be destroyed or else let. Truly with the freeness of their choice they are fulfilled with the grace of God, with which they are busily stirred to love, to speak and do good; and they are withdrawn from ill of heart, mouth, and work.

When a man is therefore perfectly turned to Christ he despises all passing things, and he fastens himself immovably to the desire only of his Maker, as far as he is let by mortality because of the corruption of the flesh. Then no marvel, manly using his might, first the heaven as it were being opened, with the eye of his understanding he beholds the citizens of heaven; and afterward he feels sweetest heat as it were a burning fire. Then he is imbued with marvellous sweetness, and henceforth he is joyed by a songly noise.

This therefore is perfect charity, which no man knows but he that receives it; and he that has received never leaves it: sweetly he lives, and sickerly shall he die.

CHAPTER XX

OF THE PROFIT AND WORTHINESS OF PRAYER AND MEDITATION

Constant prayer helps mickle to get and hold to this stableness of mind; for if it be grounded in mind it undoes the might of fiends. Though God truly knows all things, and before we ask anything He knows perfectly what we will ask, yet we ought to pray for many causes.

Because Christ gave example to us to pray when He nighted alone on the hill in prayer. And because it is the commandment of the Apostle, Sine intermissione orate. Oportet enim orare, et non deficere. Withouten ceasing pray ye. Soothly it behoves to pray, and not to fail.'

Also that we may be worthy of grace in this life, and joy in time to come: wherefore Ask and ye shall receive. He that asks receives, and to the caller it shall be opened.'

Also because the angels offer our prayers to God to help their fulfillment. Truly thoughts and desires are bare and open only to God; yet angels know when saints think worthy and holy things and are inflamed greatly with the love of eternal life, by God's showing and by the experience of their outward deeds, because they see them serve God only. Wherefore the angel said to Daniel: Vir desideriorum es. 'A man thou art of desires.'

Also because by the continuance of prayer the soul is burnt with the fire of God's love; our Lord truly says by His prophet: Nonne verba mea quasi ignis, et quasi malleus conterens petras? 'Are not my words as burning fire, and as a mallet breaking stones?' The psalm also says: Ignitum eloquium tuum vehementer; 'thy speech is hugely burned.'

But there are many now that forthwith cast out the word of God from the mouth and heart, not suffering it there to rest in them; and therefore they are not burnt with the heat of comfort but bide cold in sloth and negligence, even after innumerable prayers and meditation of scripture, because forsooth they neither pray nor meditate in mind; whiles others that put back all sloth are within a short while greatly burned, and in Christ's love full strong.

Therefore it follows full well: Et servus tuus dilexit illud; that is to say: And Thy servant has loved it.' Therefore truly is he burned because Thy word, Lord, he loved; that is to say to ponder, and after it to work. Thee he has sought sooner than Thine, and has received of Thee both Thee and Thine. Others serve Thee in order to have Thine and for Thee they care little. Truly they feign they would be under Thy service, to get worldly honour and to seem glorious among men; but whiles they joy to have found a few things, they lose many; because of Thee and Thine, and themselves and theirs.

It also behoves us to pray that we may be saved; therefore James warns, saying: Orate pro invicem ut salvemini, 'Pray for yourselves, that ye be saved.'

Also that we be not made slow, and that we be continually occupied in good: therefore it is said: Vigilate et orate ne intretis in temptationem, that is to say: Wake ye and pray, that ye enter not into temptation.' Truly we ought ever to pray or read or meditate, with other profitable deeds, that our enemy never find us idle.

But it must be taken heed to with all busyness that we wake in prayer, that is to say not be lulled by vain thoughts that withdraw the mind and make it forget whither it is bound and alway let, if they can, to overcome the effect of devotion; the which the mind of the pray-er would perceive if he prayed with wakefulness, busyness and desire.

CHAPTER XXI

THAT CONTEMPLATIVE LIFE IS WORTHIER AND MEEDFULLER THAN ACTIVE:
AND OF BOTH PRELACY AND PREACHING

By some truly it is doubted which life is more meedful and better; contemplative or active. It seems to not a few that active is meedfuller because of the
many deeds and preachings that it uses. But these err unknowingly, for they
know not the virtue of contemplative. Yet there are many active better than
some contemplative; but the best contemplative are higher than the best active.

Therefore we say the contemplative life is altogether the better, the sweeter,
the more worthy, and the more meedful as to the true meed, that is joy of the
unwrought good, because the contemplative more burningly loves God. And
more grace is asked if contemplative life be led rightly, than active.

The reason of more fervent love in contemplative life than in active is because in contemplative they are in rest of mind and body, and therefore they
taste the sweetness of eternal, before all mortal love. The active truly serve God
in labour and outward running about, and tarry but little in inward rest,
wherefore they can not be delighted save seldom and shortly; the contemplative soothly love as if they were continually within the halsing of their Beloved.

Forsooth some gainsetting say: active life is more fruitful; for it does works
of mercy, it preaches and works other such deeds; wherefore it is more merito-
rious. I say, nay, for such works belong to accidental reward, that is, joy of the
thing wrought. And so one that shall be taken into the order of angels can have
some meed that he that shall be in the order of cherubim or seraphim shall not
have; that is to say joy of some good deed that he did in this life, the which
another—that without comparison surpasses in God's love—did not. Also
ofttimes it happens that some one of less meed is good, and preaches; and
another preaches not, that mickle more loves. Is not this one better because he
preaches? No; but the one that loves more is higher and better, although he be
less in preaching he shall have some meed, because he preached not, that the
greater was not worthy of.

Therefore it is shown that man is not holier or higher for the outward
works that he does. Truly God that is the Beholder of the heart rewards the
will more than on the deeds. For the more burningly that a man loves, in so
mickle he ascends to a higher reward.

Truly, in true contemplative men, there is a full sweet heat and the plenteousness of God's love abiding, from the which a joyful sound is sent into them

with untrowed mirth; and this is never found in active men in this life, because they take not heed only to heavenly things, so that they might be worthy to joy in Jesu. And therefore active life is worthily put behind; and contemplative life, in this present and in the life to come is worthily preferred.

Wherefore in the litter of the true Solomon the pillars are of silver and the resting place of gold. The pillars of the chair are the strong upbearers and the good governors of holy kirk; these are of silver, for in conversation they are clear and in preaching full of sound. The gold resting place are contemplative men; on the which, being in high rest, Christ especially rests His Head, and they forsooth in Him singularly rest. These are of gold, for they are purer and dearer in honesty of living, and are redder in burning of loving and contemplating.

God forsooth has forordained His chosen to fulfill divers services. It is not given truly to ilk man to execute or fulfill all offices, but ilk man has that that is most according to his state. Wherefore the Apostle says: Unicuique nostrum data est gracia secundum mensuram donationis Christi; that is to say: To ilk one of us is grace given after the measure of Christ's gift.'

Some truly do alms of righteously gotten goods; others to their death defend the truth; others clearly and strongly preach God's word, and others show their preaching in their writing; others suffer for God great penance and wretchedness in this life; others, by the gift of contemplation, are only busy to God and set themselves straitly to love Christ. But without doubt, among all estates that are in the kirk, they that are become contemplative joy with a special gift; they are now worthy with singing to joy in God's love.

Truly if any man might get both lives, that is to say contemplative and active, and keep and fulfill them, he were full great; that he might fulfill bodily service, and nevertheless feel the heavenly sound in himself, and be melted in singing into the joy of heavenly love. I wot not if ever any mortal man had this. To me it seems impossible that both should be together.

Christ truly in this respect is not to be numbered among men, nor His blest Mother among women. For Christ had no wandering thoughts, and He was not contemplative in a common manner, as saints in this life are contemplative; truly He needed not to labour as we need, because, from the beginning of His Conceiving, He saw God.

No marvel by great exercise of ghostly works there comes into us a songful joy, and we receive the sweetest sound from heaven; and so henceforward we desire to stand in rest, that with great sweetness we may joy. Therefore he that serves active life well is busy to go up to contemplative life.

He who truly is raised in the manner aforesaid with the gift of heavenly contemplation, comes not down to active; unless peradventure he be compelled to take governance of Christians; that I trow has seldom or never happened. But other contemplatives can well be chosen for that, because they are less imbued with heat of love. Forsooth lesser saints are sometimes more able than greater for the office of prelacy, because they that could not rest perfectly in inward desires shall behave themselves more accordingly about outward business.

CHAPTER XXII

THE BURNING OF LOVE PURGES VICES AND SINS: AND OF THE TOKENS OF TRUE FRIENDSHIP

The burning of love truly taken into a soul purges all vices; it voids both too mickle and too little, and plants the beauty of all virtues. It never stands with deadly sin, and if it do with venial yet nevertheless the moving and desire of love in God can be so burning that they waste all venial sins, without also thinking in deed of these same venial sins: for whilst the true lover is borne to God with strong and fervent desire, all things displease him that withdraw him from the sight of God. Truly whiles he is gladdened by songly joy, his heart may not express what he feels of heavenly things, and therefore he languishes for love.

Perfect men also never bear what may be burned to the life to come, for in the heat of Christ's love all their sins are wasted. But lest any man ween himself perfect in vain when he is not, let him hear when a man has perfection in himself.

This truly is the life of the Perfect: to cast away all charge of worldly errands; to forsake father and mother and all thy goods for Christ; to despise all passing goods, for endless life; to destroy worldly desires with long labour; as far as it is possible to refrain from lechery and all unlawful movings; to burn only in the love of our Maker; after bitter sorrows and surpassing busyness in ghostly works, to feel the sweetness of heavenly contemplation: and so, I speak of men privileged, for the joy of God's love, to be taken by contemplation into ghostly song or heavenly sound, and to bide sweetly in inward rest, all disturbances being put aback, in so mickle that whiles it is lawful to the man of God to work nothing outward, he is taken within to sing the sweetness of eternal love in songs of delight and unmeasured mirth. Thus, no marvel that he shall have sweetness in mind such as the angels have in heaven; although not so mickle.

Soothly in this wise is man made perfect; and he shall not need to be purged with fire after this life, who, being in the flesh, burns burningly with the fire of the Holy Ghost. And yet this perfect love makes not a man ay not to sin, but that sin lasts not in him but is wasted forthwith by the fire of love.

Truly such a lover of Jesus Christ says not his prayers like other righteous men, for, set in righteous mind, and ravished above himself by the love of Christ, he is taken into marvellous mirth, and a goodly sound is shed into him, so that he as it were sings his prayers with notes; also offering with his mouth melody that, though hidden from human sense, is full bright to God and to himself. Strength and ghostly virtue have now truly so mickle overcome in him heaviness of the flesh that he can be ay glad in Christ; whose heart, turned into fire of love, feels verily heavenly heat, so that he can scarcely with life bear the greatness of such burning love. But the goodness of God keeps him until the time ordained; the which gave it him that he so mickle, might love, and truly say, I languish for love.'

As the Seraphim burned, he burns and loves; he signs and joys, he praises and grows warm; and the more pleasing he is, the hotter he burns in love. He not only dreads not death, but he is glad to die with the Apostle: Mihi, inquit, Christus vivere vita est, et mori gaudium, that is to say: Christ to me is life; and to die great joy'; etc.

CHAPTER XXIII

THAT PERFECT LOVE MINGLES NOTHING WITH GOD: AND WHY. AND THAT IT IS NEEDFUL TO LOVE: AND OF THE BLINDNESS OF FLESHLY LOVE

If we perfectly forsake the filth of sins and the vices of this world, we love nothing but God. How truly should God be all in all if anything were in man beside His love? No man truly has joy unless he loves the good.

The more therefore that a man loves God, no marvel the more plenteously he shall joy in Him; because the more busily and fervently we desire anything, it being gotten, the more heartily we joy. Therefore truly has a man joy because he has God; and God truly is that Joy: the which forsooth none of them have that seek anything besides God. For if I desire anything for myself, and I set not my God as the end of that desire, sicker it is that I have made a traitor of myself, and my hidden guilt is openly shown.

God truly will be loved in this wise: that no man be mingled with Him in His love. For if thou dividest thy heart and dreadest not to love another thing with Him, without doubt know well that thy love is forsaken of God; the which vouchsafes not for to behold a part of love. All the whole truly or nought He takes; for He gainbought the whole. For in the sin of Father Adam forsooth thy body and thy soul were damned; wherefore God is come down into a Maiden's body and become man, and has given the price of thy deliverance, that not only He might deliver thy soul from the power of the fiends, but also He might make thy body with thy soul blessed at the end of the world. Therefore thou hast the commandments of eternal life. If thou wilt enter the kingdom, lost, and after reparalled with Christ's blood, it behoves thee to keep God's commandments.

And truly as thou desirest after thy death to ascend into full and perfect joy, so it behoves thee in this life to have mind to love God with a whole and perfect heart. Else as now thou art not given to God's love, so then not perfect joy but endless torment shalt thou have. For truly whiles thou takest not heed to thy Maker with whole love and mind, thou art proved soothly to love some creature of God more than is honest or lawful. A soul can not be reasonable without love whiles it is in this life: wherefore the love thereof is the foot of the soul, by which, after this pilgrimage, it is borne to God or the fiend; that it may be subject to him whose will here it served.

Nothing truly can be loved but for the goodness that it has, or else seems that it has, and which is either in the loved or certainly thought to be in that that is loved. Herefore truly it is that lovers of bodily beauty or worldly riches are beguiled as it were by witchcraft; for delight is not those things the which we think we feel or see, nor the joy that is feigned, nor the good name that we give it.

No man therefore more damnably forgets his soul than he that sets his eye on woman for lechery; truly whilst the sight of the eye kindles the soul, anon from the things seen thought enters and engenders desire in the heart, and defiles the inward beauty. Wherefore suddenly with burning of a noyous fire it is umbelapped and blinded, that it may not see the sentence of the strait Judge. And thus the soul, taken from heavenly sight by evil and unclean love, stints not to show tokens of her error; and unless she may bring forth the filth that is conceived, she mistrusts of her prosperity.

Filth forsooth she conceived, that is to say wicked desire; thereby shall wickedness worthily be brought forth, because the soul the sooner slides to slippery lust inasmuch as she takes no heed to the great peril in which she errs. The dooms of God are withdrawn also from her face. Whiles truly she begins to take pleasure in fleshly desires, she sees not into how great a pit of wretchedness she casts herself.

Soothly the doom of God is that he who wilfully despised God, casting himself down into deadly sin, shall, God deeming, unwillingly be damned after this life. In the time to come truly he can not defend himself from the pains of hell, that, set in this life, would not, when he could, with all his power forsake deadly sins, and wholly hate all wickedness.

CHAPTER XXIV

OF THE STINK OF LECHERY AND THE PERIL OF TOUCHING: AND OF THE CURSEDNESS OF COVETOUSNESS: AND OF UNGODLY GLADNESS

Whiles a man weds not for pure love of God and virtue and chastity, but is busy to live in chastity and in array of all virtue, doubtless he gets to himself a great name in heaven; for as he ceases not to love God here, so in heaven he shall never cease from His praising. Wedlock soothly is good in itself; but when men constrain themselves under the band of matrimony for the fulfilling of their lust, they turn forsooth good into ill, and whereby they ween to profit, thereof they cease not to be worse. Whosoever loves wedlock for this intent, because by it he trows he may be rich, is, without doubt, busy to loose the bridle of wantonness; and overflowing in lust and riches, he joys full mickle to have found medicine for his slippery flesh.

There are forsooth froward men that love their wives unmannerly for their beauty; and the sooner their bodily strength is broken the more loose are they to fulfill their bodily lust. For the more lust they have the sooner they fail, and whiles they have prosperity they perish; and whiles they are busy to be fed with lust, they wretchedly lose strength of body and mind.

Nothing soothly is more perilous, fouler and more stinking for man than to put his mind on woman's love, and desire her as blissful rest. No marvel what before he desired with mickly anguish as great bliss, after the deed straightway waxes foul. Afterward he knows truly that he has cowardly gone wrong in such lust, when he perceives lust so short and diseases long. For it is shown that he was strongly bound with a foul band of feeble vanity. But because he would not turn to God with all his heart, he knew not his wretchedness until the time he felt it; and therefore he fell into the pit of bondage, because he beheld not the seat of joy. If truly he had felt one drop of the sweetness of eternal life, never should fleshly fairness—that is beguiling and vain grace—have appeared so sweet to his mind. But alas! he takes no heed how stinking and odious is his wretched lust in the sight of God Almighty, and in his conscience he sees not himself beguiled.

No man certainly can be given to uncleanness of the flesh unless he err from the ways of righteousness. Truly whiles the fire of earthly love ceases not to inflame man's mind, no marvel it wastes in it all the moisture of grace, and making it both void and dry, it alway increases its heat; and from the fire of covetousness kindles the fire of lechery. And so the thrall soul, marvellously mazed, covets nothing but fleshly desires, or to increase riches, and making his end in them, labours always to get new things; and he sees not those pains that he goes to because he cared not for God's words and His commandments. And because he desires only these outward joys, and is blinded to the inward and unseen, as it were sightless he goes to the fire. And truly when the unhappy soul shall pass from the body, she shall know perfectly in the Judgment how wretched she was; the which trowed herself, whiles she was in the flesh, not only guiltless, but also happy.

In ilk thing therefore cleanness of mind more than of body is to be cared for; for certain it is less wicked to touch the flesh of woman with bare hands than to be defiled with wicked lust in mind. Truly if we touch women and think nothing evil in heart it ought not to be called sin, although through it temptation of the flesh sometimes arises; for man falls not into evil whiles his mind is steadfast in God.

Whiles the heart of the toucher is caught by divers desires, or is bowed in evil sweetness, and he is not straightway refrained by the love of God and steadfastness in virtue, know without doubt that that man has the sin of un-cleanness within himself, though he be never so far not only from women but also from men. And forsooth if a true man be untied with an untrue woman, it is full near that his mind be turned to untruth. Truly it is the manner of women that when they feel themselves loved out of measure by men, they beguile men's hearts by cherishing flattery; and they draw to those things that their wicked will stirred up, the which before they assayed by open speech.

Solomon soothly was wise and true to God for a while, but afterward, for the too mickle love by which he drew to women, he failed most foully in steadfastness and in the commandments of God; the more worthy to be griev-ously smitten in that he, set in great wisdom, suffered himself to be overcome by a fond woman. Let no man therefore flatter himself, and no man presume to say of himself I am sicker, I do not dread, the world can not beguile me,' whilst thou hearest of the wisest man the unwittest deed.

Covetousness is also ghostly fornication; for the covetous heart, for the love of peace, opens his bosom to the strumpetry of the fiend. When God was loved before the love of money, as very Spouse, and afterward He is forsaken because of unclean love and wicked wooers received, what else is done but fornication and idolatry? Be we therefore busy to keep our hearts clean in the sight of God Almighty, and to destroy venomous delectations; and if anything have been done in our heart by frailty, let nothing now be shown before God but perfectness.

Sometimes truly we are hated by some men for mickle mirth, and sometimes we joy in words and laughter, and although this, and more such, may be done with a clean soul before God, nevertheless before men we know well it is taken and expounded ill; and therefore moderation is to be had; and that we keep ourselves wisely nor place ourselves where we trow we can do ought that is like evil.

It is good for the servants of Christ to be near God, because in desire for Him they receive the heat of the fire of the Holy Ghost; and they sing the sweetness of endless love with sweetest heavenly sound like to honey. Wherefore melliflui facti sunt coeli: that is to say: the heavens are made sweet as honey,' that is to mean: saints that so burningly have loved Christ, knowing that He has suffered so mickle for them. Whence truly the minds of the saints are knitted to endless love, unable to be loosed; and although ravished as it were by the sweetness of heavenly life, by a melody as it were felt before, are gladdened in that.

CHAPTER XXV

OF PERFECT LOVE: AND WHAT MUST BE HAD FOR GHOSTLY JOY: AND OF LOVE AND CORRECTION

Excellence of meed stands in greatness of love; so that a lover burns with ever burning fire and is fulfilled within with heavenly sweetness. He truly that loves most shall be set highest in heaven. For this love is in the heart, and the more it loves God the more joy it feels in itself. They err therefore that but seldom and shortly have the joy of love, and that trow they love as mickle as he that is fed, as it were all day, with the sweetness of love. Some truly love with difficulty and some with ease, but the love of God is the more blessed in that it be light; the lighter, the heartier; the quicker, the sweeter; the sweeter, the more. Truly it is greater in resters than in labourers; therefore they that continually rest and fervently love are higher than they that some time take heed to rest, and some time to other occupations.

Nothing truly is better than love, nothing sweeter than holy charity. For to be loved and to love is a sweet change; the delight of all man's life, and of angel's, and of God's; and also the meed of all blessedness. If therefore thou desirest to be loved, love; for love gainyields itself. No man has ever lost by good love who keeps in view the end of love. Soothly he that knows not to burn in love knows not to be glad. Therefore never is a man more blessed than he that is borne without himself by the might of love, and by the greatness of God's love receives within himself a songful sweetness of everlasting praising.

But this happens not anon to every man; but when a man, turned to God, marvellously exercises himself and has cast away all desire for worldly vanity; then God sheds into His lovers that unspoken praising. The mind truly disposed to cleanness, receives from God the thought of eternal love; and soothly clean thought rises up to ghostly song. Clearness of heart, certain, is worthy to have heavenly sound; and so that God's praising should bide in ghostly joy, the soul is warmed with God's fire, and is gladdened with full marvellous delight.

But although a man forsake the world perfectly; and busily take heed to prayer, waking, and fasting; and have cleanness of conscience, so that he desire to die for heavenly joy, and to be dissolved and be with Christ; unless his mind be fully knit unto Christ, and it lasts in desires and thoughts of love—the which are certain and endlessly intent—and which thoughts, wherever he be, sitting or going, he meditates within himself without ceasing, desiring nothing but Christ's love; he else soothly receives not the heavenly sound, nor in ghostly song shall he sing JESU, nor His praise, in mind or mouth.

Pride forsooth destroys many; when they trow they have done aught that others have not, anon they bear themselves before others, and they that are better than themselves they put behind. But, know it well, he himself knows not love that presumes to despise common nature in his brother; for he does wrong to his own condition that knows not his right in another. He that honours not the community of nature in his neighbour, defiles the law of man's fellowship.

In this many men err from the love of God, nor know they how to come to His love because they study not to love their brother as they are bound. And soothly they either leave the sinner uncorrected, or if they correct or rebuke the sinner, with so great sharpness and fierceness they speak that oft they that they snib are made, by their words, worse than they are. Truly with meekness they should speak, that by sweet words they might win those that sharp correcting would make worse.

CHAPTER XXVI

OF THE SIGHINGS, DESIRE, AND MEEKNESS OF A PERFECT LOVER: AND OF THE DIFFERENCE BETWEEN WORLDLY LOVE AND GODLY: AND ALSO OF MEDITATION

The voice of the soul languishing with endless love bears the likeness of the seeker of His Maker, saying: Osculetur me osculo oris sui; that is to say: the Godhead might glad me with knitting me to His Son.' Therefore for love I long; because whom I love with all my mind I desire to see in His fairness. In the meanwhile, truly, in the labour and strife of my pilgrimage, I beseech He make me glad with sweetness of His love; and unto the time I can clearly see my Beloved, I shall think of His full sweet Name, holding it, joying, in my mind.

And no marvel that he be glad thereof in this life that has lust ever to fulfill the desires of His Maker. Nothing is merrier than JESU to sing, nothing more delightful than JESU to hear. Hearing it truly mirths the mind; and song uplifts it. And truly, whiles I want this, sighing, and heavy as it were with hunger and thirst, think myself forsaken. Forsooth when I feel the halsing and kissing of my Love, with untold delight as it were I overflow; whom true lovers, for love only of His unmeasured goodness, set before all things. Coming therefore into me, He comes inshedding perfect love. My heart also He refreshes, giving continuance; He warms me, and also makes fat, all lettings to love putting away.

Who then shall say that he must fall into stinking uncleanness of flesh, whom Christ has vouchsafed to fulfill with the sweetness of heavenly contemplation. Therefore henceforward it is sung: Laetabimur in te, memores uberum tuorum super vinnum. As who says: We desire to worship and joy in Thee; in Thy gladness we are merry, forsaking the lust and riches of worldly vanity, the which so beguile their lovers, that they know not the noy they suffer. And although we may not yet see Thy face, nevertheless so hotly we desire Thee, that though we should live for ever we should seek none other love.' For the longer we live the hotter we desire Thee, and the more joy we feel in Thy love, and painfully we hasten to Thee; for to Thy lovers noyous things pass, and mirth in ghostliness follows. That soul truly good JESU that loves Thee, would rather choose to suffer a horrible death than consent to any sin.

Nor soothly does he love Christ perfectly that dreads any but Christ; whiles all things turn to good to God's lovers. Perfect love overcomes pain, and also threats, because it feels no dread of any creature; it puts away all pride, and meekly gives stead to ilk thing; whereof it is said: Recti diligunt te, that is: Righteous men love Thee.' The righteous are the meek, loving truly, forgetting nothing, and though they stand in high perfection they behave themselves most meekly in mind and deed. And so ilk true lover may say within himself; Ilk man passes me in despising the world, and hate of sin; in desire for the heavenly kingdom; in sweetness and heat of Christ's love, and brotherly charity: some flourish in virtue, some shine in miracles; some are raised by the gift of heavenly contemplation; and some seek the secrets of scripture. When I behold the worthy life of so many, methinks I am as right nought, and among all others lowest.

Therefore the righteous flee full fast all earthly encumbrances, only drawing unto everlasting joys; in desire for all temporal things they greatly fail, and they rise with a high desire in God's love. And it is worthily said they love God; for going in the right way and the plain of shining charity, they seek nor savour nothing but Christ. To whose contraries it is said by the psalmist: Obsurentur oculi corum ne videant, et dorsum corum semper incurva; that is to say: Their eyes be dim that they see not, and their back bow thou always,' so that they only take heed to earthly things; everlasting putting behind. And therefore God's wrath is shed on them and righteous vengeance, with great fierceness of umbelapping torments. The righteous forsooth putting back all feignedness of heart, mouth, and deed, endeavour to joy without ceasing in the sight of God; and they bow themselves not to the love of void vanity, that, in their pilgrimage, they be not disturbed from the path of righteousness.

He therefore that desires to please Christ will do nothing, for good nor ill, against Christ's will. Full horrible it is to go into the fire of hell; but more to be hated is it to will to have lust in sin, because of which he may lose Christ for evermore.

Forsooth a soul parted from worldly vices, and sundered from venomous sweetness of the flesh; being given to heavenly desires, and as it were ravished, enjoys a marvellous mirth; because she feels now the gladness of the Beloved's love, so that she may contemplate more clearly, and desire more likingly. Also at this time the mouth of the Spouse and His sweetest kissing she asks, saying with voice: All earthly things are irksome to me: I feel the love of my Beloved; I taste the moisture of His marvellous comfort; busily I yearn after that sweetness so that I fail not, being put far from Him by temptation; Love makes me hardy to call Him that I love best, that He, comforting me and filling me, might kiss me with the kissing of His mouth.

Truly the more I am lift from earthly thoughts, the more I feel the sweetness desired; the more fleshly desires are slakened, the truelier everlasting are kindled. I beseech He kiss me with the sweetness of His refreshing love, straitly halsing me by the kissing of His mouth so that I fail not, and putting grace in me that I may continually grow in love. As children are nourished with their mother's milk, so chosen souls, burning in love, are fed with heavenly delight, by the which they shall be brought to the sight of the everlasting clearness.

Truly the delights of Christ's love are sweeter than all the delights of the world, and of fleshly savour. Forsooth all imaginations of fleshly lust and all plenteousness of worldly riches is but wretchedness and abomination in comparison with the least sweetness that is shed by God into a chosen soul. As great difference as is betwixt the sweetness of the highest plenty of worldly riches and the greatest need of worldly poverty, so infinitely more is it betwixt the sweetness of Thy love, my God, and the lust of worldly joy that fleshly men desire and go about, and in the which only they joy: for nought of Thy love they feel, in whom alone they should be glad.

Ghostly gifts truly direct a devout soul to love burningly; to meditate sweetly; to contemplate highly; to pray devoutly, and praise worthily; to desire JESU only, to wash the mind from filth of sins; to slaken fleshly desires; and to despise all earthly things and to paint the wounds and Christ's cross in mind; and, with an unwearied desire, with desire to sigh for the sight of the most glorious Clearness.

Such are the precious ointments with which a hallowed soul is best anointed and made fair with God's love.

CHAPTER XXVII

OF TRUE MEEKNESS AND ADVERSITY: AND OF THE EXAMPLE OF THE SAINTS: AND OF THE MANNER OF GHOSTLY PROFITING: AND OF THINKING ON CHRIST'S PASSION

The very meek behold not other men's sins, but their own; and not their good deeds, but other men's they praise. The rejected truly do the reverse; for they see rather other men's sins than their own, and in comparison they count their own sins as little or none; but their good deeds—if any happen—they praise before all others, whose goodness they desire to lessen if they cannot fully destroy it.

Two things have I been heavy to hear: one was when they praised me, wretched, whom I knew only as despised; another, when I saw my neighbour, the which I loved in God and for God, reproved or with slander backbitten. Nevertheless thou that forsakest the world and art busy to follow Christ in poverty, be busy to know thyself; for truly if thou forsakest the deeds and desires of the world, thou bindest thyself to suffer worldly diseases gladly for Christ, and truly to flee wealth strongly. If, forgetting, thou takest no heed to this, thou goest beguiled from Christ's love.

Therefore marvel not though thou be noyed with divers and many temptations; for if thou withstand steadfastly, thou shalt be dearer and sweeter before God. Have in mind that God proves His own as gold is proved by fire. They truly that inwardly feel the sweetness of Christ's love, gladly halsing tribulation, seek not outward worldly solace. For the sweetness in mind of those truly loving Christ is so mickle that if the joys of the world were gathered together in one place, they were liever run to the wilderness than to once look thereon with the eye. And certain it is no marvel, for all worldly cheer seems to it heaviness rather than comfort.

Soothly the soul that is wont to be visited with the joy of Christ's love, can not be fed with vain joy, whose heart is not parted from his Beloved, for he would sooner die than offend his Maker. And that thou mayest have this grace keep thy sins in thy mind as an example of penitence and be busy to follow saints' lives; so that thou a sinner, yet turned to God's service, may rise to hope by sinners raised to heaven, and by the ransacking of the lives of righteous men refrain thyself from all pride. Truly by mind of a holier thing is the holy man's mind meeked; for whose life soever thou findest written or hearest told, alway trust it without comparison better than thine.

Such truly are called Christ's lovers that for His name receive sharp adversity from the world, and despise prosperity and vainglory. They are fulfilled with despisings, reproofs, and slanders, and in their praising they are punished, the which for God live solitary in this world, and dying are taken up to the company of angels in heaven.

Truly I fled into the wilderness because I could not accord with men; for sickerly they oft let me from joy, and because I did not as they did, they put error and indignation upon me; and therefore I have found sorrow and tribulation, but I have ay worshipped the Name of our Lord.

Therefore that we fail not in temptation let us study to be weary of all earthly comforts, and constantly to keep in mind the crown of eternal joy, that being found waking we may receive the bliss promised. In the meantime also use we such rule that fleshly desires may be utterly restrained and worldly covetousness wisely forsake the heart, so that the body may alway stand stable and strong in God's service.

He truly that for Jesu's love forsakes all things, and leaves the having of his will, and abides steadfast and profiting, says with joy, I have found that my soul loves.' Christ is truly found in the heart when the heat of endless love is felt in it, the which covets to be sought without feigning. Christ certain alights in a soul with honey sweetness and ghostly song, so that he that has this joy may boldly say: I have found my Love.' Whosoever, truly, whiles he prays, sees his mind raised high, yea lift up above this bodily heaven, if he fail not but alway more and more desires to savour everlasting things, may therefore merrily abide the meekness of Christ; for within a few years he shall feel himself ravished to behold glorious things. Wherefore with meek heart, he shall not cease advancing in profit unto the time he comes to the fellowship of everlasting rest.

If the eye of thy heart be ravished in prayer to behold heavenly things, then full near is it that thy soul, passing earthly things, be made perfect in Christ's love. He soothly that in praying is not yet raised to behold heavenly things, must not cease discreetly to meditate, pray, and wake, unto the time he may perceive higher joys; so that he, lying on the earth, be not despised with griefs and diseases.

Egredimini filiae Syon et videte regem Salomonem in diademate. That is to say: Go forth ye souls renewed, and understand Christ truly, put to death for your health. Behold Him, and ye shall see His godly head with thorns crowned; His face bespat; His full fair eyes wan by pain; His back scourged; His breast hurt; His worthy hands thirled; His sweetest side with a spear wounded; His feet nailed through, and wounds set through all His soft flesh;

as it is written: From the sole of His foot to the crown of His head there is no health in Him.'

Go forth, therefore, from your unlawful desires and see what Christ has suffered for you; that your sins be altogether cast out, and your hearts be taught the burning of love.

CHAPTER XXVIII

THAT A TRUE LOVER DESPISES WORLDLY THINGS AND DESIRES HEAVENLY: AND OF THE HATING OF PRIDE, AND HALSING OF MEEKNESS

Behold, thou wretched little man, how in the liking of fleshly lust the cruelty of endless damnation sleeps. Therefore thou oughtest to gainstand them that are busy to destroy those things—that is to say virtues—that Christ desires. Thy heart, truly, must empty out all desire for all kinds of passing vanity before it can burn with Christ's love. For the mind burning with Christ's spirit is fed only with the love of endless things, and is gladdened in a joyful song.

Truly if the sweetness of endless love be now biding in thy soul, withouten doubt it destroys all wantonness of fleshly wickedness; and delighting thee in Christ, it suffers thee to feel nothing but Christ; for neither thou fallest from Him, nor feelest anything sweet but Him. Forsooth the perfect when they die are brought anon before God and set in the seats of blissful rest, for they see that Christ is God and enjoy Him.

They that begin to love Christ, afterward in great joy of love and honeysweet burning shall not cease to sing full lovely songs to Jesu Christ. Truly no earthly thing pleases him that truly loves Christ, for by the greatness of love all passing things seem foul. With the bodily eyes fleshly things are seen, but the righteous behold heavenly things with a clean and meek heart: the which, enlightened by the flame of heavenly sight, feel themselves loosed from the burden of sin, and afterward they cease to sin in will; whose heart turned into fire halses in desire nothing earthly but always in busy to thirl high things.

They that are sickerly ordained to holiness, in the beginning of their turning, for dread of God, forsake sins and worldly vanities: and then they set their flesh under strait penance, afterward setting Christ's love before all other, and feeling a delight in heavenly sweetness in devotion of mind they profit mickle. And so they pass from degree to degree and flourish with ghostly virtues; and so, made fair by grace, they come at last to the perfection that stands in heart, and word, and deed. Christ's love certain makes him that has swallowed it as it were dead to receive these outward things: he savours what is upward, he seeks that which is above, and nought that is on earth.

No marvel the mind, sighing in desire of the heavenly kingdom, grows in love of the Spouse, and joying with gladness inshed bares itself from desire of earthly things; and fulfilled with the longing for true love tents with all his mind to see God in His fairness. Wherefore lightened with the flame of His love, it is busy only in His desire and seeks nothing but Him. Whiles a true soul, certain, desires burningly only the presence of the spouse, it is perfectly cooled from all wantonness of vainglory. For love therefore it longs, because it sets at nought all earthly things whiles it thus hies to endless joys.

He that delights himself in Christ's love, and desires to have His comfort continually, not only covets not the solace of man, but also with great desire flees it, as if it were smoke that hurts his eyes.

Like as the air is stricken by the sunbeam, and by the shining of his light is altogether shining; so a devout mind, enflamed with the fire of Christ's love and fulfilled with desire for the joys of heaven, seems all love, because it is altogether turned into another likeness; the substance abiding although it be wonderfully mirthed. For when the mind is kindled by the fire of the Holy Ghost, it is bared from all idleness and uncleanness, and it is made sweet with the spring of God's delight, alway contemplating and never failing; seeing not earthly things until it be glorified with the sight of the Lover.

Truly it behoves us to eschew all pride and swelling of heart, for this it is that has cast sad men into great wretchedness. What is more shameful? What more worthy to be punished? It is great scorn truly, and plain abomination, that the foulest worm, the worst sinner, the lowest of men, sets about to make himself great on earth, for whom the highest King and Lord of Lords has liked so mickle to meek himself. It thou wilt clearly behold Christ's meekness, of whatsoever degree thou mayest be, how mickle soever the riches or virtues thou hast, thou shalt find in this no matter of pride but of despising thyself, and a cause of meekness.

Thou therefore that despisest sinners, behold thyself, for thou makest thyself much worse than others; for truly God is more displeased with a proud righteous man than a meek sinner. When true meekness is set in thy mind, whatsoever thou doest well is done to the praise of thy Maker, so that despising thy virtue thou seekest His worship; that thou, being given to vanity, lose not thy meed everlasting.

Think therefore on Jesu with thy heart's desire; pass thy prayer to Him; be not weary ever to seek Him; care for nothing but Him alone.

Happy are the rich that have such a possession; and to have this forsake thou the vanities of the world; and He shall overcome thine enemy and bring thee to His kingdom. The fiend that noys thee shall be overcome; the flesh that grieves thee be made subject; the world that assays thee for to beguile, shall be despised, if thy heart cease not to seek Christ's love.

The man truly sits not idle the which in mind cries to Christ although his tongue be still; for the body never rests in fleshy rest whiles the mind stints not to desire heavenly things; nor is he idle that is greedy ever to covet things everlasting. Truly the thoughts of Christ's lovers are swift in going up and harmonious in course; they will not be bound to passing things nor tied to fleshly contagion, but cease not to ascend until they have come to the heavens. For whiles the body is weary in Christ's service, ofttimes the spirit being uplifted is taken up to heavenly refreshment and the contemplation of God. He truly that prays devoutly has not his heart wavering among earthly things but raised to God in the heavens. He that desires to have that he prays, busily takes heed what he prays, for whom he prays and to what end he prays, and that he loves Him Whom he prays; lest a wretch, asking reward from this life, be beguiled.

Saints forsooth have so great meekness that they think they know nought, and think themselves as those who say they do nought; they call themselves lowest of all and unworthiest, yea, like as them that they chastise with reproving. These, after God's commandment, rest in the lowest place, whose lowly sitting receives no reproof from God, but honour; not unthank nor loss of meed, but great and worthy worship, to the which meekness best disposes.

Truly this meekness gives praise to Christ, noy to the fiend, and joy to God's people; it makes Christ's servant to love more burningly, to serve more devoutly, to praise more worthily; and makes him fuller of charity. The more that a man meeks himself the more he raises God's worship on high. He that truly perseveres in the love of God and of his neighbour, and yet thinks himself unworthier and lower than others, by meekness and knowledge of himself overcomes enemies, and conquers the love of the High Judge, and shall be received into endless joy by the angels when he passes from this light.

CHAPTER XXIX

THE TEACHING OF THE BOISTEROUS AND UNTAUGHT, DESIRING TO LOVE: AND OF THE ESCHEWING OF WOMEN

A true soul, the spouse of Jesus Christ, casts out pride, for deeply she loves meekness; she abhors vainglory, for desiring only everlasting mirth, she follows Christ; she hates fleshly liking and softness, for feeling before the sweetness of the everlasting honey, she desires alway to feel love for the loveliest. Evil wrath she has not, because she is ready to suffer all things for Christ's love. She knows not envy of others, for shining with true love she joys in ilk man's profit and health.

Truly no man is envious but if he in truth be little and weens he be mickle, wherefore he raises slanders against others lest they be likened to him; or if any other among the people be called greater, fairer, or stronger, anon he is heavy, being touched with the venom of envy. But the soul the which is but a little kindled with heavenly contemplation can not seek that vainglory of slipping praise. Whereby it is plainly shown that men therefore have envy because they have not the love of God that is in ilk chosen soul. For where any are that love God, they truly desire the profit of their fellows as of themselves.

If thou wilt therefore surpass in God's love thou hatest all earthly praising. The despisings of men and their scorns thou halsest for Christ, and strongly thou spreadest thy mind to get eternal joy. Rather choose with the rejected to feel the torment of fire in pain than common in sin with them. Certain he lives sicker that loves Christ burningly, and in the joy of His love sings lustily. It is more pleasing to him to fall into everlasting fire than once to sin deadly. Forsooth there are such saints, because they live in cleanness. They despise all earthly things, and from heat and ghostly gladness joying, they sing what before they said. They burn in the love of Christ; they study after heavenly sights; they are ever busy, as much as in them is, with good works; they overflow with the likings of everlasting life; and yet to themselves them seem most foul, and among others they think themselves the last and lowest.

Therefore thou that art boisterous and untaught be busy to stand strongly against thy ghostly enemies, and to suffer no ill thought to rest in thy heart; and set thy wisdom against the waitings of the fiends. When an unclean imagination or thought, contrary to the purpose of thy mind, withstands thee, fail not but fight manly. Cry to Christ without ceasing, until thou be clad with God's armour. And if thou desire to follow the despisers of the world think not what thou forsakest but what thou despisest; with what desire thou offerest thy will to God; with how great desire of love thou presentest thy prayers; with how great heat for the sight of God thou longest to be joined to Him. If thou perfectly hate all sin; if thou desire nothing that passes; if thy soul refuses to be cheered with earthly solace; if thou savour to behold heavenly things and desire most God's Son; if thou speak mannerly and wisely, because he speaks not, except he be made, whose spirit is melted with the honey of God's love and the sweetness of the song of Jesu; behold by these, and other such, sometimes used, thou shalt come to perfection.

No marvel God approves such a despiser of the world. Truly the soul that is both sweet with the shining of conscience, and fair with the charity of endless love, may be called Christ's garden; for she is cleansed from sins, flourishes with virtues and joys with the sweetness of high song, like as with songs of birds.

Therefore set we all our mind to please and obey God, to serve and love Him, and in ilk good deed we do be we busy to come to God. What value is it to covet earthly things or to desire fleshly love? We can have nothing thereby that lasts but the Judge's wrath, that is to say everlasting pain. Soothly fleshly love stirs temptation and blinds the soul that she may not have perfect cleanness; it hides sins done, and it casts her down unwisely to new wickedness; it enflames to all cursed lusts; it disturbs all rest of the soul, and it lets, so that Christ may not be burningly loved; and wastes all virtue gotten before.

Therefore he that covets to love Christ, let not the eye of his mind look to woman's love. Women if they love men are fond, because they know not to keep measure in loving; and truly when they are loved they prick full bitterly. They have one eye for waitings, and another for true sorrow; whose love distracts the wits, perverts and overturns reason, changes wisdom of mind to folly, withdraws the heart from God and makes the soul bond to fiends. And forsooth he that beholds a woman with fleshly love—although it be not with the will to fulfill lust—keeps not himself undefiled from unlawful movings or unclean thoughts, but ofttimes defiles himself with stinking filth; and, peradventure, he feels a liking for to do worse.

Truly the beauty of women beguiles many men, through desire whereof the hearts of the righteous also are some time overturned, so that they that began in spirit end in the flesh. Therefore beware, and in the good beginning of thy conversation keep no speech with women's fairness lest receiving thereof the venomous sickness of lust for to proffer and fulfill foulness of mind, and being deceived knowingly and cowardly, thou be drawn away by the discomfits of thine enemies. Therefore flee women wisely and alway keep thy thoughts far from them, because, though a woman be good, yet the fiend by pricking and moving, and also by their cherishing beauty, thy will can be overmickle delighted in them, because of frailty of flesh.

But if thou wouldst call again Christ's love without ceasing, and have Him with dread in thy sight in all places, I trow thou shouldest never be beguiled by the false cherishing of a woman; but truly the more that thou seest thou art assayed with false flatterings—if thou despise them as japes or trifles as they are—no marvel that thou shouldest have the more joy of God's love.

Christ truly does marvellously in His lovers, the which, with a special and a perfect love He takes to Himself. Truly they desire not softness of the flesh or the beauty thereof; all worldly things they forget; they love not temporal prosperity nor dread the world's frowardness. They love full well to be by themselves that, without letting, they may fall into the gladness that they feel in God's love; full sweet they think it to suffer for Christ, and nothing hard. For he that wills worthily to honour the victory of martyrs, let him fulfill the devotion of virtue by the following of virtue. Let him hold the cause of the martyrs if that he suffer not the pain; let him keep patience, in which he shall have full victory.

A soul truly forsaking the folly of ill love enters the way of strait life, in the which is felt the earnest of the sweetness of heavenly life: which, when she feels so comfortable that she overcomes all passing liking, she prays God that He would vouchsafe such comfort to give and refresh her ghostly, and that He would give the grace of continuance lest she fail, being made weary by divers errors.

If a young man begin to do well let him ever think to continue; let him not sleep nor cease from his good purpose, but ay profit in mind, rising from less to more. Forsooth the shadow of error being forsaken, and the venomous sweetness of a wretched life despised, taking the strait life, he halses now the sweetness of full high devotion. And thus, as it were by degrees, he ascends to the height and contemplation of God by the gifts of the Holy Ghost; in the which heat of eternal love being rested and gladdened, he overflows with heavenly delights, as far as is lawful to mortal man.

Certainly a good soul umbeset with many diseases, and noyed with the heat of temptation, can not feel the sweetness of God's love as it is in itself; nevertheless she is expert in the joy of love and in stable course draws to her Lover; and though the soul may want so wonderful sweetness, yet with so great desire she loves Christ that for His love only she shall perseveringly stand.

But how mickle is His most kind help to be praised in which every true lover is expert; that it comforts all the sorry; makes sweet the forsaken; sets in peace the disturbed, and lays waste all distracting noise. The soul departed from the sins of the world, and withdrawn from fleshly desire, is purged of sin; and thereby she understands a sweetness of future mirth coming near to her, in which hope she is confirmed, and is sicker to have the kingdom. And in this life she gives to Christ a drink full likingly made of hot love, with greetings of ghostly gifts and with flowers of virtues, that Christ receives, pleased, who for love drank of the well of penance in this life.

CHAPTER XXX

OF GOD'S PRIVY DOOM: AND THAT THEY THAT FALL AGAIN BE NOT DEEMED BY US: AND OF GREAT ARGUMENTS AGAINST PURCHASOURS

But some are wont to ask how it can be that many that have led the hardest life and have utterly forsaken this world's joy, afterwards dread not to slide again into sin; and they shall not end in a good end.

If we will not err let us be in peace from proudly deeming. To us it longs not to know God's privy doom: truly after this life all things as needs shall be shown. All the ways of our Lord's dooms are merry, that is to say true and righteous; for neither He reproves one withouten very right, nor another, withouten mercy that is righteous, He chooses unto life. Therefore we ought to consider, that the clothing of His clearness is as a groundless pit; wherefore we ought, whiles we are in this way, to dread, and in no wise to presume unwisely; for man wots not whether he be worthy wrath or love, or by what end he shall pass from this life. The good ought to dread that they fall not into ill; and the ill may trow that they can rise from their malice. Forsooth if they bide in their covetousness and their wickedness, in vain they hope themselves sicker of mercy, whiles their wickedness is not left; for sin, before it be forsaken, is never forgiven; nor yet then unless satisfaction be behight and that a sinner shirk not to fulfill it as soon as he can.

But the mighty men and the worldly rich that ever hungrily burn in getting possessions of others, and by their goods and riches grow in earthly greatness and worldly power—buying with little money what, after this passing substance, was of great value—or have received in the service of kings or great lords great gifts, without meed, that they might have delights and lusts with honours: let them hear not me but Saint Job: Ducunt inquit in bonis dies suos et in puncto ad infernum descendent; that is to say: Their days they led in pleasure, and to hell they fall in a point.'

Behold, in a point they lose all that they studied all their life to get; with these worldly wisdom has dwelt that, before God, is called folly, and fleshly wit, that is enmity to God, they knew. Therefore with mighty torments they shall suffer because knowing God they glorify not God but themselves and have vanished in their thoughts; calling themselves wise they are now made fools; and they, that have felt the joy and delight of this world, are come to the deepness of stinking hell.

And yet forsooth among all that are bound with the vice of this world, in none, as I suppose, is less trust of salvation than of these the people call false purchasours. When they soothly have spent all their strength and youth in getting the possessions of another by wrong and law; and afterwards in age they rest, sickerly keeping that they with wrong have gotten. But because their conscience is feared, wickedness gives witness to condemnation only when they cease from cursed getting; they dread not to use other men's goods as if they were their own. For if they should restore all, full few should be left for themselves. And because they are proud they shame to beg; or they will not fall from their old honour, therefore they say they cannot dig or labour. Also, deceived by fiends, they choose rather to eschew worldly wretchedness that they may suffer the endless pain of hell everlastingly.

Such forsooth whiles they have lordship in this world oppress the small by the power of their tyranny; forsooth to be raised into such melody of this exile is not a matter of dread to others but rather joy; for lest God's chosen should be such they are refrained by God, David being witness: Ne timueris cum dives factus fuerit homo, etc. When man is made rich dread not, nor when joy of his house is multiplied'; for when he dies he takes not all, nor his joy goes not with him; nor the drop of water, that is to say of mercy, comes not to the tongue of the rich man burning in hell. In his dying he loses all his joy, and only sin goes with him to the land of darkness, for the which he shall be punished withouten end.

Explicit liber primus Incendii Amoris Ricardi Hampole heremite, translatus a latino in Angelicum, per fratrem Richardum Misyn heremitam, et ordinis carmelitarum, Ac sacre theologie bachalareum, Anno domini Millesimo ccccxxxv. </div3> <pb/> </div2>

BOOK II

CHAPTER I

WHY THE PERFECT CONTEMPLATIVES TAKE NO HEED TO OUTWARD SONG, AND OF THEIR ERROR THAT REPROVE THEM: AND HOW TO PROFIT IN CONTEMPLATION

Because in the kirk of God there are singers ordained in their degree, and set to praise God and to stir the people to devotion, some have come to me asking why I would not sing as other men when they have ofttimes seen me in the solemn masses. They weened forsooth I had done wrong, for ilk man, they say, is bound to sing bodily before his Maker, and yield music with his outward voice. I answered not thereof; for they knew not how I gave forth melody and a sweet voice to my Maker, but, because they could not understand by what way, they weened that no man might have ghostly song.

Truly it is fondness to trow that a man, and especially he that is perfectly given to God's service, should not have a special gift from His love that many other men have not; but many trow this because in themselves they find none such. Therefore I have thought to show some manner of answer, and not fully give stead to the reprovers. How longs the life of other men to them whose manners, as they wot, in many things surpass their life, and are far higher in things that are unseen? Whether it is lawful to God to do what He will; or their sight is wicked and God is good? Nor will they bring God's rule under their measure, for are not all men God's? And whom He will, He takes; and whom He will, He forsakes; and to whom He will and when He will, He gives what pleases Him, to show the greatness of His Goodness?

Therefore I trow they grumble and backbite because they would that others higher in devotion come down to them, and conform themselves in all things to their lowers, for they ween they be higher when they are far lower in merit. Therefore my soul has found boldness to open my music a little that is come to me by burning love; in which I sing before Jesu and sound notes of the greatest sweetness. Also the more they have stood up against me, because I fled the outward songs that are wont in the kirks, and the sweetness of the organ that is heard gladly by the people, only abiding among these either when the need of hearing mass—which elsewhere I could not hear—or the solemnity of the day asked it on account of the backbiting of the people.

Truly I have desired to sit alone that I might take heed to Christ alone that had given to me ghostly song, in the which I might offer Him praises and prayers. They that reproved me trowed not this, and therefore they would have brought me to their manner; but I could not leave the grace of Christ and consent to fond men that knew me not within. Therefore I let them speak, and I did that that was to do after the state in the which God had set me.

For this shall I say, thanking Christ's glory, that henceforward I no more fear others who be thus fond, nor that presume to deem proudly; for that I have done is not from feigning simulation, and being taken by imagination, as some say of me; and many therewith are beguiled that ween they have that they never received. But in truth an unseen joy has come to me and I have verily waxed warm within me with the fire of love; the which has taken my heart from these low things, so that, singing in Jesu, full far have I flown from outward melody to full inward.

Whence I have hated filth, and cast out vanity of words, and have not taken meats in superfluity, nor have striven unwisely to govern myself; although it were said of me I was given to rich houses, and to be fed well and live in pleasures. But by God's working I had set my soul otherwise, so that I savoured things heavenly rather than sweetness of meats; and for this cause I have loved a certain wilderness, and I chose to live away from men, only speeding the needs of the body, and so soothly I received solace of Him that I loved.

It is not to be trowed that in the beginning of his turning a man may run to the height of contemplative life or feel the sweetness thereof, when it is well known that contemplation is gotten in great time and with great labour, and is not given anon to every man, although it be had with all joy when it is gotten. Truly it is not in man's power to receive it, nor no man's labour however great is worthy it; but of the goodliness of God it is given to true lovers that have desired to love Christ above man's hoping.

Yet many after penance have fallen from innocence, afterwards gliding into idleness and to the abomination of sinners, because they were not burning in charity; seldom and so thinly have they the sweetness of contemplation that they are too weak to stand when they are tempted; or else, being weary and loathing ghostly food, they desire worldly comfort among sinners.

Truly to despise this world and desire the heavenly kingdom and desire Christ's love is full good; and, hating sin, to read busily or meditate on holy books. A devout soul being used and taught in these has a ready defence against the fiend's darts. It is truly to the devil's confusion when we spread God's word against all his temptations. Forsooth the sufferers, and bearers in patience of the burden and heat of temptation, suffer not themselves to be led into the love of deceitful sweetness; and after many tears and busy prayers they shall be enflamed with eternal love, and shall feel heat abiding in themselves withouten end, for in their meditation the fire shall wax warm.

CHAPTER II

THE TEACHING OF CONTEMPLATIVE LIFE IN PRAYING, MEDITATING, FAST-
ING, AND WAKING: AND OF THE PROUD CONTEMPLATIVE: AND OF TRUE
AND VERY GHOSTLY SONG

Therefore one chosen and alway desiring love turns himself into his love; for he has neither worldly substance nor desires to have, but following Christ by wilful poverty lives content and paid by the alms of other men, whiles his conscience is clear and made sweet with heavenly savour. All his heart shall he shed forth in love of his Maker, and he shall labour to be enlightened by daily increase in high desires. Every man forsaking this world, if he desire to be enflamed with the fire of the Holy Ghost, must busily take tent not to wax slow in prayer and meditation. Soothly by these, with tears following and Christ favouring, the mind shall be gladdened; and being glad, shall be lift into contemplative life.

The soul goes up into this height whiles soaring by excess it is taken up above itself, and heaven being open to the eye of the mind, it offers privy things to be beheld. But first truly it behoves to be exercised busily, and for not a few years, in praying and meditating, scarcely taking the needs of the body, so that it may be burning in fulfilling these; and, all feigning being cast out, it should not slacken day and night to seek and know God's love.

And thus the Almighty Lover, strengthening His lover to love, shall raise him high above all earthly things and vicious strifes and vain thoughts, so that the wicked and dying flies of sin lose not the sweetness of the ointment of grace since dead, they become as nought. And henceforward God's love shall be so sweet to him, and shall be also moistened with sweetness most liking, and he shall feel nought but the solace of heavenly savour shed into him, and token of high holiness. Truly fed with this sweetness he desires ever to wake, inasmuch as he feels verily the heat of endless love burning his heart, nor goes it away, enlightening the mind with sweet mystery. And yet some others that men trowed had been holy had this heat in imagination only. Wherefore being not in truth but in shadow, when they are called to the wedding or the feast of Christ's espousals, they are not ashamed unworthily to challenge the first place. No marvel that in the righteous examination they shall go down with shame, and shall have the lower place. Of these truly it is said: Cadent a latere tuo mille, et decem milia a dextris tuis, that is to say: From thy side a thousand shall fall, and ten thousand from thy right hand.'

But would God they knew themselves and that they would ransack their conscience; then should they not be presumptuous, nor making comparison with the deeds of their betters would they empride themselves. Truly the lover of the Godhead, whose inward parts are verily thirled with love of the unseen beauty and who joys with all the pith of his soul, is gladdened with most merry heat. Because he has continually given himself to constant devotion for God, when Christ wills, he shall receive—not of his own meed but of Christ's goodness—a holy sound sent from heaven, and thought and meditation shall be changed into song, and the mind shall bide in marvellous melody. Soothly it is the sweetness of angels that he has received into his soul; and the same praises, though it be not in the same words, he shall sing to God.

Such as is the song of the angels so is the voice of this true lover; though it be not so great or perfect, for frailty of the flesh that yet cumbers the lover. He that knows this, knows also angels song, for both are of one kind here and in heaven. Tune pertains to song, not to the ditty that is sung. This praising and song is angels meat; by which also living men most hot in love are gladdened, singing in Jesu, now when they have received the doom of endless praise that is sung by the angels of God. It is written in the psalm: Panem angelorum manducavit homo, that is to say: Man has eaten angels bread.' And so nature is renewed and shall pass now into a godly joy and happy likeness, so that he shall be happy, sweet, godly, and songful, and shall feel in himself lust for everlasting love, and with great sweetness shall continually sing.

Soothly it happens to such a lover what I have not found expressed in the writings of the doctors: that is, this song shall swell up in his mouth, and he shall sing his prayers with a ghostly symphony; and he shall be slow with his tongue, because of the great plenty of inward joy, tarrying in song and a singular music, so that that he was wont to say in an hour scarcely he may fulfill in half a day. Whilst he receives it soothly he shall sit alone, not singing with others nor reading psalms. I say not ilk man should do this, but he to whom it is given; and let him fulfill what he likes him, for he is led by the Holy Ghost, nor for men's words shall he turn from his life.

In a clear heat certain shall he dwell, and in full sweet melody, shall he be lift up. The person of man shall he not accept; and therefore of some shall he be called a fool or churl because he praises God in joyful song. For the praise of God shall burst up from his whole heart, and his sweet voice shall reach on high; the which God's Majesty likes to hear.

A fair visage has he whose fairness God desires, and keeps in himself the unmade wisdom. Wisdom truly is drawn from privy things, and the delight thereof is with the lovers of the everlasting; for she is not found in their souls that live sweetly in earth. She dwells in him of whom I spake, because he melts wholly in Christ's love and all his inward members cry to God. This cry is love and song, that a great voice raises to God's ears. It is also the desire of good, and the affection for virtue. His crying is outside of this world because his mind desires nothing but Christ. His soul within is all burnt with the fire of love, so that his heart is alight and burning, and nothing outward he does but that good may be expounded. God he praises in song, but yet in silence: not to men's ears but in God's sight he yields praises with a marvellous sweetness.

CHAPTER III

THAT GHOSTLY SONG ACCORDS NOT WITH BODILY: AND THE CAUSE AND THE ERROR OF GAINSAYERS. AND OF KNOWLEDGE INSHED OR INSPIRED; AND HOW IT DIFFERS FROM KNOWLEDGE GOTTEN BY LABOUR

But in this every man raised in holiness may know that he has the song of which I spake: if he can not sustain the cry of singers unless his inward song be brought to mind, and he has glided, so to say, into outward. That among singers and readers some are distracted from their devotion is not from perfection but from unstableness of mind, because other men's words break and destroy their prayers; and this forsooth happens not to the perfect. They truly are so stabled that by no cry or noise or any other thing can they be distracted from prayer or thought, but only cut off by such from song. For truly this sweet ghostly song is specially worth because it is given to the most special. It accords not with outward song, the which in kirks and elsewhere are used. It discords mickle from all that is formed by man's outward voice to be heard with bodily ears; but among angels' tunes it has an acceptable melody, and by them that have known it, it is commended with marvel.

See and understand and be not beguiled, for to you I have shown, to the honour of Almighty God and to your profit, why I fled strangers in the kirks, and for what cause I loved not to mingle with them, and desired not to hear organ players. Truly they gave me letting from songful sweetness, and made fail the full clear song. And therefore marvel not if I fled that that confused me; and in that I had been to blame, if I had not left what would have put me from so sweet song. Forsooth I had erred if I had done otherwise. But well I knew of whom I received it. Therefore I have alway conformed me to do His will, lest He should take from me, being unkind, that He gave to me kindly. I had great liking to sit in the wilderness that I might sing more sweetly far from noise; and with quickness of heart I might feel sweetest praise; the which doubtless I have received of His gift whom above all things I have wonderfully loved.

Truly my heart has not yearned in bodily desire, nor have I conceived this comfortable song that I have sung, singing in Jesu, from a creature. Therefore love has brought me thereto, that I should not stand in the plight in which the unthrifty are cast down; but that I should be raised above the height of all seen things, and from heaven should be kindled and lightened to praise God, whose praising is not comely in the sinner's mouth.

To whom therefore that loves not anything save one shall the window, un-thirled by all, be opened; and no marvel it were although his nature were changed into nobility of worthiness unable to be told, and made clear and free; which noble clearness no man shall know in eternity that now knows not love, and in Christ feels sweetness.

Nor doubtless ought I to cease from the best tried devotion because of backbiters that have cast evil biting into mind innocence; and I ought to cast all wickedness down, and love them that stirred me to greater ill; and thereof grace shall have been increased to the lover whiles he has not taken heed to words wavering in the wind, but with a perfect heart shall spread himself forth to his love, and unwearily pursue his purpose.

Herefore truly the desire for vanity is vanished and truthful love is risen in the mind, so that the soul of the lover shall not wax cold but shall remain in comfortable heat and the heart shall not be bruised from continual thought of his Beloved. Soothly in this steadfastness the excellence of love happens to a true lover, so that he shall be raised up to a fiery heaven and there shall be stirred to love more than may be spoken, and shall be more burned within himself than can be shown, and shall halse the degrees of grace. And hereof he has received and boldly say whatever he thinks; though before he were hold-en—or else were—a fool and unwise.

But those taught by knowledge gotten, not inshed, and puffed up with folded arguments, in this are disdainful: saying where learned he? who read to him? For they trow not that the lovers of endless love might be taught by their inward master to speak better than they taught of men, that have studied at all times for vain honours.

If in the old time the Holy Ghost inspired many, why should He not now take His lovers to contemplate the Joy of His Godhead? Some of this time are approved to be even to those of former times. I call not this approving men's allowance, for oft they err in their approving, choosing such as God despised and despising those God has chosen. But such I call allowed whom eternal love has pithily enflamed and the grace of the Holy Ghost inspires to all good; these are marked with the flower of all virtue, and continually sing in the love of God. And all that longs to the world's vain joy and the false honours of cursed and proud life they tread under the feet of their affections.

No marvel that these are outcasts of men. But in the sight of God and the holy angels they are greatly commended; whose hearts are strong to suffer all adversity, nor will they be blown about by the wind of vanity. At the last they are borne to Christ with high holiness, when they that men chose and allowed are cast down in damnation and are drawn in torments to be punished with the fiends withouten end.

CHAPTER IV

OF THE EXCELLENCE OF GHOSTLY SONG: AND THAT IT NEITHER CAN BE SAID NOR WRITTEN, NOR RECEIVES ANY FELLOWSHIP: AND OF THE CHARITY OF SPIRITUAL SINGERS: AND THE PRIDE OF THEM THAT HAVE GOTTEN KNOWLEDGE

Truly the lover of Almighty God is not raised in mind to see into high things withouten skill, and to sing the song of love that springs up in the soul, the which is ardently and openly burnt with the fire of love, and spread out in sweet devotion, abiding in songs that yield honey from our fairest Mediator. Therefore the singer is led into all mirth, and, the well of endless heat breaking forth in mirth, he is received into halsing and singular solace, and the lover is arrayed with the might of the most lovely passage and refreshed in sweet heat.

He joys, truly glistening whiter than snow and redder than a rose; for he is kindled by God's fire, and going with clearness of conscience he is clad in white. Therefore he is taken up thereto above all others; for in his mind melody abides and sweet plenty of heat tarries; so that not only shall he offer a marrow offering in himself and pay Christ praise in ghostly music, but also he shall stir others to love, so that they hie to give themselves devoutly and perfectly to God; the which vouchsafes to make glad His lovers, cleaving to Him with all their heart, in this exile also. This delight, certain, which he has tasted in loving Jesu, passes all wit and feeling. Truly I can not tell a little point of this joy, for who can tell an untold heat? Who lay bare an infinite sweetness? Certain if I would speak of this joy unable to be told, it seems to me as if I should teem the sea by drops, and spar it all in a little hole of the earth. And no marvel though I, the which scarcely tastes one drop of that same excellence, can not open to you the unmeasuredness of that eternal sweetness, nor that ye that are boisterous in wit and distracted by fleshly thoughts can not receive it; even although ye were full wise of wit and given to God's services.

Nevertheless if ye were alway busy to savour heavenly things, and if ye studied to be enflamed with God's love, withouten doubt there should come into you plenteously the liking of that love, the which fulfilling all penetrable parts of thy mind shall drop a wonderful sweetness into it. Truly the fuller ye shall be of charity, the more able ye may suppose yourselves to be receivers of that joy. The nearer truly to God shall they be endlessly that in this time have the more burningly and sweetly loved Him. They, certain, that are empty of God's love are fulfilled with worldly filth; and so being drawn to vain tales, they seek the delights in outward things that show, forgetting inward goods: whose height is hidden from mortal eye, whiles they in mind fall under worldly solace, even in their rising they vanish from a glorious perpetuity.

Therefore it seems that in the time to come covetousness shall be exiled and charity certainly reign. Contrarily, in this life it is wrought by many, forsooth by nearly all, that covetousness is brought in—yes into the King's hall; and charity, as if it were consenting to treason, is prisoned and cast out of the kingdom into exile. But yet it has found a dwelling place in the hearts of God's chosen. It goes from the proud and rests in the meek.

Many wretches are beguiled; the which feign to themselves to love God when they love Him not, trowing that they may be occupied with worldly needs and yet truly enjoy the love of Jesu Christ with sweetness. And they trow they may run about the world, and be contemplative; the which they that fervently love God and have gone into contemplative life deemed impossible. But being ignorant and not imbued with heavenly wisdom but puffed up with the knowledge that they have gotten they suppose wrongly concerning themselves; and they know not as yet how to hold God with love.

Therefore I cry and with desire I say: Salvum me fac Deus, quoniam defecit sanctus, that is to say: Lord make me safe, for thy saint is wanting.' The true lover fails: the voice of singers is at peace; there appears no heat in true lovers; ilk man goes in his evil way, and the wretchedness he has conceived in heart he ceases not to bring to deed. They waste their days in vanity and their years in haste. Alas the fire of desire has swallowed up the young man and maiden, the suckling also together with the old man.

O good Jesu, it is full good to me to be drawn to Thee, for my soul shall not come into their counsel but sitting all alone to Thee shall I sing. The whiles Thou art praised thou waxest sweet, so that it is not hard but full sweet to continually praise Thee; not bitter but merrier than to be fulfilled with all bodily and worldly delights. Delectable and desirable it is to be in Thy praise; for no marvel is it that all that is dight with so great love savours full sweet.

The lover also burning in this unbodily halsing, his wickedness being cleansed, and all his thoughts that go not unto this end vanished, and desiring to see his Beloved with his ghostly eye, has raised a cry to his Maker, bursting forth from the inner marrow of his affectuous love, as if he would cry from afar. He lifts up his inward voice, the which is not found but in the lover most burning; as far as is lawful in this way. Here I cease: for, because of the unwit and boisterousness of mind understanding, I can not describe this cry, nor yet how mickle it is or how merry to think, feel, bear; though I might in my measure. But to you I could not tell it, nor can not, for I know not how to overcome my wits except that I will say this cry is ghostly song.

Who therefore shall sing to me the ditty of my song and the joys of my desire, with burning of love and heat of my young age, that from songs of fellowly charity I might ransack my substance, and the measure of sweetness in which I was holden worthy might be known to me; if peradventure I might find myself exempted from unhappiness. And I presume not to say that by myself, because I have not yet found that I desire after so that I might rest with sweetness in the solace of my fellows. If forsooth I deemed that cry or song is alway hid from bodily ears—and that dare I well say—would God that I might find a man author of that melody the which, though not in word yet in writing, should sing me my joy, and should draw out notes of love in singing and joying in spirit, the which, in the Name most worthy, I shamed not to say before my love. This one truly should be lovelier to me than gold; and all precious things that are to be had in this exile are not like to him. Beauty of virtue dwells with him and the secrets of love he perfectly ransacks. I would love him truly as my heart, nor is there aught that I would hide from him; for he shall show me the ghostly song that I desire to understand, and shall clearly unfold the melody of my mirth. In which unfolding I shall the more joy, or else quicklier sing, because the burning of love shall be shown to me, and songful joy shall shine before me; also my clamorous thought shall not glide without a praiser, nor shall I labour thus in doubt. Now truly the longings of this heavisom exile cast me down, and heaviness grieving me scarcely suffers me to stand. And when within with unwrought heat I wax warm, without I lurk as it were wan and unhappy and without light.

O my God, to whom I offer devotion without feigning, wilt Thou not think on me in Thy mercy? A wretch I am; therefore I need Thy mercy. And wilt Thou not raise into light the longing that binds me, that I may fitly have that I desire; and the labour in which I am heavy because I trespassed, Thou shalt change into a honey sweet mansion, so that melody may last where heaviness was; and that I may see my Love in His beauty, whom I desire, and worship Him endlessly, held by His touch, for after Him I long.

CHAPTER V

THE MEDITATION OF THE LOVER IN HIS LOVE: AND THE FORSAKING OF FELLOWSHIP: AND HOW IN ORDER IT COMES TO THE FLAME OF LOVE

O Jesu, when with rejoicing, I burn in Thee, and busily the heat of love comes in so that I should halse Thee fully, O most lovely; but I am borne back, Thou sweetest one, from that I love and desire. Moreover griefs happen, and the waste wilderness forbars the way, and suffers not the habitations of the lovers to be builded in one. But would to God Thou hadst shown me a fellow in the way, that with his stirrings my heaviness might have been gladdened and the bond of sighing unloosed; if it were not forthwith cut in sunder by Thy sweet scythe, so sorely it would strain that it might gar the lover go forth from the close of the flesh for the greatness of love and be cast down before Thy Majesty.

In the meantime, certain, joying in hymns of praise, sweetly should I have rested with my fellow that Thou hadst given me, and in good speech, without strife, we should have been glad. Truly feasting together in the mirth of love we would sing lovely songs, until we be led from this outward and cumbrous prison and brought into the inward dwelling place, at the same time, receiving by lot a seat among the heavenly citizens that loved Christ in one manner and one measure.

Alas what shall I do? How long shall I suffer delay? To whom shall I flee that I may happily enjoy that I desire? Needy am I and hungry, noyed and diseased, wounded and discoloured for the absence of my love; for love hurts me, and hope that is put back chastises my soul. Therefore the cry of the heart goes up, and amongst the heavenly citizens a songly thought runs desiring to be lifted up to the ear of the most High. And when it comes there it proffers its errand and says:

O my love! O my honey! O my harp! O my psaltry and daily song! When shalt Thou help my heaviness? O my heart's rose, when shalt Thou come to me and take with Thee my spirit? Truly Thou seest that I am wounded to the quick with Thy fair beauty, and the longing relaxes not but grows more and more, and the penalties here present cast me down, and prick me to go to Thee, of whom only I trow I shall see solace and remedy. But who meanwhile shall sing me the end of my grief and the end of mine unrest? And who shall show to me the greatness of my joy and the fulfilling of my song, that from this I might take comfort and sing with gladness, for I should know the end of mine unhappiness and that joy were near? Herefore an excellent song I shall sing and my cry and voice shall soften the hardness of my Beloved also. If He should chastise He should slake, but punishing gradually, He shall not ay laugh at the pains of the innocent.

And herefore I can be called happy, and have withouten end the merriest draught of love, withouten all uncleanness; and, all griefs being cleansed away, may stand in perfectness of joy and holiness, singing worship with a heavenly symphony; when, truly, amid these needy diseases, the burning of sweet love has mirthed my mind within my secret soul as it were with music, and the sweet honeyed memory of Jesu; so that I, greatly gladdened in the song the which I received from heaven, should not feel the venomous sweetness of unworthy love—the which those that flourish in beauty of the flesh think full sweet—nor should this sturdy earthliness hold me.

O fairest and most lovely in Thy beauty, have mind that for Thy sake I dread not worldly power; and have mind also that I would cleave to Thee. All love that unwisely cherishes I have cast out, and I have fled all things that let to love Thee, God; and fleeting fairness that makes men bond and send women to malice, nor has it liked me to enjoy plays of youth, that by uncleanness make worthy souls subject to bondage of folly.

Henceforth I ceased not to give Thee my heart, touched by desire; and Thou hast withholden it so that it should not flow into divers lewdness of concupiscence and lust, and Thou hast put in me the mind of Thy Name, and hast opened to mine eyes the window of contemplation. To Thee at last devoted I have run in ghostly song; but first my heart waxed warm with the fire of love, and lovely ditties rose up within me.

If thou puttest not these things from Thy sight, the mickleness of Thy pity should move Thee; by the which Thou sufferest not Thy lovers to be taken too mickle into coldness: and I trow Thou wouldest lessen my wretchedness, and Thou wouldest not turn Thy face from my longing.

Sorrow certain and wretchedness stand in the body; longing soothly abides in the soul, until the time Thou givest that I have desired with so great heat; through love of which my flesh is made lean and foul among the beauteous of this life. And from the inflowing of it my soul has languished to see Thee whom she has burningly desired: and that in those seats she might be the secret heaven, and rest with the fellowship that she desired; and after be taken up where, among angel signers, she may worship Thee perfectly with love, withouten end.

Behold, mine inward parts have seethed up and the flame of charity has wasted the gathering of my heart that I have hated, and has put by the slippery gladness of worldly friendship; and also thoughts that were foul and to be held abominable it has drawn out. And so without feigning I have risen to mannerly love, that before had slept in divers outrays of mine errors and umbelapped with darkness; there with liking I felt the lust of devotion sweetest where I sorrow more to have trespassed. My friends I pray you hear that no man beguile you!

These, and other such words in the sight of our Maker, burst up from the fire of love; and no man that is strange to this unmeasured love should dare to use such words the which is yet disturbed with temptation to void and unprofitable thoughts, and that has not his mind continually with Christ without gainturning, or is stirred affectously in any manner about any creature: so that all the movements of his heart go not to God because he feels himself bound to earthly affection.

Full high is he in charity whose heart has sung these ditties of love, and, hid in ghostly feasting, beholds not outward fondness. Forsooth marvellously cheered with eternal desires, he raises himself to heaven by contemplation: from whence he burns with sweetest love, and is moistened by a draught from the heavenly passage; and is umbeset and truly transformed with the heat of the happiness to come, so that he shall eschew all temptation and is set in the height of contemplative life. And henceforward so continuing in ghostly song in Christ's praise he is glorified.

CHAPTER VI

OF DIVERS GIFTS OF GOD'S CHOSEN: AND HOW SAINTS COME TO LOVE IN
PRAYING, MEDITATING, LOVING, SUFFERING, ADVERSITY AND HATING VICE,
AND THAT LOVE COMES FROM GOD AND THAT HIS LOVE IS NECESSARY, AND
THAT TRUE LOVERS FALL NOT BY TEMPTATIONS OF THE FLESH, AS OTHER
IMPERFECT ONES: NOR ARE HURT BY THE DREGS OF SIN ALTHOUGH THEY
LAST

The chosen truly that are fulfilled with love, and take more heed in mind to
loving than to aught else, have wonderfully shown to us the secrets of lovers
the which, surpassing in fervour and supernaturally, have received the fire of
love, and with a wonderful desire have yearned after their Beloved Jesu. Divers
gifts truly are disposed to God's lovers: some are chosen to do; some to teach;
some to love. Nevertheless all the holy covet one thing and run to one life, but
by divers paths: for everyone chosen goes to the kingdom of bliss by that way
of virtue in the which he is most used. And if that virtue in which he surpasses
more burningly draws him to the sweetness of God's love, the which is supposed stronger in the most rest, truly when he shall come to God, he receives
for meed that dwelling-place of heavenly joy and the seat that Christ has
ordained to be had withouten end by the most perfect lovers.

The lover therefore says the glorious ditties of love he has made; and he that
is surpassingly chosen to God's love, first he cares and desires that his heart
never depart from his Beloved; so that the memory of Jesu be to him as melody
of music at a feast and is sweeter in his mouth than honey or the honeycomb.
But the longer he exercises himself in ghostly study the sweeter to him it is.
And then it withdraws his mind from vain and evil thoughts, and binds it to
the desires of his Maker, and altogether gathers it into Christ and it is stabled
in Him, the Well of love. So that he loves Him only, and he prays that he may
be glad only in Him.

Now sweet affections come into his soul, and wonderful meditations fa-
vourable only to God, the which being tasted, and spread in this mind with
intentness, affect her more than may be spoken; they lead with great liking and
sweetness of spirit to the contemplation of heavenly things, and they cleanse
from desire of worldly solace. So that God's lover seeks nothing in this world
but that he may be in the wilderness, and only takes heed to the likings of his
Maker. Afterward truly strongly and well used in praying, and given to high
rest in meditation, killing all wickedness and uncleanness, and taking a strait
way with discretion, he greatly profits in the virtue of everlasting love. And his

affection goes up on high, so that the entrance is opened, in the beholding of heavenly mysteries, to the eye of his mind. The burning also, which before he felt not, begins to kindle his soul, and whiles he is profitably occupied in that, now quicklier and now more slowly it warms—as this corruptible body suffers the soul that it heavies, and ofttimes with divers heaviness down casts. So that the same soul anointed with heavenly sweetness, and quickening with heavenly delight, cheers herself mickle to pass forth by good desire, and irks to dwell in this mortal flesh. Nevertheless she gladly suffers adversity that happens, for sweetly she rests in the joy of eternal love.

And all these things that happen can not destroy that joyful song that she had received, made glad in Jesu, nay but the fiend's falsehoods fly away ineffectual; and the beguiling vanity of worldly honours goes in despite, nor is fleshly softness sought or loved. These things are armed against God's chosen so that all they that have their conversation in heaven might together fall, unavised, to their overturning.

But it profits not to overcome them unless the holy Lover of God, in Christ's Name, resolute and as it were without strife, being glad says: Tu autem susecptor menus es: Lord, Thou art my taker,' that the malicious prickings of my froward enemies make me not unrestful. Gloria mea: my Joy, for in Thee is all my joy. Not in my virtue, for it is not sent save from Thee. Worthily is all given to Thee, nothing to me. Et exaltans caput meum: and my head,' that is to say the highest part of my soul by the which the netherer, Thee favouring, is governed. Lifting her up to ghostly song and contemplation Thou sufferest her not to be cast down or bound into the low and foul likings of this world. This soothly is the head that in the oil of ghostly gladness Thou hast made fat, that it should increase in charity and be to me a Calix inebrians: that is to say a drink of inward sweetness inebriating my soul with love of my Maker. And sleepy shall I lie, verily turned from love of temporal things; and so as it wee with sweetness, feeling nothing of earthly mirth or heaviness, I shall be led to the everlasting cleanness.

Truly in this sweetness of high love the conscience shines. For cleanness lasts there, and the heart waxes likingly warm; and the mind, mirthed with gifts, waxes hot. Nor likes she to behold the pleasures of this exile, but she halses the bitterness of this world more gladly than the sweetness to follow; for enjoying the delights that fail not, she ceases not to cleave to the love of Jesu with such burning desire, that as soon and as lightly thou mightest turn the world upside down as call back her mind from her Saviour.

All things forsooth she hates that are contrary to God's love; and she burns unweariedly to fulfill those things that she sees and knows are pleasing to God.

This certain she would not leave for any pain or wretchedness, but would hie the quicklier to do God's will if she should perceive any hard thing she might offer for that cause. Nor truly does she think or desire any other thing but to love Christ truly, and to do His will in everything without ceasing.

A mind that has received this burning will, in goodness from his Beloved, is made rich with devotion from God. Forsooth He chose her that she might be such a one that might abide Christ's perfect lover; and be a choice vessel that shall be filled with the noblest liquor of the sweetness of heavenly life. And His name which is chosen out of thousands shall continue in everlasting remembrance, and be ever withheld within the self in thought. And then by God's help she shall cast out all lettings to love and shall be glad in God. For the darts of our enemies shall not avail against such a lover, but she shall receive from her love sickerness of conscience, with untrowed cleanness of inward sweetness, and every hour shall yield up her spirit. For being in ghostly crying, she is friendlily cleansed every day by the burning of love, so that no filth of spiritual foulness may last. Whiles in continual thought she is with God, she casts out all wickedness that the malice of our enemy moves to; and the fire of love verily biding in her mind, it cleanses all the contagion of sin that is drawn out by an ungotten desire.

Truly the affection set in a great height is so sicker that it is alway ware of negligence and casts it away as a deadly enemy; and whiles it lives it leaves not busyness and dread. For the better a man is, and the more acceptable to God, the more he burns in charity, and the more he is stirred by the prickings of love to work more busily and strongly that that belongs to his degree and life. And he is alway busy that the memory of his sweetest Beloved slide not from his thought for a minute, that not only as a clothing but as deed he may have and think of Him whom he knows he is bidden to love with all his heart. And he greatly dreads lest he be drawn into these things that the least grieve Him. He certain not only busies him with all his heart to fulfill that—as he is bidden—to love Christ; but also he is taken with great delight, so that he never forgets his Beloved nor bowing to temporal liking will part himself from His love—if he might withouten pain do that he would. He is truly expert that ghostly liking is sweeter than bodily love; and therefore it were marvel if he should slip into so great wrongs; and if, forsaking ghostly cheerfulness, he would make ready to rejoice in this feigned and as it were false felicity; or overcome by fleshly beauty, would desire that which forsooth ilk holy lover of God hates.

No marvel that fleshly desire has beguiled some; and beauty shown to the sight has drawn away some wise and even devout men to unlawful halsing, because they were not perfectly grounded in charity, nor cleaved they alway to eternal love; wherefore haled by temptations, when they seemed to ascend, before they might come to height have fallen down.

But a true lover of everlasting doubtless holds himself stable among temptations, and in that strife he wins a crown, when others, unsteadfast, are slain. And Christ's lovers cease not to cut away all obstacles, and they shed forth all their heart wholly before their Maker—and not as these that have not fastened their foot in love, and, cast down from the height of their endeavour, wax lean—but rather going on without change, stand stable in the well begun, and are nourished and brought forth in the sweetness of heavenly savour; that they may give light by example of holiness to them that are without, and within they may burn sweetly with the fire of love.

Errors also of fleshly desire they shall slay by the desire of cleanness; although no man in this life can fully slaken engendered concupiscence, or be so perfect that he may live in flesh and never sin. And so neither by this nor that shall a perfect man be here perfectly healed, but in heaven where the light of joy comforts his wits to behold God; and everlasting peace shall discomfit and cast out griefs and heaviness, that now no grief of corruption be, now when everlasting bliss confirms the discomforter.

In the meantime the mind is awakened and desires to be kindled by abiding love, and it studies to eschew the liking for these seen vanities. Truly the dregs of sin abide unto death, but they and the longing of nature perish in death. So that every chosen one, abling himself to love, and strengthened by high grace against these dregs, and armed with cleanness, should exercise himself in glorious battles, and should cast down all things that hostile lovers pursue.

Herefore sickerly whiles the fighting one overcomes and is not overcome he is lift up to a marvellous mirth in which all his inward members joy. For he feels himself inspired by a mystery of love, and he ascends on high in honeysweet heat and contemplates with ghostly song the sweet praise shed forth to the lovers—hastening to death and to nothingness at the movings of the fleshly affections.

Some add hereto: saying that a sweet thing sounds in his heart, and ghostly song, wherefore, thirsting, he is ravished and gladdened. But they have not expounded it so that I could understand how their thought was changed to song and melody abides in the mind; and in what manner of praising he sings his prayers.

CHAPTER VII

THAT A TRUE LOVER ONLY LOVES HIS BELOVED: AND OF DOUBLE RAVISH-INGS, THAT IS TO SAY OUT OF THE BODY, AND OUT OF THE LIFTING OF THE MIND INTO GOD; AND OF THE WORTHINESS THEREOF

The heat of a longing spirit shows in himself a pure love for the fairness of God. For he seeks nothing but His Beloved, and all other desires he entirely slakens; and so the mind is freely borne into that it sweetly loves, and the bond of the lover's will is stably confirmed, whiles nothing happens that may let a lover from his purpose, nor that may gar him turn again to think of aught else; so that loving with great easiness he may receive his desire, and all tarrying being put back, may swiftly run to the halsing of love.

Among these delights which he tastes—burning in so sweet love—he feels a heavenly secret inshed that no man yet may know but he that has received it; and he bears in himself the lectuary that moistens all joyful lovers in Jesu, and makes them happy so that they cease not to hie to sit in heavenly seats and endlessly to enjoy the love of their Maker. After that truly they earn while abiding in heavenly sights; and set on fire inwardly, all their innermost soul is gladdened with the playful shining of light; and they feel themselves made glad with merriest love, and wonderfully melted in joyful song.

Therefore their thoughts are made sweet in His service because studying and meditating on scripture and also writing they think on their Love, and they go not from their wonted voice of praise. That forsooth shall be considered marvellous, when one mind shall fulfill and take heed to two things in one time: that is, it offers worship and love to Jesu in singing and joying in mind, and together with that, it understands that that is in books; and neither hurts the other.

But this grace is not given generally and to all, but to a holy soul inbued with the holiest, in whom the excellence of love shines, and songs of love longing—Christ inspiring—commonly burst up, and being made now as it were a pipe of love, and joying sounds more goodly than can be said, in the sight of God. The which soul knowing the mystery of love, with a great cry ascends to his Love. In wit most sharp and wise, and in feeling subtle; not spread in the things of this world, but all gathered and set in one God, that he may serve Him in clearness of conscience and shining of soul, whom he has purposed to love and himself to give to Him.

The clearer certain the love of a lover is the nearer and more present to him God is. And thereby he joys more clearly in God, and the more he feels of His sweet goodness, that is wont to inshed itself to lovers and to glide into the hearts of the meek with mirth beyond comparison. This forsooth is pure love: when desire of none other thing is mingled with it. Nor has he any inclination to the beauty of the bodily creature, but rather the sharpness of his mind being cleansed, is altogether stabled into the one desire of everlastingness; and with freeness of spirit he continually beholds heavenly things—as he that is ravished by the beauty of any whom he beholding cannot but love.

But as it is shown ravishing is understood in two ways. One manner forsooth is when some man is ravished out of fleshly feeling, so that in the time of his ravishing he plainly feels nought in the flesh, nor what is done concerning his flesh; and yet he is not dead but quick, for the soul yet gives life to the body. And in this manner saints and the chosen are sometimes ravished to their profit and other men's learning; as Paul was ravished to the third heaven. And in this manner also sinners are ravished sometimes in a vision, that they may see the joys of the saints and the pains of the damned for their own and others correction; as we read of many.

Another manner of ravishing there is, that is the lifting of the mind into God by contemplation. And this manner of ravishing is in all that are perfect lovers of God, and in none but in them that love God. And this is well called a ravishing, as the other, for it is done with a violence and as it were against nature; and truly it is above nature that of a foul sinner a child fulfilled with ghostly joy may be born unto God. This manner of ravishing is to be desired and to be loved. Truly Christ had ay the contemplation of God, but never the withdrawing from bodily governance.

Therefore it is diverse to be rapt by love in the feeling of the flesh, and to be rapt from bodily feeling to a joyful or dreadful sight. That ravishing of love I hold best in which a man may earn most meed. To see heavenly things clearly belongs not to increase of meed, but to reward.

They also are called ravished by love that are wholly and perfectly given to the desires of their Saviour, and worthily ascend to the height of contemplation. With wisdom unwrought are they enlightened, and are worthy to feel the heat of the undescried light, with whose fairness they are ravished.

This truly happens to a devout soul when all her thoughts are ordered in God's love, and all waverings of mind pass into stableness. And now she neither wavers nor hovers, but with all desires brought into one and set in full great heat she desires after Christ; reaching out and given to Him as if there were nothing but these two, that is to say, Christ and the loving soul. To Him therefore she is tied with the band of love, unable to be loosed, and by surpassing of mind—flying above the bounds of the body—she draws a marvellous moisture from heaven. To which she would never have come unless she had been ravished by God's grace from inward affections, and set in ghostly height; in which, no marvel, she receives healthful gifts of grace.

Whiles therefore she thinks only of godly and heavenly things with a free heart, not compelled, and knowingly, she sees also her mind taken above all bodily and visible things, and changed into heavenly. Withouten doubt it is near that she may verily receive unto herself and feel the heat of love, and then be molten into ghostly song and the sweetness thereof. That truly shall follow from this ravishing to him that is chosen thereto; therefore this ravishing is great and wonderful. Truly as I suppose it passes all deeds of this life, for it is trowed a foretaste of everlasting sweetness. It passes also, unless I be beguiled, all other gifts that in this pilgrimage God gives to His saints for meed. In this truly they are worthy a higher place in heaven who hereby, in this life, have loved God more burningly and restfully.

As to high rest, it is to be desired to seek and hold it. For in mickle business, or in unsteadfastness or wavering of mind, it is neither gotten nor holden. Therefore when any one is lift to this, he lives full of joy and virtue, and shall die in sicker sweetness; and after this life he shall be full worthy, and near to God among the companies of angels.

In the meantime certain he has sweetness, heat, and ghostly song—on which I have before oft touched—and by these he serves God, and loving Him, cleaves to Him without parting. But since this corruptible body grieves the soul, and this worldly dwelling casts down our mind—thinking many things—therefore he sings not ay with such busyness, nor does the soul cry at all times with evenlike ghostly song. Sometimes; certain she feels more of heat and sweetness and she sings with difficulty, sometimes truly when heat is felt less she is ravished to song with great sweetness and busyness. Oft also with great mirth she flies and passes into ghostly song, and she knows also that the heat and sweetness of love are with her.

Nevertheless heat is never without sweetness, although sometimes it is without ghostly song, the which also lets bodily song, and noise of chatterers makes it turn again into thought. In the wilderness they meet more clearly, for there the Loved speaks to the heart of the lover—as it were a shameful lover that halses not his Beloved before men nor kisses like a friend, but in common and as a stranger.

Heavenly joy comes anon into a devout soul departed, sicker in mind and body, from worldly business, and desiring only to enjoy Christ's pleasure; and

marvellously mirthing her, melody springs out to her, whose token she receives
so that from henceforward she suffers not gladly any worldly sound.

This is ghostly music that is unknown to all that are occupied with worldly
business, lawful or unlawful. There is no man that has known this but he that
has studied to take heed to God only.

CHAPTER VIII

THE DESIRE OF A LOVER AFTER GOD IS SHOWN: AND THE CURSED LOVE OF
THIS WORLD IS DECLARED BY MANY EXAMPLES: AND THAT THE MEMORY OF
GOD ABIDES NOT IN LOVERS OF THE WORLD

O sweet Jesu I bind Thy love in me with a knot unable to be loosed, seeking
the treasure that I desire, and longing I find, because I cease not to thirst for
Thee. Therefore my sorrow vanishes as the wind, and my meed is ghostly song
that no man sees. Mine inward nature is turned into sweet song, and I long to
die for love. The greatness of the gifts delights me with light, and the tarrying
of love punishes me with joy, whiles they come that receive me, and in receiving refresh.

But those things want that my Beloved shall show to me, longing: they
wound me, so that I languish, and they heal not yet my languor fully, but
rather increase it; for love growing, languor is also increased.

Sic deficit in dolore vita mea, et anni in gemitibus: thus fails my life in
heaviness, and my years in lamenting; for from my love I am put back, and
desire of death is withdrawn, and the medicine for wretches tarries; and in my
crying I arise and say: Heu mihi, quia incolatus meus prolongatus est: 'Alas,
my labour is lengthened! It is love that noys me; love that delights me; it
chastises, because it that so mickle is loved is not forthwith given; it gladdens,
for it refreshes with hope, and by this heat insheds untrowed comfort.

Great longing soothly grows when through the joy of love the ditty of
ghostly love is in the soul, and great heat gives increase to sweet love; and now
nothing is so lawful as to think death, life. For the flower in which this
thought is nourished can not have end, but the joy that continually waxes great
in the lover, and that is thought a wonder, makes of death and melody all one.
Truly when I draw nigh to death, the fullness of my blessedness, that Almighty
God whom I love shall give to me, begins in me. Soothly my seat is ordained
in the place where love cools not, nor may bow to slowness. His love certain

my heart kindles because I can feel His fire, whereby the strength in my soul knows no grief whiles I am wholly strengthened in the solace of love.

For love I faint, and I spend all my time in holy sighing; and that shall be no reproach to me before God's angels, for whose fellowship I burningly desire, and with whom also in strong hope I wait to be perfected. And the praise that gladdens a longer shall now relax, and the blissful sight that he desired and loved shall be openly shown with joy.

But woe be ay to them whose days are slipped and passed in vanity, and their years with haste are perished withouten fruit of charity; that languish in unclean love and, for the fairness of corrupt flesh—that is but the covering of filth and corruption—are led withouten sweetness to death. Upon whom also is fallen the fire of wrath and covetousness, and they have not seen the sun of everlasting light. These, following their vanity, go into exile, having made themselves as vain as were those things that they have loved. Therefore when they shall be deemed they shall see Christ sharp and intolerable to their eyes because in this life they never felt Him sweet in their hearts. They truly that here feel Him sweet in themselves, doubtless shall see Him well cheered there. Such truly as we now are to Him, such a one shall He then appear to us; to a lover certain lovely and desirable, and to them that loved not, hateful and cruel. And yet this change is not on His part but on ours. He soothly is ay one and unchangeable, but every creature shall see Him as he is worthy to see. God truly shows Himself wilfully to ilk man as He will; and therefore He shall appear pleased to the righteous, and wroth to the unrighteous, in one and at the same little part of time.

Truly the love of a reasonable soul so does that—be it good or be it ill—it shall be deemed after that it does. There is nothing so speedful to get everlasting joy as the love of Christ: nor nothing sooner brings to utter damnation as love of the world. Therefore everlasting love should enflame our minds, and cursed and hateful love of fleshly affections be put far out. May the sweetness of heavenly life moisten us, and it be not lawful to us to love the bitter sweetness of this life. For the gall of dragons, that is to say most cursed wickedness and bitterness of falsehood, is the wine of sinners, because drinking it they are so maddened that they see not what is to come to them; and venom of adders, that is killing shrewdness, is deadly drink to them, and they are unable to be healed for their malice is incorrigible.

Truly this world has delights of wretchedness: riches of vanity: wounding flatterings: deadly likings: false pleasure: mad love: hateful darkness: in the beginning midday, and at the end night everlasting. It has also unsalted salt; savourless savour: foul beauty: horrible friendship: cherishing night: bitter honey and killing fruit. It has also a rose of stink; joy of lamentation: melody of heaviness: the praising of despite: the true drink of death: the array of abomination: the beguiling leader and the prince who casts down. It also has the gem of heaviness, and scornful praise: blackness of lilies: song of sorrow, and foul beauty: discording friendship and snow's blackness; solace forsaken: and a needy kingdom. It has a nightingale roaring more than a cow: a sweet voice withouten melody: a sheep clad in a fox's skin: and a dove madder than any wild beast.

Flee we therefore bodily and worldly love, whose back has a prick although the face flatter; whose flower is anointed with gall, and the pap, though it be privily, bears adders whose savour cuts man's soul from God, and hath burns with the fire of hell; whose gold shall turn into mould, and shall shed forth the incense of fire of brimstone.

Here is love without meekness, and full liking madness; the which suffers not the soul bound to it to be joined to the seats of the saints, or have delight in God's love. To them soothly that have their desire bowed to the love of these worldly creatures, it is heavy and seems a great burden to think of God, although the memory of Him be most sweet, and waxes marvellously sweet to the thinkers. If they begin to think on Him, anon He slides from their mind, and they turn to their old thoughts in which they full long have rested. They are bound certain with their evil custom, and angels food shall not savour to minds so sick and unclean, without great and long use of ghostly thought and the casting away of fleshly imaginations. They have certain the palate of their hearts with the fever of wicked love, wherefore they can not feel the sweetness of heavenly joy. Even if it happens good thoughts come into their minds, they bide not there; but the tokens of God's inspiration being straightway put out by the roots of evil, they go from ill to worse; and they fall the more damnably in that they consented not to that good with which they were touched.

Thus they that are chosen and are utterly burned with the love of God and cleave to Christ without parting, if at any time ill thoughts should pluck their soul or do stress to enter, anon looking up to heaven, they cast them out, and slake them with the heat of their affection. And no marvel, because by good custom they raise themselves, so that they take no earthly thing, nor any other thing of venomed sweetness, in which they might have delight. Soothly he that lives in perfect charity feels no sin nor wicked lust, but rather joys in his God; and neither anger nor uncleanness heavies him.

CHAPTER IX

OF DIVERS FRIENDSHIPS OF GOOD AND ILL, AND IF THEY CAN BE LOOSED: OF
THE SCARCENESS OF FRIENDSHIP OF MEN AND WOMEN: AND OF TRUE
FRIENDSHIP, AND HOW THE CHOSEN JOY IN IT IN THIS LIFE: AND OF THE
FOLLY OF SOME THAT ABSTAIN TOO MICKLE, OR ARE NAKED: AND OF FLESH-
LY FRIENDSHIP: AND THE ARRAY OF MEN AND WOMEN

Friendship is the knitting of two wills, consenting to like things and dissenting
to unlike; and this friendship can be betwix good and betwix evil, but by divers
affections. It ought mostly to be betwix God and man's soul; the which is
bound to conform her will to God's will in all things, so that what God wills
she wills, and what God wills not neither she wills. Thus soothly shall full
friendship be betwix them.

But in human affections where true friendship is God forbid that the sundering of bodies should make the parting of souls, but rather the unloosed
knot of cleaving friendship shall comfort the heaviness of bodily sundering, so
that the friend shall think he is with his friend, whiles he sees the steadfastness
of their will is unloosed. It is true friendship certain when a friend behaves him
to his friend as to himself; when he thinks his friend is himself in another
body; and he loves his friend for himself, and not for the profit that he trows
he may have from him.

But it is asked, if the one friend err whether shall friendship cease? Some
say friendship is not perfect unless it be betwix them that are like in virtue; but
how was that perfect that might be broken? The one erring is not now perfect,
and so gradually it can go to nought; which is against reason in true friendship
where a man is loved for himself and not for profit or liking.

Soothly it is not necessary for friends that the one be changed on account of
the changing of the other; but it is impossible that friendship—since it is
virtue—be voided in any man without his changing. Wherefore it is not
broken on account of the error of the one, but—and it be true friendship—it
shall be the more busy to call him that erred back again. And thus it behoves
that friendship by which he wills and gets good for his friend as for himself be
called love; and, whiles they live, for no error can it be broken.

Friendship certain is lightly loosed when that wherefore they should be
loved is not found in the friends; that is to say when the friendship for which
now the friends are loved is not profitable nor pleasing. And such friendship is
feigned, for it can not last save whilst pleasure and profit bide. But that is the
cause wherefore true friendship is not dissolved in friends whiles they live.

Therefore true friendship is not broken whiles they are, but the one can be erring yet both live. And therefore though one err yet friendship lasts if it be true, because they love each other according to what they are—that is as they are good—and by that it behoves to be understood goodness not of manners but of nature.

Nature truly gars a man seek him a true friend, for nature desires to keep kindness and faith. And it works nothing in vain. Wherefore that friendship that is natural shall not be loosed—nature being lasting—unless it be to the great wrong of nature that the nature loved gainstands; and that can nature in no wise do unless it be oppressed by corrupt manners. Therefore friendship that kindles anything that is not the same as that that is loved slakes, and is slakened when the things that stirred the love are not had; so that if by manners or riches or fairness friendship be had, with ill manners, sliding riches, and wasted fairness be had, with ill manners, sliding riches, and wasted fairness friendship vanishes also, and it is said of him that had it, there is nothing unhappier than to have been happy.

But friendship that nature works in friends is cast out by no poverty, nor with any error done away, and with no foulness of body ended, whiles the nature lasts that is the cause of this friendship. Such friendship is purely natural and therefore it is worthy neither meed nor unmeed, unless it conflicts ought against God's commandments. It has also a great delight knit with it, in which it earns neither meed nor unthank. True friendship can not be without mutual liking betwix friends, and their speech is desirable and their cheer comfortable. And this friendship—if it be informed with God's grace and be altogether in God and if it be given to Him—so then it is called holy friendship and is full meedful. But if on account of this friendship anything be done by the friends against God's will, it is perverse and wrong and foul friendship, and unclean and unmeedful.

I wot not soothly by what unhap it now befalls that scarcely or seldom is found a true friend. Ilk one seeks his own, and no man has a friend of whom he says, he is myself in another body. They bow to their own profits and likings and shame not to fulfill guile in their friends. Thereof it is deemed that they are not true friends but feigned, because they love not men but either they covet their goods or they strive after false flatteries and favours.

Yet, forsooth, friendship betwix men and women may be perilous, for fair beauty lightly cherishes a frail soul, and temptation seen sets fleshly desire on fire and ofttimes brings in the sin of body and soul; and so the company of women with men is wont to happen to the destruction of virtue. And yet this friendship is not unlawful but meedful; if it be had with good soul, and if it be loved for God and not for the sweetness of the flesh.

If women truly saw themselves despised by men, they would complain of God that made them such as men should disdain, and they would peradventure mistrust of health; for they trow themselves forsaken if they receive not the counsel or help of men. Reason certain is less quick in them, therefore they are lightly beguiled and soon overcome and therefore they mickle need the counsel of good men. They are drawn truly from ill to ill. For mickle readier are they to the likings of lust than to the clearness of holiness.

There is also a natural love of man for woman and woman for man that wants to no man, not even the holy, for it was ordained by God first in nature; by the which being together, and according by the stirring of nature they are fellowly made glad. This love also has its pleasures; as in speech and honest touching and goodly dwelling together, by the which man gets no meed unless it be mingled with charity; nor gets he unthanks, unless it be defiled with sin. If ill movings arise by which they think of lust, and they go towards it, doubtless they are guilty of death, because they sin against God.

Therefore they foully trespass that say that all our deeds, inward or outward, are meedful or unmeedful; for they would—or at the least they strive—to deny natural deeds and likings to be in us; and thus they are not ashamed to bring in confusion to noble nature.

Certain, that friendship, and companionship of men and women is unlawful and forbidden in which they accord to fulfill all their desire of covetous and foul lust; and putting the everlasting behind they seek to flourish intemporal solace and bodily love. They also sin grievously, and most, that have taken holy orders and go to women as wooers, saying that they languish for their love, and nearly faint with great desire and strife of thought; and so they lead them, light and unstable, to wretchedness in this life, and also in the endless. But they shall not be left unpunished, for they bear their damnation with them; of whom it is said by the psalmist: Sepulcrum patens est guttur corum, etc. That is to say: Their throat is an open grave, with their tongues they have wrought falsely, deem them God.'

God certain wills that women be not despised of men, nor be beguiled by vain flattery; but that they be taught truly and charitably in all holiness that longs to body and soul. But seldom is he found now that so does; but rather—what is to sorrowed for—either to get their gifts or their beauty they study to inform them. Wherefore ofttimes it happens that if they teach them in one thing, in another they destroy them; and they will not, or they dare not, forbid those things, although they be evil, that women please to use, so that they be not grieved.

True friendship certain is the sadness of lovers, and comfort of minds; relief of grief, and putting out of worldly heaviness; reformation of sinners; increase of holiness; lessening of slander, and multiplying of good meed. While a friend is drawn from ill by his friend by healthful counsel and is inflamed to do good when he sees in his friend the grace that he desires to have. Holy friendship therefore that has medicine for all wretchedness is not to be despised. From God it truly is that amid the wretchedness of this exile we be comforted with the counsel and help of friends, until we come to Him. Where we shall all be taught of God, and sit in eternal seats; and we shall be glad without end in Him that we have loved, and in whom and by whom we have friends.

From this friendship I can except no man, be he never so holy, but he needs it; unless there be any such to whom not man but angels serve. There are some that joy in God's love and are so moistened with His sweetness that they can say: Renuit consolari anima mea: My soul gainsays to be comforted' with worldly cheer with which worldly lovers refresh themselves. Nevertheless it behoves that in these things that, according to nature and grace, are needful to their body, and in men they be delighted. Who eats or drinks or takes recreation from heat or cold, withouten liking? Who has a friend, and in his presence and speech and dwelling with him and taking part in his good, is not glad? Sickerly none but the mad and they that want reason, for in these things and others like is the life of man comforted—although it be the holiest—and joys most quickly in God.

Therefore, My soul gainsays to be comforted,' is not to be understood of such comfort, but of stinking and unclean and unlawful comfort of worldly things. And afterwards he said: Delectasti me domine in factura tua; et in operibus mannum tuarum exultabo. 'Lord in Thy work thou hast gladdened me; and in the work of Thy hands I shall be joyful.' Who denies that he shall receive comfort that says he is mirthed in God's works? Vir insipiens non cognoscet, et stultus non intelliget hoc. 'But the unwise man shall not know this nor a fool understand.'

Some truly have the love of God, but not after knowledge; the which, whiles they study to put by superfluities are also unwisely led to cut away their necessities, supposing that they can not please God unless they chastise themselves by too mickle abstinence and unmeasured nakedness. And although paleness of face be the beauty of solitary man, nevertheless their service is not rightly ordered; for if they be hidden to chastise their bodies and bring them into the service of the spirit, yet ought they not to slay their bodies but keep them for the honour of God, to the time He sunders the soul from the body to which He has joined it. Therefore such are sharp to men and bitter in themselves, and they know not the keeping of friendship, nor keep the way thereof.

Forsooth love of kinsmen, if it be unmannered, is called fleshly affection, and it is to be broken because it lets from God's love: and if it be mannered it is called natural, and lets not from God's service; for in that it is nature it works not against the Maker thereof.

Next the women of our time are worthy of reproof that in such marvellous vanity have found new array for head and body, and have brought it in, so that they put beholders to both dread and wonder. Not only against the sentence of the apostle in gold and dressing of the hair, in pride and wantonness, they go serving, but also against the honesty of man and nature ordained by God, they set broad horns upon their heads, and a horrible greatness of wrought hair that grew not there, some of whom study to hide their foulness or increase their beauty and with painting of beguiling adultery they colour and whiten their faces. Newly carven clothing also both men and women use full fondly, not considering what beseems nature, but what tidings, that are newly noised, and vain novelties they can bring by the fiend's stirring.

If any should snib such things—yea even full seldom—he is laughed to scorn; and they consider more a fond tale than their amends. Therefore they go, and are taken and also snared by those things—these ladies and women that are called worthy, that desire to be fair for a time, and everlasting to be foul. For after this joy they, that have not loved Christ in this life but the foulest vanity of this world, shall feel hell pain, having crowned themselves with roses before they withered. But let us pass now to other things.

CHAPTER X

THAT GOD'S LOVE IS TO BE MINGLED WITH ILK TIME AND DEED NOR FAILS NOT FOR WEAL OR WOE, AND OF THE WORTHINESS AND THE GAINING THEREOF: AND OF TEARS TURNED TO SONG

Love of the Godhead that perfectly thirls a man, and truly enflames with fire of the Holy Ghost, takes the soul to itself with marvellous gladness and from memory of so great love allows her not to wander for a moment. It binds the mind of the lover, so that it may not turn to vain things; and he continually goes after his Love.

We can forsooth if we be true lovers of our Lord Jesu Christ, think upon Him when we walk, and hold fast the song of His love whiles we sit in fellowship; and we may have mind of Him at the broad and also in tasting of meat and drink. At every morsel of meat and draught of drink we ought to praise God, and in time of our meat taking and the space betwixt morsels to yield Him praising with honey sweetness and a mental cry, and to yearn with desire while at meat. And if we be in labour of our hands what lets us to lift our hearts to heaven and without ceasing to hold the thought of endless love? And so in all time of our life, being quick and not slow, nothing but sleep shall put our hearts from Him.

O what joy and gladness glides into the love? O with how happy and truly desireable sweetness it fulfills his soul? Love certain is life without end, abiding where it is set and made firm in Christ. When this love after loving desire is rooted in the heaven, neither prosperity nor adversity may change it, as the wisest men have written. Then no marvel it shall turn the night to day, darkness to light, heaviness to melody, noy to solace, and labour to sweet rest.

This love truly is not of imagination or feigned, but true and perfect, and given to Christ without parting, yielding angel's song with melody to Jesu. And forsooth if thou love in this manner as I have said, full glorious shalt thou be—with the best and worthiest in the Kingdom of God—near to that quickening light. Meantime all the impugnations of the fiend's movings that arise from fleshly friendship and the coveting of worldly things thou shalt well overcome in the heat of love and virtue of prayer. Thou shalt also overcome the likings of fairness; showing that thou wilt not be defiled once on account of all things that can be thought. With that also thou shalt be filled with ghostly food, and the delight of endless love; so thou shalt know the sign in sickerness and as it were in very knowledge, that thou art the lover of the Everlasting King.

Nevertheless this happens to no man unless either God says it to him, or that in this life he feels a great part of the meed to come biding in him. But whereto do I speak of them with the others, which although they be chosen have not yet tasted this holy lectuary? Sometimes I marvel at myself that I have spoken of the excellence of God's lovers, as who should say, whoever wills might come to it. And yet it is not for ilk runner nor willer, but of the lover, lifter up, and taker of Christ. The smallness of my mind certain knows not how to open that which as a blabberer, I am busy to show. Yet I am compelled to say somewhat, although it be unable to be spoken, that hearers or readers may study to follow it; finding that all love of the fairest and loveliest worldly thing, in comparison to God's love, is sorrow and wretchedness.

Therefore consider and know well with your understanding that our Lord makes His lover marvellous and raises him on high and suffers him not to be cast down with unworthy love of vain hope, but keeps him stably in Himself for the sweetest love. Love truly is continual thought with great desire for the fair, the good and lovely: for if the thing I love be fair and not good, I show myself unworthy to love it, if it be good it is to be loved. Truly love of the creature, though it be good and fair, is forbidden to me, so that I should offer and keep all my love for the Well of goodness and fairness, that He that is my God and my Jesu be my Love. He only has fairness and goodness of Himself, and He is the same fairhead and goodness. Other things, whatever they be, are neither fair nor good but of Him, and the nearer to Him the fairer and better they are. Therefore He is most worthily loved that in Himself contains all things that are worthy to be loved and to be sought of a lover, wherefore He withholds nothing on His part save that He might be loved most burningly. Truly if I love aught else my conscience bites me that I love not right. I dread that that I love loves me not again; and yet if I dread not on this account I should be fearful on account of death that departs ill lovers and wastes all their vanity.

Ofttimes also other noys happen that disturb the gayness and sweetness of lovers; but he that truly loves God with all his heart is so much the clearer in his conscience as he knows himself the more burning in the love of God. Therefore he knows his loveliest Love from whose sweetness death departs not, but when he passes from this world then he finds his Love perfectly, and to Him most sickerly is joined, so that never after shall he be put from Him, but busily he runs in merriest halsing and, openly seeing Him he has loved and coveted, shall be glorified without end.

This love I liken to fire unslakened, the which no power of enemies can cast down, no softness of flattery can overcome. This love cleanses us from our sins, and burns in unmeasured heat the obstacles that might let to love, and in the hottest flame of God's love makes us clearer than gold and brighter than the sun. This love brings us ghostly medicine; and I suppose there is no thing among all others that can be numbered by clerks that may succour us so mickle and cleanse us and from all dregs of wickedness clear us, as fervent love of the Godhead and continual thought of our Maker. Tears are wont to wash us from defaults and heaviness of hearts puts by damnation, but burning love passes all other things more than can be thought, and makes man's soul shine most excellently. Therefore before all things that we can do it gets the heart of the Everlasting King, and is worthy to be contemplated in joyful song.

I say not greeting is unprofitable, nor sorrow of heart uncomely or not to be loved in this exile, and I marvel that any so highly ravished in song of love can not greet in his devotion or praying or meditation. Rather I say that the prayer and meditation of such a lover is turned into song and molten into melody of heavenly sweetness, so that he gives the sound of angels rather than of man; anointed by which honied heat he is taken not to heaviness but to joy and, his tears as it were wiped away, he is mirthed in the spring of endless and true joy.

Our doctors say: the perfect ought to weep, and the more perfect the more plenteous they should be of tears because of the wretchedness of this life and the delay of the heavenly life. To me certain a wonderful longing in God's love was near, and noy of bodily greeting has ceased for the greatness of inward sweetness. He certain that is not burned with endless love needs to be purged with tears. Love is enough to chastise him that languishes in everlasting love; there is no wound greater and sweeter than of love. If such a one forsooth would weep he is not greatly suffered in privy devotion, in that the Holy Ghost uprising him, he is rapt in mind, and with angel's sweetness he sings to God his praises and loving thoughts.

The seat of love is lift on high for into the heavens it runs, and on earth also methinks it subtly and craftily makes men, sometime lovely, wan and pale. It makes them to wither that afterward they may wax green, and to fail that they may be strong. Therefore he draws near to the rest of endless joy, and dreadless himself, mingles with those singing to his Maker; for the more burningly he loves the sweeter he sings and the more delicious he feels that that he strongly desired. And if the way seem sharp and long to them that love not, love nevertheless couples God to man, and with short labour fulfills the abiders.

CHAPTER XI

THAT PERFECT LOVE BINDS TO GOD WITHOUT LOOSING AND MAKES MAN MINDFUL OF HIS GOD; BUT LOVE OF THE WORLD FALLS TO NOUGHT. AND OF THE NATURE OF TRUE LOVE, STABLE AND AY-LASTING, SWEET, SOFT, AND PROFITABLE: AND OF FALSE LOVE; VENOMOUS, FOUL, AND UNCLEAN

This work is perfect if we depart our minds pithily from love of creatures and join them truly to God without departing. And in this work the more perfect we be the better we are. This deed is above all others, for all that we do is referred to this end, so that we be knitted and oned perfectedly to God. And from this onehead many things draw; that is to say, liking beauty of this world, vanity of men and women, riches and honours, praise and favour of people. Therefore we must exercise ourselves to fulfill this work, putting back and forgetting all things that might let us.

Certain the love to which we ascend in this work is quicker than a burning coal, and shall produce its effect in us, for it shall make our souls both burning and shining. This is the love that can not be beguiled by a creature or scorned in heaven nor put from meed. We could long suffer the flame of this fire if it should ay last in one measure; but ofttimes it is tempered, lest it waste nature that through the body corrupts and grieves the soul; for the corruptible flesh suffers not our mind to be continually borne to God.

Certain the heat of very devotion is sometimes hindered as by sleep, and the misuse of the body or labour; and yet the burning is not slaked, but it is not felt as it was before. It comes again to us truly whiles we turn again to God, and makes us mend from sickness of mind and gives sweetness. It delivers the body also from many sicknesses, and whiles it keeps us in temperance and soberness it raises our souls to heavenly desires so that we have no delight in low things.

This is the love that ravishes Christ into our hearts and makes our minds sweet, so that within we burst out in songs of praise, and as it were in spiritual music we sing. I suppose no delight he like to this, for it moistens with clear sweetness and gladdens with holy liking. The soul that receives it is purged with blessed fire and in it bides no rust nor filth, but it is altogether thirled with heavenly joy, so that our inward nature seems turned into godly joy and song of love. Thus forsooth everlasting love gladdens and insheds plenteous delight, so that the friends thereof are not compelled to bow to any desire for a creature of this world but they may freely melt in praise and love of Jesus Christ.

Learn therefore to love thy Maker if thou desire to live when thou passest hence; so do that thou mayest love God in thy life if thou wilt live after thy death. Give all thy mind to Him that He may keep it from temporal and eternal sorrows. Beware that thy heart be not sundered from Him though thou be set in adversity or wretchedness; for so shalt thou be worthy to have Him with joy, and to love Him withouten end. If thou suffer not the memory of God to slip whether prosperity come or grief; in that certain thou showest thyself a true lover.

O good Jesu, that gavest me life, lead me desiring into Thy love. Take unto Thee all mine intent so that Thou mayest be all my desire, nor nothing beyond

Thee shall my heart desire. Sorrow certain and all heaviness would pass from me, and that I desire come to me, if my soul had received or heard the song of Thy praise. Thy love would ever unwearily bide in us, so that we can perceive it. Take therefore my mind into Thy power and make it stable that it come not to nought with vain and unprofitable fantasies, nor be scorned by errors, nor be bowed to earthly felicity or love or praise, but my mind being so settled in Thee may in Thy love so burn that by no sudden nor avised chance it may be cooled.

If certain I love any creature of this world that shall in all kinds please my wish and set my joy and the end of my solace in it, when it should come to me I well might have dread of the burning and bitter parting. For all felicity that I have in such love is but greeting and sorrow in the end, and that pain, when it draws near, most bitterly will punish the soul. All pleasure also that men have beholden in this exile is likened to hay that now flourishes and waxes green, but suddenly vanishes as if it had not been.

No marvel that to them that behold rightly, the joy of this world thus seems; and to them following the solace of those bound in sin; it never abides in one estate but passes until it come to nought. Nevertheless all stand in labour and grief, and no man can eschew that. The nature certain of true love and not feigned is this, that it stands ay stable and is changed by no new thing.

Therefore the life that can find love and truly know it in mind, shall be turned from sorrow to joy unspoken and is conversant in the service of melody. Song certain it shall love, and, singing in Jesu, shall be likened to a bird singing to the death. And peradventure in dying the solace of charitable song shall not want,—if it happen to him to die and not go swiftly to his love. After this passage forsooth he shall be marvellously lifted up into the praise of his Maker, and singing shall overflow with delights more than may be trowed, and into the song of the seraphim shall forthwith rise, so that in praising he shall give light, and continually and endlessly burn. There shall be halsing of love, and the sweetness of lovers shall be coupled in heart, and the joining of friends shall stand for ever. The sweet mouth shall give liking kisses and their love shall never cease.

The presence of my Love begets to me gladness unmeasured and sickerness, and with him I have mind of no heaviness; all adversity vanishes and all other desires appear not, but are stilled and dispersed; and He alone, that my mind has alone burningly desired, wholly refreshes and in-laps me. Truly if thou love Christ with all thy will, thou hatest all filth of wickedness, and thou givest thy heart to Him that bought it so that He may be thy Lord by grace and not the fiend by sin. As Christ has truly and unfeared sought thy soul, and would not cease in seeking until the time thou foundest Him, so to endless joy thou shalt be led and be near to God in a blessed seat. Therefore I counsel Thee to love as I have expounded, and take thy place with the angels.

Beware thou sellest not this joy and honour for foul vanity of fleshly lust; wisely consider that the love of creatures exclude thee not from the love of God. Hate thou no wretchedness on earth except that they thy pure love can cast over and disturb; for perfect love is strong as death, true love is hard as hell. Love forsooth is a light burden, not charging but lightening the bearer; the which makes glad the young with the old; in the which the discomfiters of fiends joy, having taken their prey; in which fighters are defended against the flesh and the world. Love is ghostly wine moistening the minds of the chosen and making them bold and manly, so that they have forgotten the venomous likings of the world nor have no care thereof but rather great scorn.

Therefore by holy love no lover can lose but needs win mickle if he keep it truly in his heart. Love without pain bides in the soul of a lover, as lovers have shown, for love makes perfect and pain destroys. Making perfect and destroying are contrary, therefore the heart, loving perfectly, feels no pain nor heaviness, nor is it sorry nor disturbed. Thus soothly perfect love and wretched heaviness stand not together. Moreover, that that is done gladly is not done painfully. Soothly a lover works wilfully and gladly, therefore he has no wretchedness in his work but he is happy; not constrained, not heavy, but ay showing himself glad and merry.

Love therefore is the sweetest and most profitable thing that ever reasonable creature received. Love is most acceptable and liking to God; it not only binds the mind with bands of sweetness and wisdom and joins to God, but also it constrains flesh and blood that man slip not into beguiling sweetness and into divers desires of errors. In this love our life should stand and wax mighty and strong. A better dwelling place nor sweeter found I never, for it has made me and my love one, and made one out of two.

Yet worldly love shall grow and perish as the flower of the field in summer, and shall be joying no more but as it were one day, so sickerly shall it last a short while, but after that end in sorrow. And so doubtless it shall be bitter to fond lovers. Their pride and play in false beauty shall be cast into filth, that shall be with them endlessly when they are downcast into torments. These shall not pass; as did their false felicity and the joy they had in shining beauty, which have gone into voidness, and all that they enjoyed has swiftly vanished.

God truly gives fairness to men and women not that they should burn together in love despising their Maker—as all nearly do now—but, knowing it as God's gift, they should glorify and love Him unceasingly with all their heart, and should continually desire that heavenly beauty, in comparison to which all worldly beauty is nought. For if a lovely form is shown in the servants of this world, what shall be the beauty of God's children set in heaven? Therefore let us love burningly, for if we love we shall sing in heavenly mirth to Christ with melody, whose love overcomes all things. Therefore let us live and also die in love.

CHAPTER XII

OF THE FELICITY AND SWEETNESS OF GOD'S LOVE: AND OF THE NIGHTIN-GALE'S SONG: AND PRAYER FOR PERSEVERANCE OF TRUE GHOSTLY SONG THAT WORLDLY LOVERS HAVE NOT

Sweeter delight I know not than in my heart to sing Thee Jesu, whom I love, a song of Thy praise. A better and more plenteous felicity I know not then to feel in mind the sweet heat of love. Of all things I hold it best to set Jesu in my heart and desire no other thing. He truly has a good beginning of love that has loving tears, with sweet longing and desire for things everlasting.

Truly Christ as it were languishes in our love, whiles He to get us hied to the Cross with so great heat; but it is well said in play love goes before and leads the dawn.' It was nought but love that put Christ thus low.

Come my Saviour to comfort my soul; make me stable in Thy love so that I never cease to love Thee. Do away sorrow when I must pass, for there is none such a sinner that can not joy if he be perfectly turned to Thee. O sweetest Jesu have mind of Thy mercy, so that my life may be light and fulfilled with virtue that I may overcome my strong enemy. I pray Thee give me health in this wise that I be not lost with the child of damnation.

Truly since my soul was incensed with holy love, I am set in longing to see Thy Majesty. Therefore made the bearer of poverty I despise earthly dignity and care for no honour; my joy truly is friendship. When I began to love Thy love took my heart and suffered me to desire nothing but love. And then Thou, God, madest my soul burn in sweet light, therefore in Thee and by Thee I can die and feel no heaviness. Delectable heat is also in the loving heart, that has devoured heavy grief in the fire of burning love. And from hence is sweetness given, principally music going betwixt and softening the soul, where Thou my God and my Comfort hast ordained Thy temple.

That joy certain is full delicious after which I yearn, and no man may be more covetous in such desire. Wherefore my loving soul as it were arraying a spouse for the King of the high Empire, says thus: Love holds my heart with unloosened bands, and sets it in such governance and binds it so greatly with a marvellous maistry that it is pleased to think rather to die than to live.' This flower certain can not end for my friend is so burning in love, he sings the melody and joy of death.

In the beginning truly of my conversion and singular purpose I thought I would be like the little bird that languishes for the love of his beloved, but is gladdened in his longing, when he that it loves comes and sings with joy, and in its song also languishes, but in sweetness and heat. It is said that the night-ingale is given to song and melody all night, that she may please him to whom she is joined. How mickle more should I sing with greatest sweetness to Christ my Jesu, that is Spouse of my soul through all this present life that is night in regard to the clearness to come, so that I should languish in longing and die for love. But in dying I shall wax strong, and in heat I shall be nourished; and I shall joy and in joying sing the likings of love with mirth, and hot devotion as it were from a pipe shall issue and my soul shall yield angels melody, kindled within, to the most high, and offered by the mouth at the altar of God's praise. Thus my soul shall alway be greedy to love and never fail with heaviness or sloth from the desire she received.

Soothly holiness of mind, readiness of will, heat of very desire and turning to God by continuance of thought, that are in holy souls, suffer them not to sin mortally; and if they sin through frailty or ignorance, anon they are raised up to true penance by those pricks, nor shall they bide long in sin although they cleave to the liking. The venial sin forsooth that they do, they waste in the fire of love—unless any be cast down by such negligence that they ween that that in which they trespass by no sin—and charity is not enough to put away all the pain merited; or else they have no tribulation wherewith their sin may be purged. Certain in the coming of love the lover's heart is burned. Hotter than fire is this marvellous heat, the which most sweetly gladdens the mind and tempers and shadows from the heat of sins.

Good Jesu, give me the organ-like and heavenly song of angels that in that I may be ravished and Thy worship continually sing; that Thou gavest to me unknowing and unwise, now to me expert and asking, give again. Cherish me in my last end I may be found full of fire. Show me sweet cherishing in Thy good will that my defaults may be here punished and cleansed in that wise that, in Thy mercy, Thou hast known for him cleaving to Thee; not as in Thy wrath Thou cherishest those flourishing in this world, to whom Thou givest temporal prosperity and keepest endless pains. Worldly lovers soothly may know the words, or the ditties of our song but not the music of our songs; for they read the words, but they can not learn the notes and tone and sweetness of the songs.

O good Jesu Thou has bound my heart in the thought of Thy Name, and now I can not but sing it; therefore have mercy upon me, making perfect that Thou hast ordained. Thy true and busy lover is ravished into ghostly song of mind, that it is impossible any such sweetness be of the fiend, or such heat from any creature, nor such song from man's wit: in which if I abide I shall be safe.

It behoves truly we be not glad to do small sins that will to perfectly eschew great sins. He truly that wilfully and knowingly falls into the least, ofttimes shall unavised fall into greater. It longs truly to love to desire to fall into great wretchedness rather than sin once. It is nought needful to him, but scornful, to seek delight, riches, strength, or fairness, that in the doom of the everlasting King shall be made a knight, with perfect beauty of members and clearness of colour; where in the heavenly hall there shall neither be too mickle nor too little, where he shall serve the Emperor in the world of worlds.

Explicit liber de Incendio Amoris, Ricardi Hampole heremite, translatus in Anglicum instancijs domine Margarete Heslyngton, recluse, per fratrem Richardum Misyn, sacre theologie bachalaureum, tunc Priorem Lyncolniensem, ordinis carmelitarum, Anno domini M. CCCCxxxv in festo translacionis sancti Martini Episcopi, quod est iiij nonas Iulij, per dictum fratrem Richardum Misyn scriptum & correctum. </div3> </div2> <pb/> </div1>

THE MENDING OF LIFE

THE MENDING OF LIFE OR RULE OF LIVINGAS TRANSLATED BY RICHARD MISYN IN 1434 FROM DE EMENDATIONE VITAE' BY RICHARD ROLLE OF HAMPOLE: AND NOW DONE INTO MODERN ENGLISH

CHAPTER I

FIRST OF CONVERSION

Tarry thou not to our Lord to be turned, nor put it off from day to day; for ofttimes the cruelty of death ravishes the wretched, and bitterness of pains suddenly devours them that now irk to be turned. It may not be numbered by us how many of the worldly wicked presumption has beguiled.

Truly it is a great sin to trust in God's mercy and not cease from sin, trowing God's mercy be so mickle that He will not give righteous pain to sinners. Work ye therefore whiles it is day, the night truly comes in which no man may work.' Light or day' he calls this life, in which we ought never to cease from good working, knowing that death to us is sicker, the hour of death truly unsicker. The night' he calls death, in the which our members are bound, and wits put by, and we may not now work any healthful thing, but shall receive joy or tormentry according to our works. In a point we live, yea less than a point; for if we would liken all our life to the life everlasting, it is nought.

Therefore how waste we our life in love of vanity, not without grievous damnation; and all day negligent, without repenting, we stand idle. Lord, therefore turn us and we shall be turned; heal us and we shall be healed. Many truly are not healed, but their wounds rot and fester; for today turned to God, tomorrow are turned from Him; today doing penance, tomorrow turning to their ill. Of such it is said: we have cured Babylon and it is not healed, for to Christ it is not truly turned.

What is turning to God but turning from the world and from sin; from the fiend and from the flesh? What is turning from God but turning from unchangeable good to changeable good; to the liking beauty of creatures; to the works of the fiend; to lust of the flesh and the world? Not with going of feet are we turned to God, but with the change of our desires and manners.

Turning to God is also done whiles we direct the sharpness of our minds to Him, and evermore think of His counsel and His commandments, that they may be fulfilled by us; and wherever we be, sitting or standing, the dread of God pass not from our hearts. I speak not of dread that has pain, but that that is in charity, with which we give reverence to the presence of so great a Majesty, and alway we dread that we offend not in any little thing. Soothly, thus disposed, to God we are truly turned because we are turned from the world.

To be turned from the world is naught else but to put aback all lust, and to suffer the bitterness of this world gladly for God; and to forget all idle occupations and worldly errands, in so mickle that our soul, wholly turned to God, dies pithily to all things loved or sought in the world. Therefore being given to heavenly desires they have God evermore before their eyes, as if they should unwearily behold Him, as the holy prophet bears witness: Providebam Dominum in conspectu meo semper, that is to say In my sight I saw our Lord evermore before me.' Not only the space of an hour; as do they that set all fair or lovely earthly things before the eyes of their hearts, which they behold and in which they delight and desire for love to rest. And after the prophet says: Oculi mei semper ad Dominum; quoniam ipse evellet de laqueo pedes meos, that is: Mine eyes evermore are to our Lord, for he shall deliver my feet from the snare.' By this is shewed that except our inward eyes to Christ unwearily be raised we may not escape the snares of temptation. And there are many lettings so that the eyes of our heart may not be fixed on God; of which we put some: abundance of riches; flattering of women; the fairness and beauty of youth. This is the threefold rope that scarcely may be broken; and yet it behoves to be broken and despised that Christ may be loved.

Truly he that desires to love Christ truly, not only without heaviness but with a joy unmeasured he casts away all things that may let him. And in this case he spares neither father nor mother, nor himself; he receives no man's cheer; he does violence to all his letters; and he breaks through all obstacles. Whatever he can do seems little to him so that he may love God. He flees from vices as a brainless man and looks not to worldly solace, but certainly and wholly directed to God, he has nearly forgotten his sensuality. He is gathered all inward and all lifted up into Christ, so that when he seems to men as if heavy, he is wonderfully glad.

But there are many that say they will turn to God, but they can not yet, they say, for they are holden back by this occupation or other; whose cold mind sorrowingly we reprove. For withouten doubt and they were touched with the least spark of Christ's love, anon with all busyness they would seek which way they might come to God's service, and in seeking they would not cease until they had found.

Ofttimes they feign excuses, which the rather accuses them more. Riches forsooth withdraws many, and the flattering of women beguiles them; and they that have long done well sometimes are drowned, by them, in the worst dykes. For fairness is soon loved; and when it feels itself loved, it is lightly cherished;

and the chosen one is cast down, and after turning or conversion, he is made worse than he was before. Then his name is blackened, and he that before was worthy, now is despised of all men and hated of all.

I saw a man truly of whom they said that he chastised his body with marvellous sharpness for fifteen years, and afterwards he lapsed into sin with his servant's wife, nor might he be parted from her until his death. In his dying truly they said that he cursed the priests that came to him, and refused to receive the sacraments.

Therefore the newly turned ought for to flee the occasion of sinning; and with their will avoid words, deeds, and sights stirring to ill. The more unlawful a thing is, the more it is to be forsaken.

The feind also strongly upbraids against them which he sees turned from him and turned to God, and ceases not to kindle fleshly and worldly desires. He brings to mind lusts done before, and the desolation of the contrite; and unprofitable desires that were slaked before stir themselves. Among these it behoves the penitent manfully to use himself, and to take ghostly armour to gainstand the devil and all his suggestions; and to slake fleshly desires and ever to desire God's love; and to go not from Him, despising the world: of the which now we will speak.

CHAPTER II

OF THE DESPISING OF THE WORLD

To despise this world is to pass through this life without the love of all temporal and passing things; to seek nothing in this world but God; for all vainglory and solace not to care; scarcely to take thy necessaries, and if they sometimes want, to bear it goodly. This is the despising of this world. Have this in mind if thou wilt not be slain through love of it. Thus is the world despised and not loved.

All soothly that we love, we worship; it is also foul to worship dirt, that is to love earthly things. Therefore these rich niggards bind themselves thrall in most foul filth and stink, and joy to be called lords of men, though they be servants of sin. If a man be lord of men, that is not of nature but of fortune. That man is subject to vice is from a froward will. Put away therefore thy wicked will, and thou shalt be free from the fiend and from sin and made the servant of righteousness that teaches thee not to love earthly things.

Covetousness of the world and the love of God truly are contrary, and rest not together in one soul. The place is so strait, that one falls out. The more soothly thou castest out covetousness the more thou tastest God's love. The more covetousness, the less charity.

O wretched soul, what seekest thou in this world where thou seest that all things are deceitful and passing? They soonest beguile thee that most flatter thee. Why busiest thou thyself for mortal things? Why yearnest thou with great desire for the things that shall perish? Seest thou not that they perish sooner than they are gotten? But I wot where thou dwellest, where Satan's seat is; that has blinded thine eyes and by his falsehoods has scorned thee: so that thou shouldest desire fleeting things, and love hateful things, and despise abiding things, and be drawn to things vanishing. And so thou settest thyself on a false ground, and when thou weenest to stand thou fallest into the fire.

The dwellers in temporal plenty are beguiled by five things that they love: by riches; by dignity; by will; by power; and by honours. These bind them in sin, and constrain them in defaults; with these lusts they are overcome, and never are loosed but by death; but their loosing is too late when there is no more save endless pain. This lets them from despising the world; from God's love; from knowledge of themselves; from the desire for the heavenly kingdom. No man may be saved unless he cease to love the world with all that is therein. Cease therefore whiles heat is in the body and the fair age of youth yet abides.

What things shall delight him that disposes himself to love Christ? He will despise youth and will keep his strength for God; riches he counts for nought; he will take heed that this fairness is vain, and grace deceitful. Whereto shall I run on one by one? He shall perfectly despise all things that in this world pass as a shadow.

O lover of the flesh, what findest thou in thy flesh wherefore thou so delightest in it? Does the form or shape please thee, or hast thou now thy joy in a skin? Why takest thou not heed what is hid under the skin? Or knowest thou not that fleshly fairness is the covering of filth, and the dregs of corruption, and oft the cause of damnation? Therefore be it enough for thee, all other things being despised, to love God; to praise God; with God to be; in God to joy; and from Him not to part; but to cleave to Him with unslakened desire.

The world itself compels us to despise the world that is so full of wretchedness; in which is abiding malice, destroying persecution, swelling wrath, fretting lust, false blaming for sin, and bitterness of slander; where all things are confused and withouten order; where neither righteousness is loved nor truth approved; where faithfulness is unfaithful, and friendship cruel, that stands in prosperity and falls in adversity.

There are yet other things that should move us to the despising of the world: the changeableness of time; shortness of this life; death sicker; the chance of death unsicker; the stableness of everlastingness and the vanity of things present; the truth of the joys to come.

Choose what thou wilt. If thou love the world, with it thou shalt perish; if thou love Christ, with Him thou shalt reign.

CHAPTER III

OF POVERTY

If thou wilt be perfect, go, sell all that thou hast and give it to the poor and come and follow Christ. In the forsaking of worldly things and in the following of Christly things, it is shown there is perfection. Forsooth all that have forsaken their goods follow not Christ, for many are worse after the forsaking of their good than they were before. Then certain they serve backbiting, and they dread not to withdraw the good fame of their neighbours. Then they swell with envy; they gnash with malice; they set themselves before all others; they praise their state, all others they either dispraise or condemn. Trowest thou how that the fiend has beguiled such, that neither have the world nor God, whom by divers wiles he leads to endless tormentry.

Thou that understandest that I have said, take thy poverty another way. When He says go and sell' He marks the changing of thy desire and of thy thought, as thus: he that was proud now be lowly; that was wrathful now be meek; he that was envious now be charitable; before covetous, now generous and discreet. And if he were unclean, now let him abstain not only from all ill but from all likeness of ill. And if before he exceeded in meat or drink, now by fasting let him amend. He soothly that loved the world too mickle, now let him gather himself altogether in Christ's love; and fasten all the waverings of his heart in one desire for things everlasting. And so no marvel that willful poverty shall be fruitful to him, and the noy that he suffers for God be a glorious crown. Beati pauperes spiritu, quoniam ipsorum est regnum coelorum. That is to say: Bless be they that are poor in spirit, for theirs is the kingdom of heaven.'

What is poverty of spirit but meekness of mind, by the which a man knows his own infirmity? Seeing that he may not come to perfect stableness but by the grace of God, all things that might let him from that grace he forsakes, and he sets his desire only in the joy of his Maker. And as of one root spring many branches, so of wilful poverty, taken in this wise, proceed virtues and marvellousness untrowed. Not as some that change their clothes and not their souls; soothly it seems they forsake riches, yet they cease not to gather innumerable vices.

What is worse than a proud poor man? What more cursed than an envious beggar? If thou truly forsake all things for God, see more what thou despisest than what thou forsakest. Take heed busily how thou followest Christ in manners. Discite, inquit, a me quia mitis sum, et humilis corde. 'Learn of me,' He says, for I am meek and lowly of heart.' He says not learn of me for I am poor. Truly by itself poverty is no virtue but rather wretchedness; nor for itself praised, but because it is the instrument of virtue and helps to get blessedness, and makes many eschew many occasions of sinning. And therefore it is to be praised and desired. It lets a man from being honoured, although he be virtuous; but rather it makes him despised and over-led, and cast out among lovers of the world. To suffer all which for Christ is highly needful.

Therefore Christ to our example led a poor life in this way, for He knew that for them that abound in riches and liking it is hard to enter into heaven.

Therefore so that men should desire poverty more greedily He has promised high honour and the power of justice to them that forsake all things for Him, saying: Vos qui reliquistis omnia et secuti estis me, sedebitis super sedes duodecim, judicantes duodecim tribus Israel, that is to say: Ye that have forsaken all things and followed me, shall sit on twelve seats, deeming the twelve tribes of Israel.'

They soothly that have wilful poverty and want in the meekness and lowliness that Christ teaches, are more wretched than they that have plenty of all riches, nor shall they take the apostles places of worthiness in the day of doom; but they shall be clad with the doublet of confusion, that is damnation of body and soul. They soothly that shine in meekness and lowliness, though they have mickle riches, yet shall they be set on the right hand of Christ when He deems.

Some men soothly say: we can not leave all, we are sick; it behoves us to keep our necessaries that we may live, and that is lawful. But they are the less worthy, for they dare not suffer anguish, poverty and neediness for God. Yet by the grace of God they may come to the height of virtue, and lift themselves to the contemplation of heavenly things, if they forsake secular occupations and errands, and unwearily rise to meditate and pray; and hold not the goods they have with full love, but having them, forsake them.

Take heed also: to seek more than enough is foul covetousness; to keep back necessaries is frailty; but to forsake all things is perfectness. Therefore whiles they see high things that they can not reach, they empride not nor presume because of the small things that they have, so that they may mannerly ascend to the ordering of man's life: of which now follows.

CHAPTER IV

OF THE SETTING OF MAN'S LIFE

So that a man may be righteously directed to the worship of God and to his own profit and the profit of his neighbour, four things are to be said.

First: what is it that defiles a man. There are three sins, or three kinds of sin; that is to say of thought, of mouth and of work. A man sins in thought when he thinks aught against God. If he occupies his heart not with the praise and loving of God, but suffers it to be abstracted or stirred with divers thoughts, and to go void in the world. In mouth he sins when he lies; when he forswears; when he curses; when he backbites; when he defends a wrong; when he uses fond speech, or foul speech; or brings forth vain things or idle. In deed he sins many wise: by lechery; touching sinfully, or kissing; defiling himself wilfully; or, without great cause, procuring or sustaining occasions by which he trows he might be defiled; in robbing; stealing; beguiling; smiting; and other such.

Secondly: which are they that cleanse a man? And they are three, against the three aforesaid, that is to say: Contrition of thought and pulling out of desires that belong not to the praise or worship of God and love of Him. Confession of mouth, that ought to be timely, bare, and whole. Satisfaction of deed, that has three parts, that is to say: Fasting because he has sinned against himself; prayer because he has sinned against God; alms because he has sinned against his neighbour. Yet I say not he should do alms of other men's goods, but he should restore; for sin is not forgiven unless that that is withdrawn, be restored.

Third: which things keep cleanness of heart? And they are three: lively thought of God, that there be no time in which thou thinkest not of God except in sleep that is common to all; busy keeping of thine outwards wits, that tasting, savouring, hearing, and seeing they may wisely be restrained under the bridle of governance. The third is honest occupation, as reading of holy writ, speaking of God, writing, or some other good deed doing.

There are three things also that save cleanness of mouth: avisedness of speech; to eschew mickle speech; and to hate lying.

Also three things keep cleanness of working: moderation in meat; fleeing ill company; and oft to mind of death.

The fourth: which things are they that allure us to conform us to God's will? And there are three. First, the example of creatures, that is had by consideration; the goodliness of God, that is gotten by meditation and prayer: and mirth, of the heavenly kingdom, that is felt in a manner by contemplation.

The man of God set to live in this wise shall be as a tree that is set by running waters—that is the flowing of grace—so that he shall always be green in virtue and never be dry by sin; and shall give fruit in time; that is, he shall give good works as an example, and good words to the worship of God, and these he shall not sell for vainglory. He says in time' against them that give example of fasting in time of eating, and the reverse way also; and against covetous men that give their fruit when it is rotten; or else they give not until they die.

Therefore he prays wisely who says: Bonitatem et disciplinam et scientiam doce me, that is to say: goodliness, discipline and knowledge teach me.' What is discipline but the setting of, or correcting, of manners? First therefore we are taught righteousness, and corrected of ill by discipline; and after that we know what we should do, or what we should eschew. At the last we savour not fleshly things, but everlasting heavenly and godly.

And when a man with all busyness has dressed himself to the will of his Maker and grown in virtue, and has passed another that peradventure went before, in steadfastness of living and desire of Christ, he ought not thereof to joy nor give praise to himself, nor trow himself better than others—although they be low—but rather hold himself as the foulest and most wretched. He shall deem no man but himself, and all others set before himself; he shall not desire to be called holy of men, but worthy to be despised. When he comes amongst men, he should procure to be last in number and least in opinion; for the greater thou art the more shouldest thou meek thyself in all things and then thou shalt find grace before God to be made high. For the might of God is great, and honoured by the meek; therefore it is despised by the proud, for they seek their own joy not God's worship.

Truly if thou takest with gladness the favour of the people and the honour of men that is done to thee for thy holiness and good fame in this life, know it well thou hast received thy meed. And if thou seemest marvellous in penance and chastity whiles thou joyest more in man's joy than in angels' in the time to come nought but tormentry shall be for thee. Therefore thou oughtest perfectly to despise thyself, and entirely to forsake all joy of this world, and to think nor do nothing but in the sight of God's love, that all thy life, inward and outward, may cry the praise of God.

In meat and drink be thou scarce and wise. Whiles thou eatest or drinkest let not the memory of thy God that feeds thee pass from thy mind; but praise, bless, and glorify Him in ilka morsel, so that thy heart be more in God's praising than in thy meat, that thy soul be not parted from God at any hour. Thus doing, before Christ Jesu thou shalt be worthy a crown, and the temptations of the fiend, that in meat and drink awaits most men and beguiles them, thou shalt eschew. Either soothly by immoderately taking of food they are cast down from the height of virtue, or by too mickle abstinence they break down that virtue.

Many truly there are that always fluctuate in eating, so that over little or over mickle they always take; and the form of living they never keep whiles they trow that now this, now that, be better. The unwise and untaught, which have never felt the sweetness of Christ's love, trow that unwise abstinence be holiness; and they trow they can not be worthy of great meed with God unless they be known as singular of all men by scarceness and unrighteous abstinence.

But truly abstinence by itself is not holiness, but if it be discreet it helps us to be holy. If it be indiscreet it lets holiness, because it destroys discipline, without which virtues are turned to vice. If a man would be singular in abstinence he ought to eschew the sight of men and their praising, that he be not proud for nought and so lose all: for men truly ween they be holiest that they see most abstinent, when in truth ofttimes they are the worst.

He certain that has truly tasted the sweetness of endless love shall never deem himself to pass any man in abstinence, but the lower he supposes himself in abstinence with himself, the more he shall be held marvellous with men. The best thing, and as I suppose pleasing to God, is to conform thyself in meat and drink to the time and place and estate of them with whom thou art; so that thou seem not to be wilful nor a feigner of religion.

Know it truly, without doubt, if one or two think well of him, yet others will call him an hypocrite or a feigner. But there are some covetous of vainglory that in no wise will be holden as common men; for either they eat so little that they always draw the speech of men to them, or they procure other manner of meats to be seen diverse from others: whose madness and obstinacy be far from me.

Truly it is wholesome counsel that they that fast little give preference to them of greater abstinence, and since they may not do so great abstinence be sorry in mind. And they that are of great abstinence should trow others higher in virtue; whose virtue, in which they surpass, is hidden to men, whiles their virtue, that is to say abstinence, is praised of many. But unless it be dight with meekness and charity before Christ, it is nought.

It behoves him truly to be strong that will manfully use the love of God. The flesh being enfeebled with great disease ofttimes a man cannot pray, and then mickle more he cannot lift himself to high things with hot desire. I would rather therefore that a man failed for the greatness of love than for too mickle fasting; as the spouse said of herself: Nunciate dilecto quia amore langueo; that is: Show thyself to my love, for I long for love.'

Be thou therefore steadfast in all thy ways and dress thy life after the rule shown to thee, and if thou may not get that thou desirest in the beginning mistrust not, but abide; for by long use and time thou shalt come to perfection.

If thou be a pilgrim and rest by the way, whatever thou dost in this life to God ever have an eye. Let not thy thought go from Him; think that time lost in which thou thinkest not of God. In the night praise Him and desire His love, that sleep may not find thee in any other wise occupied than praying or thinking of God. See that thou flow not with vain thoughts, nor give thyself to many charges, but study to get and hold this steadfastness of mind so that thou dread not the wretchedness of this world nor desire the goods thereof unmannerly. He that dreads to suffer adversity knows not yet how it behoves us to despise the world; and he that joys in earthly things is far from everlasting things.

To the virtue of strength truly belong all adversities and prosperities; and also to despise death for endless life. And charity is to desire only heavenly things. A perfect lover forsooth joys to die, and suffers life meekly. To which perfection if thou ascend by the gift of Christ, yet shalt thou not be without tribulation and temptation: to show which our words shall turn.

CHAPTER V

OF TRIBULATION

When the fiend sees one man out of thousands perfectly turned to God; following the steps of Christ; despising this present world; loving and seeking only the things unseen; taking perfect penance; and purging himself from all filth of mind and body: he devises a thousand beguilings of annoyance and a thousand crafts of fighting to cast him from the love of God to the love of the world, and to fill him again with the filth of sin so that at the least with lecherous thoughts he should be made hateful to God. He raises against him persecution, tribulation, slander, false blame for sins, and all kinds of hatred; so that pain may slay and break him that prosperity could not beguile.

Now sharpness, now cherishing, he puts before him, and he brings to mind images of bodily things; he gathers together fantasies of sin; he gaincalls old shrewdness and delights of past love; he inflames heart and flesh with lecherous fire. He begins with the least but he comes to the greatest flame of wickedness. And with as great busyness he studies to blow against us all kinds of temptation, tormentry and tribulation, as he sorrows that we, by the mercy of God, have escaped from his cheeks.

He seeks nothing but that he might depart us from the unbodily embrace, sweetest and most chaste, of everlasting love; and afterward defile us in the pit of wretchedness. That were more wretched for us than I can tell.

Who can think his madness that from the delicacies of kings would come down to swine's meat? And yet is he more mad that forsakes the delicious meat of unwrought wisdom and puts himself under the filth of the flesh. Is not gluttony and lechery swinish filth, and they that do such, feed they not fiends?

Therefore how we must do against the tribulation and temptations of our enemies, and how to gainstand, shall patience teach us; of which now we will speak.

CHAPTER VI

OF PATIENCE

The children of God disdain to come down to the meat of unreasonable beasts, but truly they despise all unlawful lusts and worldly solace for the love of Christ. He truly that is fed with the bread that comes from heaven inclines not his desire to those things that are moved by the devil. When temptations arise or tribulation, ghostly armour is to be taken and it is time to go to battle.

Temptations truly are overcome with steadfastness of faith and love; tribulation truly with patience. What is patience but goodly and wilful suffering of adversity? He therefore that is patient murmurs in no grief, but rather at all times with the prophet praises God. The more patient a man is in his noys the more glorious shall he be in heaven.

Gladly therefore are tribulations to be suffered in adversity, noys and bitterness, pains and sickness and thirst; for by these and such other our sins are cleansed and meeds increased. Truly it either behoves us in this life [to be burnt with the fire of God's love and of tribulation, or else after this life] with the fire of purgatory or hell to be most bitterly crucified and punished. Choose therefore; we shall not escape the one. Here truly with little pain, yea with joy, if we cleave to God, we may eschew all pain to come.

Therefore tribulations are sent to us to call us from the love of the world, that we be not punished more grievously in the other life. With sorrow truly it behoves us to be cleansed of that ill we did in lust. If sinners build upon our backs, they noy us not, if we suffer it patiently, but themselves; for if they put us to a little pain for us they work a crown, but for themselves tormentry.

The sinful truly are suffered to pass this life withouten great tribulations; for in the time to come no joy is kept for them. Therefore holy men love tribulations, for they wot by them to win to endless life. Contrarily the rejected always murmur in adversity, and flee all that they can; for whiles they are given too mickle to seen things, they are deprived of the hope of things everlasting. In outward things only they find solace, because they have fully lost the savour of heavenly.

There is no reasonable soul here abiding but either she loves creatures, or the Maker of creatures. If she loves creatures she loses God and goes, with the good loved, to death. Truly such love in the beginning is labour and fondness; in the middle languor and wretchedness; and in the end hatred and pain.

He soothly that loves his Maker forsakes omnia quae that is in the world, and he thinks it full sweet of Him and with Him to speak; his refreshment is to think on Him. He bolts his outward wits that death ascend not by the windows; and that he be not unprofitably occupied in vanity. And sometimes despisings, reproofs, scorns, and slanders are raised against him, and therefore it is needful to take the shield of patience and be readier to forget wrongs than to know them. He shall pray for their turning that hate him and cast him down, and shall care not to please man, but dread to offend God.

If thou be tempted in the flesh make it subject, that the spirit be not overcome. Temptation truly that we consent not to is a matter for using virtue. For no man wots whether he be weak or strong until the time he be assayed. Likewise in peace no man is called patient, but when he is pulled with wrong; then he should see if he have patience. Many seem patient when they are not pricked, but when a soft blast—I say not of wrong but of correction—touches them, anon their mind turns to bitterness and wrath; and if they hear one word against their will they give again two more ungodly: into whose counsel my soul comes not.

Therefore the darts of our enemy are to be slakened with the meekness and sweetness of Christ's love; nor is place to be given to temptation, although it be grievous. For the greater battle the worthier victory and higher crown, as says the psalm: Beatus vir qui suffert tentationem, quoniam cum probatus fuerit accipiet coronam vitae, etc.; that is to say: Blest be the man that suffers temptation, for when he is proved a crown of life he shall receive that God behested to His lovers.'

Doubt not that thou art in the perfect life if despising be to thee as praising, poverty as riches, hunger as meat; so that thou sufferest them with even soul, and if thou fall in nought from height of mind. Flee and hate as mickle as thou canst the praise of man; for it is most praiseworthy to be worthy of praising, and not to be praised of men. The tongues of flatterers beguile many, and also the tongues of backbiters destroy many. Despise thou therefore favour, worship, and all vainglory; suffer meekly wraths, hatreds, and detractions; and so by slander and good fame, by tribulations and anger cease not to make haste to the heavenly kingdoms.

Ofttimes we fall, so that taught by many chances we should stand more strongly. The strong dread not, nor are the patient heavy, in adversity, as it is written: Non tristabit justum quicquid ei acciderit. Whatever happens to the righteous man it shall not heavy him.' Thus disposed, no marvel thou shalt overcome all temptation and slake all malice; thou shalt see thy noyers more wretched than thee, and with all thy mind thou shalt cleave to Christ.

CHAPTER VII

OF PRAYER

If thou be set in temptation or tribulation, to prayer anon run. Truly if thou prayest clearly thou shalt have help. Distractions sometimes come and waverings of heart, and thoughts of divers things ravish the heart and suffer it not to stand in the praising of God. Then peradventure it were good a while to think of holiness, until the mind is more stabled, and so thy prayers are fulfilled.

Truly if any have left all worldly occupations for the love of God, and always are given to holy prayer and holy meditation, I trow that by God's grace within a short space they shall find their heart is stabled to love and pray. They should not waver now to this and now to that, but rather abide in rest and endless peace. Full mickle it strengthens to get stableness of heart to be busy in frequent prayers, and devoutly to sing psalms. With busy prayers truly we overcome fiends, and we loosen their waitings and stirrings. They are enfeebled and as it were without strength, whiles we, strong and not overcome, bide in prayer.

Truly those men that have it in custom with long exercise to pray, sometimes find more sweetness and more fervent desire of prayer. Therefore whiles that sweetness and heat last it is good not to cease from prayers. When they cease—that often happens because of the corruptible flesh—they may turn to read holy scripture, or do some other profitable thing, that they suffer not their thought to waver from God, so that when they rise to pray again they may be quicker than they were before.

Truly then we pray well when we think of no other thing, but all our mind is dressed to heaven and our soul is enflamed with the fire of the Holy Ghost. Thus truly a marvellous plenteousness of God's goodness is found in us; for from the innermost marrow of our hearts shall the love of God rise, and all our prayer shall be with desire and effect; so that we overrun not the words, but nearly every syllable with a great cry and desire we shall offer to our Lord. Our heart being kindled with hot fire our prayer is also kindled, and in the savour of sweetness is offered by our mouth in the sight of God, so that it is great joy to pray. For whiles in prayer a marvellous sweetness is given to the one praying, the prayer is changed to song.

Here some are reproved that rather take heed to meditation than to prayer, not knowing that God's speech is fired; and with it the filth of sin is cleansed, and the minds of prayers are enflamed with love. They say that they will first meditate and so stable their hearts; but they are stabled the later in that they are not comforted by prayer.

Although we can not gather our hearts together as we would yet may we not leave off, but little by little we should study to grow in prayer, that at the last Jesu Christ may stable us. To which meditation helps if it pass not measure and manner.

CHAPTER VIII

OF MEDITATION

The meditation of Christ's passion and His death is good; and oft to recall what pain and wretchedness He freely took for our health in going about and preaching, in hunger, thirst, cold, heat, reproaches, cursings, and sufferings; so that it be not grievous to an unprofitable servant to follow his Lord and Emperor.

He truly that says he dwells in Christ ought to walk as He did. Christ says truly by Jeremy: Have mind of my poverty and of my passage, of wormwood and gall; that is to say, of sorrow and bitterness, by which I went from the world to the Father.

Truly this mindfulness or meditation overcomes the fiend and destroys his crafts; it slakes fleshly temptation and kindles the soul to Christ's love; it raises and cleanses, and also purges the mind. I trow this meditation is most profitable of all others to them that are newly turned to Christ. For there truly is shown the manhood of Jesu Christ, in the which man should be repeatedly glad; in which he has matter for joy and also mourning. Joy for the sickerness of our gainbuying; heaviness for the filth of our sinning, on account of which it is to be grieved for that so worthy an offering is offered. For the boisterous and fleshly soul is not ravished into the contemplation of the Godhead unless all fleshly lettings be wasted away by ghostly meditation and contemplation of the manhood.

Truly when a man begins to have a clean heart, and no image of bodily things can beguile him, then sickerly he is admitted to high things, that in love of the Godhead he may be wonderfully made glad. Some think truly on the joy of the blessed angels and holy souls joying with Christ; and this thought belongs to contemplation. Some think on the wretchedness of man's condition and his filth, and they dispute in their thoughts about man's folly that for the vanities of this life forgets the joys unseen. Others thus dispose their thoughts: that they will nothing but the praise and desire of their Maker, so that they love Him as much as is possible for men in this life. To this meditation no man comes but he that is mickle used in these things before rehearsed. For truly it is a more excellent manner than others and makes a man most contemplative.

Therefore as the works and uses of saints are divers, so are their meditations divers. Yet all, because they come of one spring, go to one end, and they come or lead to one bliss; but by divers ways, through the one charity, that is more in one than another. Therefore the psalm says: Deduxit me super semitas justitiae; that is, He has led me upon the paths of righteousness;' as if to say, there is one righteousness and many paths by which we are led to the joy of the life everlasting; because whiles all are one in being, they are of divers needs, and in one righteousness they are led to God by divers paths. Some go by a low path, some by a mean, and some by a high. The higher path is given to him that is ordained from eternity to love Christ more, not because he works more than others, or gives more or suffers more, but because he loves more. Which love is heat and sweetness, and it seeks rest in all men.

No man may set himself in any of these paths; but he takes to that which God chose him. Sometimes they that seem in the higher are in the lower, and the reverse; for that is only inward in soul before God, not in anything that may be done outward of man. According to the disposition and desire of their meditation they are dressed to this path or to that. By outward works no man may be known who is more or who less before God. Therefore it is folly to deem of the chosen and say: he passes him; or, his merits are far below the meeds of this one, when plainly they know not their minds; the which if they knew they might lawfully deem.

Therefore truly God wills it to be secret from all creatures, that they despise not some too mickle, or honour some too mickle. For doubtless if they saw men's hearts, many that they honour they would despise as stinking and foul, and others that they set not by, nor yet desire to see, they would honour as most lovely, and as the holy angels.

Good thoughts also and meditations of the elect be of God, and such by His grace He sheds forth to each one as best accords to their state and condition. Therefore I can tell thee my meditations, but which is most effectual for thee I cannot opine, for I see not thy inward desires. I trow truly that those meditations in thee most please God and most profit thee that God by His mercy sheds in thee.

Nevertheless in the beginning thou mayest have the words of other men; that I know well by myself. Truly if thou despise the teachings of doctors and trow that thyself mayest find something better than they teach thee in their writings, know forsooth that thou shalt not taste Christ's love. For truly it is a fond saying: God taught them, why therefore shall He not teach me?' I answer thee: because thou art not such as they were. Thou art proud and sturdy, and they were lowly and meek; and they asked nothing of God presuming, but meeking themselves under all, took knowledge from the saints. He taught them therefore so that we should be taught in their books.

If truly thou now desirest the love of Christ in thy meditations, or to re-sound His praises—as meseems—thou art well disposed. But the thoughts in which thou feelest more sweetness in God profit thee more. To meditate well without sweetness profits thee little, except in that case when the need for sweetness is not felt.

CHAPTER IX

OF READING

If thou desire to come to the love of God, and be kindled in thy desire for heavenly joys, and be brought to the despising of earthly things, be not negli-gent in meditating and reading holy scripture; and most in those places where it teaches manners, and to eschew the deceits of the fiend, and where it speaks of God's love, and of contemplative life. Hard sayings may be left to disputers and to wise men used for a long time in holy doctrine.

It helps us truly mickle to profit in good. By this we know our defaults and good deeds; in which things we sin, and in which not; what we should do, and what forbear; and the most subtle deceits of our enemies are opened to us. They kindle to love, and prick to weeping. If we have delight in them as it were in all riches, they prepare us a table of delights.

But let not covetousness of the honour or favour or praise of men kindle us to knowledge of scripture, but only the intent to please God; that we may know how we should love Him, and teach our neighbour the same. We ought not to be holden wise anent the people but rather hide our knowledge than show it so as to be praised, as it is said: In corde meo abscondi eloquia tua, ut non peccem tibi, that is: In my heart thy words, that I sin not towards thee,' in void or vain showing.

Therefore the cause of our speaking should be only the praise of God and the edification of our neighbour, that it may be fulfilled in us: Semper laus ejus in ore meo. Alway His praise be in my mouth,' and that is, when we seek not our own honour and we speak not against His praise.

CHAPTER X

OF CLEANNESS OF MIND

By these nine degrees before touched upon man comes to cleanness of mind, where God is seen. Cleanness, I say, that may be had in this life. How may perfect cleanness be gotten here where so oft man, with venial sins at least, is defiled? The feet of saints are to be washed for they draw the dust of the earth.

Who may truly say, I am clean from sin?' Truly none in this life; for as Job says: Si lotus fuero aquis nivis, et effulserint velut munditiae manus meae, tamen sordibus intinges me, et abominabuntur me vestimenta mea; that is to say: If I be washed with snow water,' that means true penance, and if my hands shine with cleanness,' because of works of innocence, yet shalt thou touch me with filth,' because of venial sins that can not be eschewed; and my clothes shall abhor me,' that is to say my flesh makes me abhor myself; and sensuality that is so frail, slippery, and ready to love the liking beauty of this world, ofttimes makes me sin. Therefore the apostle says: Non regnet peccatum in nostro mortali corpore. 'Sin reigns not in our mortal body,' as who should say: Sin may un-reign in us, but it may not un-be.

What cleanness therefore can man have in this life? Truly worthy and great if he rightly use himself in the study of reading, prayer, and meditation, as it is before noted. Truly although he sometimes sin venially yet forthwith, because his whole mind is dressed to God, it is destroyed. The heat truly of charity wastes in him all rust of sin, as it were a drop of water put into a great fire.

The virtue therefore of a cleansed soul is to have the mind busy to God, for in this degree all the thought is dressed to Christ; all the mind, although he seems to speak to others, is spread unto Him. Truly in a clean conscience nothing is bitter, sharp, or hard, but all is sweet and lovely. Out of cleanness of heart rises a song of joy, sweet ditty and joyful mirth. Then full oft a wonderful joy of God is given, and heavenly song is inshed. In this state a man may know that he is in charity that he shall never lose; he lives not without great dread— not lest he should suffer tormentry but that he offend not his Lover.

I spare to say more here for I seem to myself a full great wretch. For oft my flesh is noyed and assayed. Although forsooth the love of God and contemplative life is contained in these things beforesaid, yet somewhat of them is more specially to be said to your need and profit.

CHAPTER XI

OF THE LOVE OF GOD

O sweet and delectable light that is my Maker unmade; enlighten the face and sharpness of my inward eye with clearness unmade, that my mind, pithily cleansed from uncleanness and made marvellous with gifts, may swiftly flee into the high mirth of love; and kindled with Thy savour I may sit and rest, joying in Thee, Jesu. And going as it were ravished in heavenly sweetness, and made stable in the beholding of things unseen, never, save by godly things, shall I be gladdened.

O Love everlasting, enflame my soul to love God, so that nothing may burn in me but His embraces. O good Jesu, who shall grant me to feel Thee that now may neither be felt nor seen? Shed Thyself into the entrails of my soul. Come into my heart and fill it with Thy clearest sweetness. Moisten my mind with the hot wine of Thy sweet love, that forgetful of all ills and all scornful visions and imaginations, and only having Thee, I may be glad and joy in Jesu my God. Henceforward, sweetest Lord, go not from me, continually biding with me in Thy sweetness; for Thy presence only is solace to me, and Thy absence only leaves me heavy.

O Holy Ghost that givest grace where Thou wilt, come into me and ravish me to Thee; change the nature that Thou hast made with Thy honeyed gifts, that my soul fulfilled with Thy liking joy, may despise and cast away all things in this world. Ghostly gifts she may take of Thee, the Giver, and going by songful joy into undescried light she may be all melted in holy love. Burn my reins and my heart with Thy fire that on Thine altar shall endlessly burn.

O sweet and true Joy, I pray Thee come! Come O sweet and most desired! I pray Thee come! Come O sweet and most desired! Come my Love, that art all my comfort! Glide down into a soul longing for Thee and after Thee with sweet heat. Kindle with Thy heat the wholeness of my heart. With Thy light enlighten my inmost parts. Feed me with honeyed songs of love, as far I may receive them by my powers of body and soul.

In these, and such other meditations be glad, that so thou mayest come to the pith of love. Love truly suffers not a loving soul to bide in itself, but ravishes it out to the Lover; so that the soul is more there were it loves, than where the body is that by it lives and feels.

There are soothly three degrees of Christ's love, by one or another of which he that is chosen to love profits. The first is called, unable to be overcome; the second, unable to be parted; the third is called singular.

Then truly is love unovercomeable when it can not be overcome by any other desire. When it casts away lettings, and slakes all temptations and fleshly desires; and when it patiently suffers all griefs for Christ, and is overcome by no flattery nor delight. All labour is light to a lover, nor can a man better overcome labour than by love.

Love truly is undeparted when the mind is kindled with great love, and cleaves to Christ with undeparted thought. Forsooth it suffers Him not to pass from the mind a minute, but as if he were bound in heart to Him it thinks and sighs after Him, and it cries to be holden with His love that He may loose him from the fetters of mortality, and may lead him to Him Whom only he desires to see. And most this name JESU he in so mickle worships and loves that It continually rests in his mind.

When therefore the love of Christ is set so mickle in the heart of God's lover and the world's despiser that it may not be overcome by other desire of love, it is called high. But when he holds undepartedly to Christ, ever thinking of Christ, by no occasion forgetting Him, it is called everlasting and undeparted. And if this be high and everlasting, what love can be higher or more?

Yet there is the third degree that is called singular. It is one thing to be high, and another to be alone; as it is one thing to be ever presiding, and another to have no fellow. Truly we may have many fellows and yet have a place before all.

Truly if thou seekest or receivest any comfort other than of thy God, and if peradventure thou lovest the highest, yet it is not singular. Thou seest therefore to what the greatness of worthiness must increase, that when thou art high thou mayest be alone. Therefore love ascends to the singular degree when it excludes all comfort but the one that is in Jesu; when nothing but Jesu may suffice it.

The soul set in this degree loves Him alone; she yearns only for Christ, and Christ desires; only in His desire she abides, and after Him she sighs; in Him she burns; she rests in His warmth. Nothing is sweet to her, nothing she savours, except it be made sweet in Jesu; whose memory is as a song of music in a feast of wine. Whatever the self offers to her besides it or comes into mind, is straightway cast back and suddenly despised if it serve not His desire or accord not with His will. She suppresses all customs that she sees serve not to the love of Christ. Whatever she does seems unprofitable and intolerable unless it runs and leads to Christ, the End of her desire. When she can love Christ she trows she has all things that she wills to have, and withouten Him all things are abhorrent to her and wax foul. But because she trows to love Him endlessly she steadfastly abides, and wearies not in body nor heart but loves persevering-ly and suffers all things gladly. And the more she thus lives in Him the more she is kindled in love, and the liker she is to Him.

No marvel loneliness accords with such a one that grants no fellow among men. For the more he is ravished inwardly by joys, the less is he occupied in outward things; nor is he let by heaviness or the cares of this life. And now it seems as if the soul were unable to suffer pain, so that not being let by anguish, she ever joys in God.

O my soul, cease from the love of this world and melt in Christ's love, that always it may be sweet to thee to speak, read, write, and think of Him; to pray to Him and ever to praise Him. O God, my soul, to Thee devoted, desires to see Thee! She cries to Thee from afar. She burns in Thee and languishes in Thy love. O Love that fails not, Thou hast overcome me! O everlasting Sweet-ness and Fairness Thou hast wounded my heart, and now overcome and wounded I fall. For joy scarcely I live, and nearly I die; for I may not suffer the sweetness of so great a Majesty in this flesh that shall rot.

All my heart truly, fastened in desire for JESU, is turned into heat of love, and it is swallowed into another joy and another form. Therefore O good Jesu have mercy upon a wretch. Show Thyself to me that longs; give medicine to my hurt. I feel myself not sick, but languishing in Thy love. He that loves Thee not altogether loses all; he that follows Thee not is mad. Meanwhile therefore be Thou my Joy, my Love, and Desire, until I may see Thee, O God of Gods, in Syon.

Charity truly is the noblest of virtues, the most excellent and sweetest, that joins the Beloved to the lover, and everlastingly couples Christ with the chosen soul. It reforms in us the image of the high Trinity, and makes the creature most like to the Maker.

O gift of love, what is it worth before all other things, that challenges the highest degree with the angels! Truly the more of love a man receives in this life, the greater and higher in heaven shall he be. O singular joy of everlasting love that ravishes all His to the heavens above all worldly things, binding them with the bands of virtue.

O dear charity, he is not wrought on earth that—whatever else he may have—has not Thee. He truly that is busy to joy in Thee, is forthwith lift above earthly things. Thou enterest boldly the bedchamber of the Everlasting King. Thou only art not ashamed to receive Christ. He it is that thou hast sought and loved. Christ is thine: hold Him, for He cannot but receive thee, whom only thou desirest to obey. For withouten thee plainly no work pleases Him. Thou makest all things savoury. Thou art a heavenly seat; angels fellowship; a marvellous holiness; a blissful sight; and life that lasts endlessly.

O holy charity, how sweet thou art and comfortable; that remakest that that was broken. The fallen thou restorest; the bond thou deliverest; man thou makest even with angels. Thou raisest up those sitting and resting, and the raised thou makest sweet.

In this degree or state of love is love chaste, holy, and wilful; loving what is loved for the self, not for goods, and fastening itself altogether on that that is loved. Seeking nothing outward, pleased with itself: ardent, sweet-smelling, heartily binding love to itself in a marvellously surpassing manner. In the loved one joying; all other things despising and forgetting; thinking without forgetfulness; ascending in desire; falling in his love; going on in halsing; overcome by kissing; altogether molten in the fire of love.

Thus truly Christ's lover keeps no order in his loving nor covets no degree, because however fervent and joyful he be in the love of God in this life, yet he thinks to love God more and more. Yea, though he might live here evermore yet he should not trow at any time to stand still and not progress in love, but rather the longer he shall live the more he should burn in love.

God truly is of infinite greatness, better than we can think; of unreckoned sweetness; inconceivable of all natures wrought; and can never be comprehended by us as He is in Himself in eternity. But now, when the mind begins to burn in the desire for its Maker, she is made able to receive the unwrought light, and so inspired and fulfilled by the gifts of the Holy Ghost—as far as is lawful to mortals—she has heavenly joy. Then she overpasseth all things seen, and is raised up in height of mind to the sweetness of everlasting life. And whiles the soul is spread with the sweetness of the Godhead and the warmness of Creating Light, she is offered in sacrifice to the everlasting King, and being accepted is all burned up.

O merry love, strong, ravishing, burning, wilful, stalwart, unslakened, that brings all my soul to Thy service and suffers it to think of nothing but Thee. Thou challengest for Thyself all that we live; all that we savour; all that we are.

Thus therefore let Christ be the beginning of our love, whom we love for Himself. And so we love whatever is to be loved ordinately for Him that is the Well of love, and in whose hands we put all that we love and are loved by. Here soothly is perfect love shown: when all the intent of the mind, all the privy working of the heart, is lift up into God's love; so that the might and mirth of true love be so mickle that no worldly joy, nor fleshly merchandise, be lawful nor liking.

O love undeparted! O love singular! Although there were no torments for the wicked, nor no meed in heaven should be trowed for chosen souls, yet shouldst thou never the sooner loose thee from thy Love. More tolerable it were to thee to suffer an untrowed grief than once to sin deadly. Therefore truly thou lovest God for Himself and for no other thing, nor thyself except for God; and thereof it follows that nothing but God is loved in thee. How else should God be all in ilk thing, if there be any love of man in a man?

O clear charity, come into me and take me into thee and so present me before my Maker. Thou art savour well tasting; sweetness well smelling, and pleasant odour; a cleansing heat and a comfort endlessly lasting. Thou makest men contemplative; heaven's gate thou openest; the mouths of accusers thou sparrest; thou makest God be seen and thou hidest a multitude of sins. We praise thee, we preach thee, by the which we overcome the world; by whom we joy and ascend the heavenly ladder. In thy sweetness glide into me: and I commend me and mine unto thee withouten end.

CHAPTER XII

OF CONTEMPLATION

Contemplative life or contemplation has three parts: reading, prayer and meditation. In reading God speaks to us; in prayer we speak to God. In meditation angels come down to us and teach us that we err not; in prayer they go up and offer our prayers to God, joying in our profit; that are messengers betwixt God and us.

Prayer certain is a meek desire of the mind dressed in God, with which, when it comes to Him, He is pleased. Meditation on God and godly things, in which is the halsing of Rachel, is to be taken after prayer and reading.

To reading belongs reason or the inquisition of truth, that is as a goodly light marked upon us. To prayer belongs praise, song, surpassing in beholding, and marvel; and thus contemplative life or contemplation stands in prayer. To meditation belongs the inspiration of God, understanding, wisdom and sighing.

If it be asked what is contemplation it is hard to define. Some say that contemplative life is nought else but knowledge of things to come and hidden: or to be void of all worldly occupation: or the study of God's letters. Others say that contemplation is the free sight into the visioned truths of wisdom, lift up with full high marvel. Others say that contemplation is a free and wise insight of the soul all spread about to behold His might. Others say, and say well, that contemplation is joy in heavenly things. Others say, and say best, that contemplation is the death of fleshly desires through the joy of the mind upraised.

To me it seems that contemplation is the joyful song of God's love taken into the mind, with the sweetness of angels praise. This is the jubilation that is the end of perfect prayer and high devotion in this life. This is the ghostly mirth had in mind for the Everlasting Lover, with great voice outbreaking. This is the last and most perfect deed of all deeds in this life. Therefore the psalmist says: Beatus vir qui scit jubilationem, that is to say: Blest be the man that knows jubilation,' in contemplation of God. Truly none alien to God can joy in Jesu, nor taste the sweetness of His love. But if he desire to be ever kindled with the fire of everlasting love, in patience, meekness, and gentle manners; and to be made fair with all cleanness of body and soul, and dight with ghostly ointments; he is lift up into contemplation. Let him unceasingly seek healthful virtues, by which in this life we are cleansed from the wretchedness of sins, and in another life, free from all pain, we joy endlessly in the blessed life: yet in this exile he thus shall be worthy to feel the joyful mirth of God's love.

Therefore be not slow to chastise thyself with prayer and waking, and use holy meditations; for doubtless with these ghostly labours, and with heaviness and weeping from inward repenting, the love of Christ is kindled in thee, and all virtues and gifts of the Holy Ghost are shed into thy heart. Begin therefore by wilful poverty, so that whiles thou desirest nought in this world, before God and man thou livest soberly, chastely and meekly. To have nothing is sometimes of need, but to will that you may have nought is of great virtue. We may have mickle desires and yet will to have right nought, when we hold that we have to our need and not to our lust. Right as he sometime that hath nought coveteth to have many things; right so he that seemeth to have many things hath right nought, for that that he hath he loveth it not, save only for his bodily need.

Truly it behoves the most perfect to take necessaries, else were he not perfect if he refused to take that whereof he should live.

This is the manner for perfect men to keep: all worldly goods for God to despise, and yet to take of the same meat and clothing; and if this want at any time, not to murmur but to praise God; and as much as they may to refuse superfluities. The warmer a man waxes with the heat of everlasting light, the meeker shall he be in all adversities. He that is truly and not feignedly meek holds himself worthy of being despised, and neither by harm nor reproof is provoked to wrath. Wherefore lowing himself to continual meditation, it is given him to rise to the contemplation of heavenly things, and the sharpness of his mind being cleansed as the sickness of the flesh suffers, it is given him to sing sweetly and burningly with inward joys. And truly when he goes to seek any outward thing, he goes not with a proud foot, but only joying in high delights anon with the sweetness of God's love is as it were ravished in trance, and being ravished is marvellously made glad.

Such forsooth is contemplative life if it be taken in due manner. By long use in ghostly works we come to contemplation of things everlasting. The mind's sight is truly taken up to behold heavenly things, yet by shadowly sight and in a mirror, not clearly and openly: whiles we go by faith we see as it were by a mirror and shadow. Truly if our ghostly eye be busy to that spiritual light it may not see that light in itself as it is, and yet it feels that it is there whiles it holds within the savour and heat of that light unknown. Whereof in the psalm it is said: Sicut tenebrae ejus, ita et lumen ejus; that is: And as the darkness thereof, so the light thereof.'

Although truly the darkness of sin be gone from an holy soul, and murk things and unclean be passed, and the mind be purged and enlightened, yet whiles it bides in this mortal flesh that wonderful joy is not perfectly seen. Forsooth holy and contemplative men with a clear face behold God. That is either their wits are opened for to understand holy writ; or else the door of heaven is opened unto them: that is more. As one might say: all lettings betwixt their mind and God are put back, their hearts are purged, and they behold the citizens of heaven. Some truly have received both these.

As we, standing in darkness, see nothing, so in contemplation that invisibly lightens the soul, no seen light we see. Christ also makes darkness His resting place, and yet speaks to us in a pillar of a cloud. But that that is felt is full delectable. And in this truly is love perfect when man, going in the flesh, cannot be glad but in God, and wills or desires nothing but God or for God. Hereby it is shown that holiness is not in crying of the heart, or tears, or outward works, but in the sweetness of perfect charity and heavenly contemplation. Many truly are molten in tears, and afterwards have turned them to evil; but no man defiles himself with worldly business after he has truly joyed in everlasting love. To greet and to sorrow belong to the newly converted, beginners and profiters; but to sing joyfully and to go forth in contemplation belongs but to the perfect.

He therefore that has done penance for a long time, whiles he feels his conscience pricking for default knows without doubt that he has not yet done perfect penance. Therefore in the meantime tears shall be as bread to him day and night; for unless he first punish himself with weeping and sighing he cannot come to the sweetness of contemplation.

Contemplative sweetness is not gotten but with full great labour; and with joy untold it is possessed. Forsooth it is not of man's merit but God's gift. And yet from the beginning to this day a man might never be ravished in contemplation of everlasting love unless he before had perfectly forsaken all the vanity of the world. Moreover he ought to be used in healthful meditation and devout prayer before he come truly to the contemplation of heavenly joys.

Contemplation is sweet and desirable labour. It gladdens the labourer, and hurts not. No man has this but in joying: not when it comes, but when it goes, he is weary. O good labour to which mortal men dress them! O noble and marvellous working that those sitting do most perfectly! It behoves that he take great rest of body and mind whom the fire of the Holy Ghost truly enflames.

Many truly know not how to rest in mind, nor yet to put out void and unprofitable thoughts, and cannot fulfill what is bidden in the psalm: Vacate, et videte quaniam ego sum Deus; that is to say: Be void from worldly vanity and see, for I am God.' Truly the void in body, and wavering in heart, are not worthy to taste and see how sweet our Lord is—how sweet the height of contemplation.

Truly ilk man contemplative loves solitariness so that the more fervently and oftener, in that he is letted of no man, he may be exercised in his affections.

Then, therefore, it is known that contemplative life is worthier and fuller of meed than active life. And all contemplatives by the moving of God love solitary life, and because of the sweetness of contemplation are especially fervent in love. It seems that solitary men raised by the gift of contemplation are high and touch the highest perfection. Unless it happen there be some in such state that they have come even with the height of the contemplative life, and yet they cease not to fulfil the office of the preacher. They pass these other solitaries—highest in contemplation and only given to godly things, not to the needs of their neighbours—their degrees being like, and for their preaching they are worthy a crown that is cleped aureola.

Truly a very contemplative man is set towards the light unseen with so great desire that ofttimes he is deemed by man as a fool or unwise; and that is because his mind is enflamed from its seat with Christ's love. It utterly changes his bodily bearing, and his body departing also from all earthly works it makes God's child as a man out of his mind.

Thus truly whiles the soul gathers all the self into endless mirth of love, withholding herself inwardly she flows not forth to seek bodily delights. And because she is fed inwardly with liking pleasure, it is no marvel though she say sighing; Who shall give thee me, my brother, that I may find thee without, and kiss thee?' That is to say: loosed from the flesh I may be worthy to find Thee, and seeing Thee face to face, be joined with Thee withouten end. And now man despises me.'

A devout soul given to contemplative life and fulfilled with love everlasting despises all vainglory of this world, and, joying only in Jesu, covets to be loosed. For why she is despised by these that savour and love this world, not heaven, and grievously languishes in love, and greatly desires with the lovely company of the angels to be given to the joys that worldly adversity can not noy.

Nothing is more profitable, nothing merrier, than the grace of contemplation that lifts us from these low things and offers us to God. What is this grace but the beginning of joy? And what is the perfection of joy but grace confirmed? In which is kept for us a joyful happiness and happy joy, a glorious endlessness and everlasting joy; to live with the saints and dwell with angels. And that which is above all things: truly to know God; to love Him perfectly; and in the shining of His majesty to see Him and, with a wonderful song of joy and melody, to praise Him endlessly.

To whom be worship and joy, with deeds of thankfulness, in the world of worlds. Amen.

THE FORM OF PERFECT LIVING AND OTHER PROSE TREATISES

RICHARD ROLLE

E-BOOK ALSO AVAILABLE IN PAPERBACK.

BY RICHARD ROLLE, OF HAMPOLE, A.D. 1300–1349

RENDERED INTO MODERN ENGLISH BY GERALDINE E. HODGSON, D.LITT., LECTURER IN
EDUCATION IN THE UNIVERSITY OF BRISTOL

LONDON:

THOMAS BAKER, 72, NEWMAN STREET, W.

1910

"Love is a life, joining together the loving and the loved."
"Truth may be without love, but it cannot help without it."
RICHARD ROLLE
(The Form of Perfect Living, ch. x.).

THE FORM OF PERFECT LIVING
AND OTHER PROSE TREATISES

PREFACE

THIS book is not intended for those who are acquainted with Anglo-Saxon and Middle English; but for those who care for the thought, specially the religious and devotional thought, of our forefathers. My one aim has been to make a portion of that thought accurately intelligible to modern readers, with the greatest possible saving of trouble to them. When I could use the old word or phrase, with certainty of its being understood, I have done so. When I could not, I have replaced it with the best modern equivalent I could find or invent. In extenuation of the occasional use of Rolle's expression, "by their lone," I may urge its expressiveness, the absence of an equivalent, and the fact that it may still be heard in remote places. Where possible, I have retained the archaic order of the original Text. Such irregular constructions, as e.g., the use of a singular pronoun in the first half of a sentence, and of a plural in the second half, I have left unaltered; for the meaning was perfectly clear. In short, I have endeavoured to make Richard Rolle as he was as significant as possible to English men and women of to-day as they are, when they are not professed students of English language. In such an undertaking, it is obvious that I must have presented endless vulnerable places to the learned. I can only repeat that the book was never meant for them, but for those who will perhaps forgive me if I describe them as specialists in religious thought rather than in English Language.

The rendering is made from the texts printed by Professor Horstman in his Library of Early English Writers: Richard Rolle of Hampole an English Father of the Church.

GERALDINE E. HODGSON.
The University, Bristol,
S. Mary Magdalene, 1910.

INTRODUCTION

RICHARD ROLLE of Hampole is the earliest in time of our famous English Mystics. Born in or about 1300, he died in 1349, seven years after Mother Julian of Norwich was born. Walter Hilton died in 1392.

An exhaustive account of Rolle's life is given in Vol. ii. of Professor Horstman's Edition of his works, a book unfortunately out of print. The main facts are recorded in a brief "Life" appended to Fr. R. Hugh Benson's A Book of the Love of JESUS. Therefore, it will suffice to say here that Richard Rolle seems to have been born at Thornton, near Pickering, in Yorkshire, in or about 1300; that, finding the atmosphere of Oxford University uncongenial, he left it, and for some four years was supported, as a hermit, by the Dalton Family. By the end of that time, through prayer, contemplation and self-denial, he had attained the three stages of mystical life which he describes as calor, dulcor, canor; (heat, sweetness, melody.) The next period of his life was less easy. Having left the protection of the Daltons, and being without those means of subsistence which are within the reach of priest or monk, this hermit depended for his daily bread on other men's kindness. Not that he was a useless person: apart from the utility of a life of Prayer, he could point to counsel and exhortation given; to the existence of converts consequent upon his ministrations. To add to his difficulties, he preached a doctrine of high pure selflessness with which, the average man, in all times, seems to have no abundant sympathy: and to crown all he was endowed by nature with a sensitive temper. His remarkable gifts forced him into public notice; his cast of thought and his temperament were not calculated to win him ease or popularity. Professor Horstman is peculiarly severe to those among his enemies and detractors "who called themselves followers and disciples of Christ." The insertion here of this painful passage would introduce a jarring note; moreover, the raked embers of past controversy seldom tend to the spiritual improvement of the present. An interesting judgment by Professor Horstman on Rolle's place in mysticism is too long for quotation; but the following sentence may be taken as the pith of it:—"His position as a mystic was mainly the result of the development of scholasticism. The exuberant luxuriant growth of the brain in the system of Scotus called forth the reaction of the heart, and this reaction is embodied in Richard Rolle, who as exclusively represents the side of feeling as Scotus that of reason and logical consequence; either lacking the corrective of the other element."

It is consoling to know that Rolle's last years were passed in peace, in a cell, near a monastery of Cistercian nuns at Hampole, where the nuns supported him, while he acted as their spiritual adviser.

In the book mentioned above, Fr. Hugh Benson has translated some of Richard Rolle's Poems, and certain devotional Meditations. In this Volume, four of his Prose Treatises have been selected from the rest of his works, in the belief that they may supplement those parts of Rolle's writings with which, those who are interested in these phases of thought, are already familiar.

The first, The Form of Perfect Living, is a Rule of Life which he wrote for a nun of Anderby, Margaret Kirkby, of whom Professor Horstman writes: "She seems to have been his good angel, and perhaps helped to smooth down his ruffled spirits. This friendship was lasting—it lasted to their lives' ends."

This treatise was written of course to meet the requirements of the "religious" life. It has seemed expedient, because supplementary, then, to put next to it his work on Our Daily Life, which was meant for those who are "in the world"; and which may give pause to some who might otherwise criticise the first hastily, perhaps condemning it as unpractical, or even objectionable in a world where, after all, men must eat and drink and live, and where some, therefore must provide the necessary means. Most intensely practical is this second treatise, and perhaps nowhere more so than when it meets the needs of those who are inclined to split straws over the definition of the word "good." What is a good action?—such people love to inquire, and like "jesting Pilate," sometimes do not "stay for an answer." Richard Rolle has no manner of doubt about his reply. An action must be good in itself, i.e., so he would tell us, pleasing to GOD in its own nature. But the matter by no means ends there for him. This good action must be performed,—and it is this which is, now palpably, now subtly, hard—entirely for the sake of goodness, without the slightest taint of self-seeking, of vanity, of secret satisfaction that we are not as other men are, not even as this Pharisee or this Publican.

Such a motive, inspiring each person's whole work, would surely go far to remove what is known as the Social Problem. It would make many a house the dwelling of peace, many a business-place an abode of honour. If we could get back to Richard Rolle's simplicity and to his unmovable faith, then, his goal, even the acquisition of perfect love, might seem to all of us less distressingly remote.

The present rendering has been taken from the longer and more elaborate of the two MSS. containing the Treatise. The shorter form of his work On Grace and the Epistle have been added in the hope that they may meet the need of all, contemplative or active as they may chance to be.

There is, among his voluminous writings, a curious and interesting Revela-tion concerning Purgatory, purporting to be a woman's dream about one, Margaret, a soul in Purgatory. Amidst much natural horror, not however exceeding that described by Dante, there are many quaint side-lights thrown upon our forefathers' ways of thought; as e.g., when Margaret's soul is weighed in one scale, against the fiend, "and a great long worm with him," in the other; the worm of conscience, in fact. But the work has not been included in this volume, lest it should prove wholly unprofitable to a generation which if it be not readily disturbed by sin, is easily and quickly shocked by crude suggestions concerning its possible consequences and reward. They will find enough, perhaps, in the treatise on Daily Work.

If any one should think that there, and in one portion of the treatise on Grace, Rolle has dwelt harshly on considerations of fear, rather than on those of love, he must not make the mistake of concluding that these admonitions represent the whole of Catholic teaching on the point. Men's temperaments differ, and teachers, meeting these various tempers, differ in their modes of helping them. Side by side with Richard Rolle may be put the words of S. Francis Xavier, in what is perhaps the most beautiful of Christian hymns:—

My GOD, I love Thee; not because
I hope for heaven thereby,
Nor yet because who love Thee not
Are lost eternally.
Not for the hope of gaining aught,
Not seeking a reward;
But as Thyself hast loved me,
O ever-loving Lord!

Moreover, no reader of the Epistle on Charity can entertain any doubt as to whether our English Mystic understood the mystery of limitless love.

It is no doubt, easy to complain, as we read certain passages, that Richard Rolle's recommendations are neither new nor original: but if instead of dis-missing them as familiar, we tried to put them into practice, we should perhaps have less leisure for idle criticism of others, and ourselves be less evil and tiresome people.

On the other hand, the accusation may be brought that he proposes an im-possibly high aim. No doubt, in such a pitch of devotion as is suggested, e.g., in ch. viii. of The Form of Perfect Living, some may think they find extrava-gance: but no doubt it was this same spirit which inspired SS. Peter and Paul, and the other Apostles; which built up the Early Church; which made Saints, Martyrs and Confessors; which suggested such apparently forlorn hopes as that of S. Augustine of Canterbury, when, to bring them the Gospel of JESUS Christ, he bearded the rough Men of Kent, and (according to Robert of Brunne) reaped, as his immediate reward, a string of fishtails hung on his habit, though later, the conversion of these sturdy pagans. It was doubtless, too, the spirit which inspired the best men and women in the English Church, before they began to confuse the spheres of Faith and Reason, and to disregard S. Hilary's warning about the difficulty of expressing in human language that which is truly "incomprehensible,"—incomprehensible in the old sense, as in the Athanasian Symbol, "Immensus Pater, immensus Filius, immensus Spiritus sanctus"; till, indeed, men forgot, for all practical purposes that infinity transcends the grasp of finite minds (in fact, as well as in placidly accepted and then immediately neglected theory); and can be apprehended only, and that imperfectly, by the best aspirations of a heart, set of fixed purpose on that high goal.

To the modern Englishman, immersed in business anxieties, imperial interests and domestic cares, the invitation repeated so often by Richard Rolle, to love GOD supremely, may seem incalculably unreal and remote, even though he might hesitate to confess it baldly. But what if the Englishman who so loved GOD, were also the greater Englishman? And what answer does history return to that plain question?

"Richard Rolle," Professor Horstman does not hesitate to write "was one of the most remarkable men of his time, yea, of history. It is a strange and not very creditable fact that one of the greatest of Englishmen has hitherto been doomed to oblivion. In other cases, the human beast first crucifies, and then glorifies or deifies the nobler minds, who swayed by the Spirit, do not live as others live, in quest of higher ideals by which to benefit the race; he, one of the noblest champions of humanity, a hero, a saint, a martyr in this cause has never had his resurrection yet—a forgotten brave. And yet, he has rendered greater service to his country, and to the world at large, than all the great names of his time. He rediscovered Love, the principle of Christ. He reinstalled feeling, the spring of life which had been obliterated in the reign of scholasticism. He re-opened the inner eye of man, teaching contemplation in solitude, an unworldly life in abnegation, in chastity, in charity … He broke the hard crust that had gathered round the heart of Christianity, by formalism and exteriority, and restored the free flow of spiritual life."

This passage, to those who feel that there has been no age since the Birth of Christ when the great principles of religious life have been wholly lost, and who remember that Richard Rolle lived in the age of Dante, may seem overstated. But it shews sufficiently at least, and for that reason is quoted here, what a great Englishman he was, and what a debt his unaware countrymen owe him; a debt which they could pay in the way most grateful to him, by listening to his words.

It may be remarked, by the way, that Rolle is not inclined to substitute individualism for the authority of the Church; a change which has been brought against some mystics. There is immense emphasis laid, all through his writings, on the importance of conduct. The penetrating analysis, in ch. vi, of The Form of Perfect Living, of the possible sins humanity can commit on its journey through the wilderness of this world, hardly leaves a corner of the heart unlighted; lets not one possible shift, twist or excuse of the human conscience go free. But it all has the Church as its immediate background; the Mystical Body, not the individual soul in isolation, is everywhere taken for granted. Man lives not to himself nor dies to himself, even though he be Richard Rolle the hermit, or Margaret Kirkby the recluse, that is the plain teaching of these plain-speaking pages. And all through them too is a tough common sense, and an unusually alert power of observation; and there is perhaps an element of that business capacity, which some of the Saints and Mystics have shewn, in his inclusion among "sins of deed" of "beginning a thing that is above our might"; for in that there is not only pride, but a kind of stupid incapacity surely.

It is quite possible that Rolle's tendency to repetition may tire any one who reads him "straight on," as the phrase is. But it is doubtful whether that be the best means of approach. If he be read in bits, he will prove far more effective: and his ability to hit the right nail on the head, and to hit it wonderfully hard, may occasionally bring his words home to our immediate circumstances with an appositeness that may be more than a coincidence.

In the past, the learned and ignorant alike have been guilty of the operation which may be described as cutting man up into parts: i.e., they have been inclined to treat him now as if he were all intellect, then as if he were all feeling; while to the will a kind of intermediate part has generally been allotted, as if it were the handmaid instead of the master of the other two. And there is still, in some quarters, a tendency to relegate the will and the feelings to an inferior plane, if indeed they be allowed any place at all. In other quarters, the onslaught is made on intellect. Men are bidden to be humble, to become as little children; as if there were any humility in thinking incorrectly or not at all; as if the odd, though suppressed, assumption that children have no intellects had any ground in fact. It is surely a true apostrophe—

"GOD! Thou art mind! Unto the master-mind,
Mind should be precious."

The Angelic Doctor himself paid a tribute to the importance and special difficulties of intellect, and also to the necessity of uniting it with will:—"the martyrs had greater merit in faith, not receding from the faith for persecutions; and likewise men of learning have greater merit of faith, not receding from the faith for the reasons of philosophers or heretics alleged against it." Richard Rolle, following on the same lines as S. Thomas Aquinas, has nothing of this spirit of division: the whole being is what he would fain see offered to GOD, whether it be so by Margaret Kirkby, or by those who are "in the world," for whom Our Daily Work was written. In the image of GOD was man made, and therefore GOD suffices for all the needs of man's nature: that, at least seems to be the underlying idea when Rolle writes:—"GOD is light and burning. Light clarifies our reason, burning kindles our will." May we not say here too?—"What GOD has joined together, that let not man put asunder."

Above all things, Rolle aims at a perfect balance, culminating in a harmony ruled by one power, and that the greatest in the world, Love. Real love, he asks; not the degraded things to which men give that great name, as to every passing gust of feeling, to every unworthy untamed emotion: but the divine quality, when to the "lastingness," which he requires, is also joined that which is the inner essence of Love, viz., sacrifice. "Love is a life," he writes, "joining together the loving and the loved." And then he remembers the other great gift to men, intellectual sincerity, which has inspired all "who follow Truth along her star-paved way"; and he gives to that its place and due: "Truth may be without love: but it cannot help without it." Even then, the whole tale is not complete; the way of the Saints is not "Primrosed and hung with shade." Love, with Rolle, is no easy sentimentality: it involves definite sacrifice in more directions than one; it demands thought, perseverance, supernatural strength, natural strenuousness; it is not a selfish enjoyment of a circumambient atmosphere wrapping humanity, without responsibility or effort of its own: "Love is a Life."

"Love," he writes, "is a perfection of learning; virtue of prophecy; fruit of truth; help of sacraments; establishing of wit and knowledge; riches of pure men: life of dying men. So, how good love is. If we suffer to be slain; if we give all that we have (down) to a beggar's staff: if we know as much as men may know on earth, all this is naught but ordained sorrow and torment." Then, with that sound sense, which is not the least element in the sum of his attractiveness, he utters a subtle warning against that all too common sin, judging one another: "If thou wilt ask how good is he or she, ask how much he or she loves: and that no man can tell. For I hold it folly to judge a man's heart, that none knows save GOD."

After this it cannot be necessary to say that Rolle is a true mystic. "Many," so he tells us in this same chapter x., "Many speak and do good, and love not GOD." But that will not suffice his exacting demands. A man is not "good" until his interior disposition be all filled and taken up with pure love of GOD. And as he analyses the Christian Character, there is a pleasant blunt directness about this holy man:—"he that says he loves GOD and will not do what is in him to shew love, tell him that he lies."

It is possible that the alarming list of sins of the heart, in chapter vi., may give the heedless and even the heedful matter for grave thought, as each one finds himself ejaculating with spontaneous fear—"Who can tell how oft he offendeth? Cleanse thou me from my secret faults."

Surely no one need fear that the outcome of a study of Richard Rolle will be effeminacy. Not that that indeed is the special temptation of the English: a chill commonplace acquiescence in a convenient, if baseless, hope that somehow "things will come all right," is far more likely to lead them astray than any "burning yearning to GOD with a wonderful delight and certainty." Is not George Herbert's cry apposite still?

"O England, full of sin, but most of sloth!"

Nor can any one argue fairly that this absorption of the mystic is just selfish idleness. It is, so it seems, as we read Rolle's injunctions, of the nature of hard exacting toil. No doubt, there must be those who do the material work of the world; who gain, among other things, those "goods" which go to support the Mystics. But there will be no lack of such workers, through the inroads of religion; the broad ways of daily life are in no danger of contracting suddenly in to the path to the strait gate. Moreover, natural life itself is a poor thing unsupported by an unseen stream of spiritual refection. Here, as elsewhere in the ordered economy of things, two forms of life are found to be complementary. It is true, as Dr. Bigg once wrote:—"If Society is to be permeated by religion, there must be reservoirs of religion like those great storage places up among the hills which feed the pipes by which water is carried to every home in the city. We shall need a special class of students of GOD, men and women whose primary and absorbing interest it is to work out the spiritual life in all its purity and integrity." It is indeed the idlest of criticism that condemns such people as slothful or selfish.

There is one charm in our own Mystics which we may miss in S. John of the Cross or S. Teresa for example; viz., that with all their zeal, there is also an amazing reality and simplicity down at the bottom of it, which may seem to us not present in the rhapsodies of more southern lovers; though in all probability such seeming is purely racial. Nevertheless, we may be thankful if we find the antidote to our national prosaic ways in the sane zeal of others of our nation.

Lastly, as men read, they may be overcome perhaps by despair. This pure untainted selflessness of which Richard Rolle writes almost glibly, how can it be possible here and now? How can men and women, fixed in and condemned to the dusty ways of common life, unable as they are to leave the world even if they would, how can they so much as dream of such unattainable heights? Is there no help for them in the often quoted lines of a later English Mystic?—

"Who aimeth at the sky
Shoots higher much than he who means a tree."

For plain men and women, the key to the problem may lie in the question put by Robert Browning into the mouth of Innocent XII.:—

"Is this our ultimate stage, or starting place
To try man's foot, if it will creep or climb,
'Mid obstacles in seeming, points that prove
Advantage for who vaults from low to high,
And makes the stumbling-block a stepping-stone?"

Even though the goal be not reached, to have willed deliberately here the first step may prove to have been not wholly unavailing.

The Form of Perfect Living
by
Richard Rolle

CHAPTER I

IN every sinful man and woman that is bound in deadly sin, are three wretchednesses, the which bring them to the death of hell. The first is: Default of ghostly strength. That they are so weak within their heart, that they can neither stand against the temptations of the fiend, nor can they lift their will to yearn for the love of GOD and follow thereto. The second is: Use of fleshly desires:—for they have no will nor might to stand, they fall into lusts and likings of this world; and because they think them sweet, they dwell in them still, many till their lives' end, and so they come to the third wretchedness. The third is, Exchanging a lasting good for a passing delight: as who say they give endless joy for a little joy of this life. If they will turn them and rise to penance, GOD will ordain their dwelling with angels and with holy men. But because they choose the vile sin of this world, and have more delight in the filth of their flesh than in the fairness of heaven, they lose both the world and heaven. For he that hath not JESUS Christ loses all that he hath, and all that he is, and all that he might get. For he is not worthy of life, nor to be fed with swine's-meat. All creatures shall be stirred in His vengeance in the day of Doom. These wretchednesses that I have told you of are not only in worldly men and women, who use gluttony, lust, and other open sins: but they are also in others who seem in penance and godly life. For the devil that is enemy to all mankind, when he sees a man or a woman among a thousand, turn wholly to GOD, and forsake all the vanities and riches that men who love this world covet, and seek lasting joy, a thousand wiles he has in what manner he may destroy them. And when he can not bring them into such sins which might make all men wonder at them who knew them, he beguiles many so privily that they cannot oftentimes feel the trap that has taken them.

Some he takes with error that he puts them in. Some with singular wit, when he makes them suppose that the thing that they say or do is best; and therefore they will have no counsel of another who is better and abler than they; and this is a foul stinking pride; for such man would set his wit before all other. Some, the devil deceives through Vain-glory, that is idle joy; when any have pride and delight in themselves, of the penance that they suffer, of good deeds that they do, of any virtue that they have; are glad when men praise them, sorry when men blame them, have envy of them who are spoken better of than they. They consider themselves so glorious, and so far surpassing the life that other men lead, that they think that none should reprehend them in anything that they do or say; and despise sinful men, and others who will not do as they bid them. How mayst thou find a sinfuller wretch than such a one? And so much the worse is he because he knows not that he is evil, and is considered and honoured of men as wise and holy. Some are deceived by over-great lust and liking in meat and drink, when they pass measure and come into excess, and have delight therein; and they know not that they sin, and therefore they amend them not, and so they destroy virtues of soul. Some are destroyed with over-great abstinence of meat and drink and sleep. That is often temptation of the devil, for to make them fall in the midst of their work, so that they bring it to no ending as they should have done, had they known reason and had discretion; and so they lose their merit for their frowardness. This snare our enemy lays to take us with when we begin to hate wickedness, and turn us to GOD. Then many begin a thing that they can never more bring to an end: then they suppose that they can do whatsoever their heart is set on. But oftentimes they fall or ever they come midway; and that thing which they supposed was for them is hindering to them. For we have a long way to heaven, and as many good deeds as we do, as many prayers as we make, and as many good thoughts as we think in truth and hope and charity, so many paces go we heavenwards. Then, if we make us so weak and so feeble that we can neither work nor pray as we should do, nor think, are we not greatly to blame that fail when we had most need to be stalwart? And well I wot that it is not GOD'S will that we so do. For the prophet says: "Lord, I shall keep my strength to Thee," so that he might sustain GOD'S service till his death-day, and not in a little and a short time waste it, and then lie wailing and groaning by the wall. And it is much more peril than men suppose. For S. Jerome says that he makes an offering of robbery who outrageously torments his body by over-little meat or sleep. And S. Bernard says: "Fasting and waking hinder not spiritual goods, but help, if they be done with discretion; without that, they are vices." Wherefore, it is not good to torture ourselves so much, and afterwards to have displeasure at our deed. There have been many, and are who suppose it is naught all that they do unless they be in so great abstinence and fasting that all men speak of them who know them. But oftentimes it befalls that the more outward joy or wondering they have (on account) of the praising of men, the less joy they have within of the love of GOD. By my judgment, they should please JESUS Christ much more if they accepted for His sake—in thanking and praising Him, to sustain their body in His service and to withhold themselves from great speech of men—whatsoever GOD sent them in time and place, and gave themselves since entirely to the love and the praising of that Lord JESUS Christ: Who will stalwartly be loved, and lastingly be served, so that their holiness were more seen in GOD'S eye than in man's. For all the better thou art, and the less speech thou hast of men, the more is thy joy before GOD. Ah! how great it is to be worthy of love, and to be not loved. And what wretchedness it is, to have the name and the habit of holiness, and be not so; but to cover pride, ire or envy under the clothes of Christ's childhood. A foul thing it is to have liking and delight in the words of men who can no more deem what we are in our soul than they wot what we think. For ofttimes they say that he or she is in the higher degree that is in the lower; and whom they say is in the lower, is in the higher. Therefore I hold it to be but madness to be gladder or sorrier whether they say good or ill. If we be trying to hide us from speech and praise of this world, GOD will shew to us His praise, and our joy. For that is His joy when we are strength-full to stand against the privy and open temptation of the devil, and to seek nothing but the honour and praise of Him, and that we might entirely praise Him. And that ought to be our desire, our prayer and our intent, night and day, that the fire of His love kindle our hearts, and the sweetness of His grace be our comfort and our solace in weal and woe. Thou hast now heard a part how the fiend deceives, with his subtle craft, unknowing men and women. And if thou wilt do by good counsel and follow holy teaching, as I hope that thou wilt, thou shall destroy his traps, and burn in love's fire all the bands that he would bind thee with; and all his malice shall turn thee to joy, and him to more sorrow. GOD suffers him to tempt good men for their profit, that they may be the higher crowned, when they, through His help, have overcome so cruel an enemy, that oftentimes, both in body and soul, confounds many men.

In three manners, the devil has power to be in a man. In one manner, hurting the good they have by nature, as in dumb men, and in others, staining their thoughts. In another manner, snatching away the good that they have of grace: and so he is in sinful men whom he has deceived through delight of the world and of their flesh, and leads them with him to hell. In the third manner, he torments a man's body, as we read that he has done (to) Job. But wit thee well, if he beguile thee not within, thou needst not dread what he may do to thee without, for he may do no more than GOD gives him leave to do.

CHAPTER II

BECAUSE thou hast forsaken the solace and the joy of this world, and taken thee to solitary life, for GOD'S sake to suffer tribulation and anguish here, and afterwards to come to that bliss which never more ceases, I trow truly that the comfort of JESUS Christ, and the sweetness of His love, with the fire of the Holy Ghost, that purges all sin, shall be in thee, and with thee, leading thee and teaching thee how thou shalt think, how thou shalt pray, what thou shalt work, so that in a few years thou shalt have more delight to be by thy lone, and to speak to thy Love and thy Spouse JESUS Christ, Who is high in heaven, than if thou wert lady here of a thousand worlds. Men suppose that we are in torture and in penance great; but we have more joy and more very delight in a day than they have in the world all their life. They see our body: but they see not our heart where our solace is. If they saw that, many of them would forsake all that they have, for to follow us. Therefore, be comforted and stalwart, and dread no annoy or anguish: but fasten all thine intent in JESUS, that thy life be good and convenient; and look that there be nothing in thee that should be displeasing to Him that thou dost not soon amend it. The state which thou art in, which is solitude, is most able of all other to revelation of the Holy Ghost. For when S. John was in the Isle of Patmos, then GOD shewed him His secrets. The goodness of GOD it is that He comforts them wonderfully that have no comfort of the world, if they give their heart entirely to Him, and covet not nor seek but Him: then He gives Himself to them in sweetness and delight, in burning of love, and in joy and melody and dwells aye with them, in their soul, so that the comfort of Him departs never from them. And if they any time begin to err, through ignorance or frailty; soon He shews them the right way; and all that they have need of, He teaches them. No man to such revelation and grace on the first day may come; but through long travel and carefulness to love JESUS Christ, as thou shall here-afterward. Nevertheless, then he suffers them to be tempted in sore manners, both waking and sleeping. For aye the more temptations and the grievouser they stand against and overcome, the more they shall joy in His love when they are passed. Waking, they are sometimes tempted with foul thoughts, vile lusts, wicked delights, with pride, ire, envy, despair, presumption and other many. But their remedy shall be: Prayer: Weeping: Fasting: Waking. These things, if they be done with discretion, they put away sin and filth from the soul, and make it clean to receive the love of JESUS Christ, Who may not be loved, but in cleanness. Also, sometimes the fiend tempts men and women, who are solitary, by their love in a quaint manner and a subtle: he transfigures himself in the likeness of an angel of light, and appears to them, and says he is one of GOD'S angels come to comfort them, and so he deceives fools. But they that are wise and will not quickly trust to all spirits, but ask counsel of knowing men, he can not beguile them. Also, I find written of a recluse, that was a good woman, to whom the ill-angel oft-times appeared in the form of a good angel, and said that he was come to bring her to heaven. Wherefore, she was right glad and joyful. But nevertheless, she told it to her Shrift-father, and he, as a wise man and wary, gave her this counsel. When he comes, he said, bid him that he shew thee our Lady, S. Mary. When he has done so, say Ave Maria. She did so. The fiend said: "Thou hast no need to see her; my presence suffices to thee." And she said by all means she would see her. He saw that it behoved him either to do her will, or she would despise him: so quickly, he brought forth the fairest woman that might be as to her sight, and shewed to her. And she set her on her knees and said, Ave Maria. And so quickly all vanished away, and for shame never after came he to her. This I say not, because I hope he shall have leave to tempt thee in this manner, but because I will that thou beware, if any such temptation befall thee sleeping or waking, that thou trust not over quickly till thou knowest the truth. More privily he transfigures himself into an angel of light—that commonly all men are tempted with—when he hides ill under the likeness of good. And that is in two manners. One is, when he eggs us on to over-great ease and rest of body, and softness to our flesh, for need to sustain our nature. For such thoughts he puts in us: that unless we eat well, and drink well, and sleep well, and lie soft and sit warm, we can not serve GOD, nor last in the labour that we have begun. But he thinks to bring us to over-great pleasure. Another is, when under the likeness of ghostly good, he entices us to sharp and over-great penance, for to destroy ourselves; and says thus: "Thou wot'st well that he who suffers most penance for GOD'S love, he shall have most meed. Therefore eat little, and feeble meat; and drink less, the thinnest drink is good enough to thee. Reck not of sleep: wear the hair-shirt and the habergeon. All thing that is affliction for thy flesh, do it; so that there may be none that can pass thee in penance. He that speaks thee thus, is about to slay thee with over-great abstinence; as he that said the other to slay thee with over-little. Therefore, if we will be rightly disposed, it behoves us to set ourselves in a good mean, and that we may destroy our vices and hold our flesh under, and nevertheless that it should be stalwart in the service of JESUS Christ. Also, our enemy will not suffer us to be in rest when we sleep, but then he is about to beguile us in many manners. Sometimes, with ugly images, for to make us afraid and to make us hateful of our state: sometimes with fair images, fair sights and that seem comfortable; for to make us glad in vain, and make us think we are better than we are. Sometimes, tells us we are holy and good, for to bring us into pride; [sometimes says we are wicked and sinful for to make us fall into despair.] But He Who is Ordainer of all things, suffers not that our sleep be without reward to us, if we dress our life to His Will. And wit thou well, thou sinnest not sleeping, if waking thou beest evermore without excess of meat and drink, and without ill-thoughts. But many a one the devil has deceived through dreams, when he has made them set their heart on them. For he has shewn them some truth, but afterwards beguiled them with one that was false. Therefore says the wise man that many cares follow dreams; and they fell that hoped in them. Wherefore that thou beest not beguiled with them, I will that thou wit that there are six manners of dreams. Two are, that no man, holy or other, may escape: they are, if their stomach be over-empty or over-full; then many vanities, in sore manners, befall them sleeping. The third is of illusions of our enemy. The fourth is, of thought before and of illusions following. And the fifth through the revelation of the Holy Ghost, that is done in many a manner. The sixth is, of thoughts before that are due to Christ or Holy Church, revelation coming after. In thus many manners, the image of dreams touches men when they sleep. But so much the less shall we give faith to any dream, because we can not wit which is truth, which is false; which is of our enemy, which is of the Holy Ghost. For where many dreams are, there are many vanities. And many they may make to err, for they set up unwise men, and so deceive them.

CHAPTER III

I KNOW that thy life is given to the service of GOD. Then is it shame to thee, unless thou beest as good, or better, within thy soul, as thou art seeming in the sight of men. Turn therefore thy thoughts perfectly to GOD, as it seems that thou hast done thy body. For I will not that thou shouldest ween that all are holy that have the habit of holiness, and are not occupied with the world. Nor that all are ill who discourse of earthly business. But they only are holy, what state or degree they be in, the which despise all earthly things, that is to say, love it not; and burn in the love of JESUS Christ; and all their desires are set to the joy of heaven, and hate all sin, and cease not from good works, and feel a sweetness in their heart of the love without end: and nevertheless, they think themselves vilest of all, and hold themselves wretchedest, least and lowest. This is holy men's life; follow it and be holy. And if thou wilt be in the Apostles' reward, think not what thou for-sookest, but what thou despisest. For they who follow JESUS Christ in willing poverty, and in meekness, and in charity, and in patience, forsake as much as they can covet who follow Him not. And consider with how great and how good will thou presentest thy vows before Him: for on that He has set His eyes, and if thou with great desire offerest thy prayers, with great fervour desirest to see Him, and seekest no earthly comfort, but the savour of Heaven, and in contemplation thereof hast thy delight. Wonderfully JESUS works in His lovers, those whom he reaves from the pleasure of flesh and blood through tender love. He makes them to will no earthly thing, and makes them rise to the solace of Him, and to forget vanities and fleshly loves of the world, and to dread no sorrow that may fall: to diminish over-great bodily ease: to suffer for His love, seems to them joy; and to be solitary they have great comfort: so that they be not hindered of that devotion. Now mayst thou see that many are worse than they seem, and many are better than they seem, and namely among those that have the habit of holiness. Therefore force thyself, in all that thou mayest, that thou mayest be no worse than thou seemest. And if thou wilt do as I teach thee in this short form of living, I hope, through the grace of GOD, that if men hold thee to be good, thou shalt be well better.

CHAPTER IV

AT the beginning then, bow thee entirely to thy Lord JESUS Christ. That turning to JESUS is naught else but turning from all the covetousness and the liking and the occupations and business of worldly things and of fleshly lust and of vain love: so that thy thought, that was ever downward, burrowing in the earth, whilst thou wert in the world, now should be aye upward like fire; seeking the highest place in heaven, right to thy Spouse, where He sits in His bliss. To Him thou art turned, when His grace illumines thine heart; and forsakes all vices, and conforms it to virtues and good manners, and to all manner of compliance and debonairness. And that thou mayst last and grow in the goodness that thou hast begun without slowness, and sorriness, and irking of thy life; four things shalt thou have in thy thought, till thou beest in perfect love. For when thou art come thereto, thy joy and desire will aye be burning in Christ. One is: the measure of thy life here, that it is so short that scarcely is it anything. For we live but in a point—that is the least thing that may be. And soothly, our life is less than a point, if we liken it to the life that lasts aye. Another is: uncertainty of our ending. For we wot never when we shall die, nor where we shall die, nor how we shall die, nor whither we shall go when we are dead; and that GOD wills that this be uncertain to us, for He wills that we be aye ready to die. The third is: that we shall answer before the righteous Judge, for all the time that we have been here, how we have lived, what our occupation has been and why, and what good we might have done when we have been idle. Therefore said the prophet: "He has called thee times again," that is every day He has lent us here for to spend in good use, and in penance, and in GOD'S service. If we waste it in earthly love and in vanities, full grievously must we be condemned and punished; for that is one of the greatest sorrows that may be: unless we try manfully in the love of GOD, and do good to all that we may, while our short time lasts. And every time that we think not on GOD we may count it as the thing that we have lost. The fourth is: that we think how great the joy is that they have who last in GOD'S love to their ending. For they shall be brethren and fellows with angels and holy men, loving and thanking, praising and seeing the King of Joy in the beauty and in the shining of His majesty. The which sight shall be reward and food, and all delights that any creature may think, and more than any can tell, to all His lovers, without end. It is much easier to come to that bliss than to describe it. Also think what pain and what sorrow and tormenting they shall have who love not GOD above all things that one sees in this world, but defile their body in the pleasures and lusts of this life, in pride and greed and other sins; they shall burn in the fire of hell with the devil whom they served, as long as GOD is in heaven with His servants, that is evermore.

CHAPTER V

I WILL that thou beest aye climbing to JESUS-ward, and increasing thy love and thy service to Him; not as fools do; they begin in the highest degree and come down to the lowest. I say not that if thou hast begun unreasonable abstinence that thou hold it; but for many who were burning at the beginning and able to (capable of) the love of JESUS Christ, through over-great penance they have hindered themselves, and made themselves so feeble that they cannot love GOD as they should. In the which love that thou mayest wax aye more and more is my coveting and my admonition. I consider thee never of the less merit if thou beest not in so great abstinence; but if thou set all thy thought how thou mayest love thy Spouse JESUS Christ more than thou hast done, then dare I say that thy reward is waxing not waning.

CHAPTER VI

WHEREFORE, that thou may'st be rightly disposed both for thy soul and thy body, thou shalt understand four things. The first thing is: what thing defiles a man. The second thing: what makes him clean. The third: what holds him in cleanness. The fourth: what thing draws him for to ordain his will entirely at GOD'S will. For the first, wit thou that we sin in three things that make us foul: that is with heart and mouth and deed. The sins of the heart are these: Ill-thought: ill delight: assent to sin: desire of ill; wicked will: ill suspicion: unde-votion: if thou lettest thine heart any time be idle, without occupation of the love, of the praising of GOD: ill dread: ill love: error: fleshly affection to thy friends or to other that thou lovest: joy in any man's ill-faring, whether they be enemy or none: contempt of poor or sinful men: to honour rich men for their riches: unsuitable joy in any world's vanity: sorrow of the world: impatience: perplexity, that is doubt what to do and what not, for every man ought to be secure (about) what he shall do and what he shall leave: obstinacy in ill: annoyance (at having) to do good: sorrow that he did no more ill, or that he did not have that pleasure or that will of his flesh which he might have done: unstableness of thought: pain at penance: hypocrisy: love to please men: dread to displease them: shame of good deed: joy of ill deed: singular wit: desire for honour or dignity, or to be holden better than another, or richer, or fairer, or more to be dreaded: vain glory of any good of nature, of happening, or of grace: shame of poor friends: pride of rich or of gentle kin, for all we alike are free before GOD'S face, unless our deeds make any better or worse than another, in spite of good counsel and of good teaching. The sins of the mouth are these: to swear oftentimes: forswearing: slander of Christ or of any of His Saints; to name His name without reverence; gainsaying and strife against truthfulness; murmuring against GOD for any anguish or trouble or tribulation that may befall on earth: to say GOD'S Service undevoutly and without reverence: backbiting; flattering: lying: abusing: cursing: defaming: quarrelling: threatening: sowing of discord: treason: false-witness: ill counsel: scorn: unbuxomness in speech: to turn good deeds to ill: to make them be holden ill who do them: (we ought to wrap up our neighbours' deeds in the best not the worst); exciting any man to ire: reprehending in another what one does one's self: vain speech: much speech: foul speech: to speak idle words: or to speak words not needful: praising: polishing of words: defending sin: shouting with laughter: making grimaces at any man: to sing secular songs and to love them: to praise ill-deeds: to sing more for the glory of men than of GOD. The sins of deed are these: gluttony: lechery: drunkenness: simony: witch-craft: breaking of the holy-days: sacrilege: to receive GOD'S Body in deadly sin: breaking of vows: apostasy: dissipation in GOD'S service: to set example of ill deeds: to hurt any man in his body, or in his goods, or in his fame: theft: rapine: usury: deceit: selling of righteousness: to hearken ill: to give to harlots: to withhold necessaries from the body, or to give it to excess: to begin a thing that is above our might: custom to sin: falling often into sin: feigning of more good than we have: for to seem holier, more learned and wiser than we are: to hold office that we do not suffice to: or to hold one that cannot be held without sin: to lead dances: to bring up new fashions: to be rebellious against one's Sovereign: to insult those who are less: to sin in sight, in hearing, in smelling, in touching,

in handling, in swallowing: in means: in signs: in beggings: writings. To receive the circumstances, that is to say time, place, manner, number, person,
dwelling, knowledge, age, that makes thee sin more or less. To desire a sin or
to be tempted: to constrain one to sin. Other many sins there are of omission,
that is, of leaving good undone: when men leave the good they should do. Not
thinking about GOD, nor dreading, nor praising Him, nor thanking Him for
His gifts: to do not all that one does for love of GOD: to sorrow not for one's
sins as one should do: not to dispose one's self to receive grace. And if one have
taken grace, not to use it as one ought; not to keep it: to turn not to the inspiration of GOD: to conform not one's will to GOD'S will: to give not attention to one's prayers, but mutter on and never reck save that they be said; to
do negligently what one was bound by vow to do, or by command, or else
enjoined in penance: to draw out at length what should be done soon: having
no joy at one's neighbour's profit as at one's own; not sorrowing at his ill-
faring: standing not against temptations: forgiving not those who have done
one harm: keeping not faith with one's neighbour as one would that he did to
one's self: and yielding not a good deed for another if one can. Amending not
those sins before one's eyes: not appeasing strifes: not teaching them that are
unlearned: not comforting them that are in sorrow, or in sickness, or in poverty, or in penance, or in prison. These sins, and many others make men foul.
The things that cleanse us of that filth, are three, against these three manners
of sins. The first is: sorrow of heart against the sin of thought: and that it
behoves (thee to) be so perfect that thou beest in full will never to sin more.
And that thou mayest have sorrow for all thy sins. And that all joy and solace,
except of GOD and in GOD, be put out of thine heart. The second is: shrift
of mouth; against the sin of mouth. And that shall be hasty, without delaying.
Naked, without excusing. Whole, without parting. Also (not) for to tell one sin
to one priest and another to another. Say all that thou wottest to one, or else
thy shrift is not worth. The Third is, Satisfaction; that has three parts, Fasting,
Prayer, and Alms-Deed. Not only to give poor men meat and drink: but to
forgive them that do thee wrong and pray for them: and inform them who are
at the point to perish what they shall do. For the third thing, thou shalt wit
that cleanness behoves to be kept in heart, in mouth and in work. Cleanness of
heart, three things keep: one is, watchful thought and stable about GOD.
Another is, care to keep thy five wits, so that all the wicked stirrings of them be
closed out of the flesh. The third, honest and profitable occupation. Also,
cleanness of mouth, three things keep: one is that thou should'st bethink thee
before thou speakest. Another is that thou beest not of great but of little
speech; and specially ever till thine heart be established in the love of JESUS

Christ: so that men think thou ever lookest on Him, whether thou speakest or not. But such a grace may'st thou not have on the first day: but with long travel and great care to love Him from habit, so that the eye of thine heart be aye upward, shalt thou come thereto. The third, that thou for nothing, not even for meekness, shalt lie to any man. For every lie is sin and ill: and not GOD'S will. Thou needest not tell all the truth always, unless thou willest. But hate all lies. If thou sayest a thing of thyself that seems to thy praise, but thou sayst it to the praise of GOD and help of another, thou dost not unwisely for thou speakest truth. But if thou will have aught private, tell it to none but such a one that thou beest secure that it should not be shewed (disclosed) but only to the praise of GOD, of whom is all goodness, and who makes some better than others, and gives them special grace, not only for themselves, but also for them that will do well after their example. Cleanness of work, three things keep. One is: a careful thought of death: for the wise man says; "Bethink thee of thy last ending, and thou shalt not sin." The second: flee from ill fellowship, that gives more example to love the world than GOD, earth than heaven, filth of body than cleanness of soul. The third is: temperance and discretion in meat and drink: that it be neither to excess, nor beneath suitable sustenance for thy body. For both come to one end: excess and over-great fasting: for neither is GOD'S, will—and that many will not suppose, for anything one may say. If you take sustenance of such good as GOD sends for the time and the day, whatever it be, I take out no manner of meat that Christian men use; with measure and discretion, thou dost well; for so did Christ and His Apostles. If you leave many meats that men have, not despising the meat that GOD has made for man's help, but because thou thinkest thou hast no need thereof, thou dost well: if thou seest that thou art stalwart to serve GOD, and that it breaks not thy stomach. For if thou hast broken it with over-great abstinence, appetite for meat is reft from thee: and often shalt thou be in tremblings, as if thou wert ready to give up the ghost. And wit thou well, thou didst sin that deed. And thou may'st not wit soon whether thine abstinence be against thee, or with thee. For the time thou art going, I counsel thee that thou should'st eat better and more, as it comes, that thou beest not beguiled. And afterward, when thou hast proved many things, and overcome many temptations, and knowest better thyself and GOD than thou didst, then if thou seest that it be to be done, thou mayst take to greater abstinence. And meanwhile thou mayst do privy penance which all men need not know. Righteousness is not all in fasting or in eating. But thou art righteous, if contempt and praise, poverty and riches, hunger and need or delights and dainties be all alike to thee. If thou takest these with love of GOD, I hold thee blessed and high before JESUS.

Men who come to thee, they love thee because they see thy great abstinence, and because they see thee enclosed: but I may not love thee so lightly for anything I see thee do without, but if thy will be conformed entirely to GOD'S will. And set not by their praise and blame, and never give thou heed if they speak less good of thee than they did; but that thou shouldest be more burning in GOD'S love than thou wert. For one thing I warn thee: I hope that GOD has no perfect servant in earth without enemies of some men—For only wretchedness has no enemy. For to draw us that we conform our will to GOD'S will: are three things. One is, example of holy men and women, who were intent, night and day, to serve GOD, and dread Him and love Him. If we follow them on earth, we must be with them in heaven. Another is the goodness of our Lord, which despises none, but gladly receives all that come to His mercy: and He is homelier to them than brother or sister, or any friend that they most love, or most trust in. The third is the wonderful joy of the kingdom of heaven, which is more than tongue may tell, or heart may think, or eye may see, or ear may hear. It is so great that, as in hell nothing might live for great pain but that the might of GOD suffers them not to die; so the joy in the sight of JESUS in His GOD-head is so great that they must die of joy, if it were not for His goodness, who wills that His lovers should be living aye in bliss: also His righteousness wills that all who loved Him not, be aye living in fire, which is horrible to any man that thinks: look then what it is to feel. But they who will not think of it and dread it now, they shall suffer it evermore. Now hast thou heard how thou mayst dispose thy life, and rule it to GOD'S will. But I wot well that thou desirest to hear some special point of the love of JESUS Christ, and of contemplative life, which thou hast taken to thee in all men's sight. (According) As I have grace and knowledge, I will teach thee.

CHAPTER VII

A MORE LANGUEO. These two words are written in the Book of Love, that is called the Song of Love, or the Song of Songs. For he that loves greatly, lists often to sing of his love, for joy that he or she has when they think on that they love, specially if their love be true and loving. And this is the English of these two words: "I languish for love." Separate men on earth have separate gifts and graces of GOD, but the special gift of those who lead the solitary life, is for to love JESUS Christ. Thou sayest to me, 'All men love Him who keep

His commandments.' That is Truth. But all men who keep His bidding keep not also His Counsel. And all that do His Counsel are not all fulfilled by the sweetness of His love, nor feel the fire of burning love of heart. Therefore, the diversity of love makes the diversity of holiness and of need. In heaven, the angels who are most burning in love, are nearest to GOD. Also, men and women that have most of GOD'S love, whether they do penance or none; they shall be in the highest degree in heaven: they who love Him less, in the lower order. If thou lovest Him much, great joy and sweetness and burning thou feelest in His love, that is thy comfort and strength night and day. If thy love be not burning in Him: little is thy delight. For Him may no man feel in joy and sweetness, unless they be clean and filled with His love; and thereto shalt thou come with great travail in prayer and thanking, having such meditations as are all on the love and the praising of GOD. And when thou art at thy meal, ever love GOD in thy thought, at each moment, and say thus in thine heart: Loved be Thou, King: and thanked be Thou, King, and blessed be Thou, King, JESU all my joying, of all Thy good gifts: Who for me spilt Thy blood, and died on the rood. Do Thou give me grace to sing the song of Thy praise. And think it not only whiles thou eatest, but both before and after, and ever when thou prayest or speakest. Or if thou hast other thoughts, that thou hast more sweetness in and devotion than in those that I teach thee, thou may'st think them. For I hope that GOD will put such thoughts in thine heart, as He is pleased with, and as thou art ordained for. When thou prayest, look not how much thou sayest, but how well: that the love of thine heart be aye upward, and thy thought on what thou sayst as much as thou canst. If thou beest in prayers and meditations all the day, I wot well that thou must wax greatly in the love of JESUS Christ, and feel much of delight, and within short time.

CHAPTER VIII

THREE degrees of love I shall tell thee, for I would that thou mightest win to the highest. The first degree is called Insuperable. The second Inseparable. The third is, Singular. Thy love is Insuperable, when nothing that is contrary to GOD'S love overcomes it: but it is stalwart against all temptations; and stable, whether thou beest in ease or in anguish, or in health or in sickness: so that men think that thou wouldest not, even to have all the world without end, make GOD angry at any time: and thou wert liefer, if so it should be, to suffer all the pain and woe that might come to any creature, before thou wouldst do the thing that should displease Him. In this manner shall thy love be Insuperable that nothing can bring it down, but it may aye spring on high. Blessed is he or she who is in this degree: but yet are they blesseder who might hold to this degree and turn to the other, that is to Inseparable. Inseparable is thy love, when all thine heart, and thy thought, and thy might is so wholly, so entirely and so perfectly fastened, set and established in JESUS Christ, that thy thought comes never from Him, never departs from Him, sleeping excepted: and as soon as thou awakest, thine heart is on Him, saying Ave Maria, or Gloria Tibi, Domine, or Pater Noster, or Miserere mei, DEUS, if thou hast been tempted in thy sleep; or thinking on His love and His praise as thou didst waking. When thou canst at no time forget Him, waking or sleeping, whatso thou dost or sayst, then is thy love Inseparable. Full great grace have they that be in this degree of love. And methinks that thou, who hast nothing else to do but for to love GOD, mayst come thereunto if any may get it.

The third degree is highest and most wondrous to win. That is called Singular, for it has no peer. Singular love is when all comfort and solace is closed out of thine heart, but of JESUS Christ alone. Other joy it delights not in. For the sweetness of Him in this degree is so comforting, and lasting in His love, so burning and gladdening, that he or she who is in this degree can as well feel the fire of love burning in their soul, as thou canst feel thy finger burn if thou puttest it in the fire. But that fire, if it be hot, is so delectable and so wonderful, that I cannot tell it. Then, thy soul is loving JESUS, thinking of JESUS, desiring JESUS; in covetousness of Him breathing; to Him singing: of Him burning; in Him resting. Then the song of praise and of love has come. Then, thy thought turns into song and into melody. Then it behoves thee to sing the psalms which before thou said'st. Then must thou be long over a few psalms. Then, thou wilt think death sweeter than honey, for then thou art full of sighs to see Him whom thou lovest. [Then mayst thou boldly say "I languish for love."] Then mayst thou say "I sleep, and my heart wakes."

In the first degree, men may say "I languish for love," or "I long in love." And in the second degree also: for languishing is when men fail for sickness, and they who are in these two degrees fail from all the covetousness of this world, and from lust and liking of sinful life, and set their will and their heart to the love of GOD—therefore they may say "I languish for love," and much more that are in the second degree than in the first. But the soul that is in the third degree is all burning fire, and like the nightingale that loves song and melody, and fails for great love: so that the soul is only comforted in praising and loving GOD; and till Death come, is singing ghostly to JESUS, and in

JESUS, and JESUS; not crying bodily with the mouth—of that manner of singing I speak not, for both good and evil have that song. And this manner of song have none unless they be in this third degree of love: to the which degree it is impossible to come, but in a great multitude of love. Therefore, if thou wilt wot what kind of joy that song has, I tell thee, that no man wots, save he or she who feels it, who has it, and who loves GOD singing therewith. One thing tell I thee, it is of heaven, and GOD gives it to whom He will, but not without great grace coming before. Who has it, he thinks all the song and all the minstrelsy of earth naught but sorrow and woe (compared) thereto. In sovereign rest shall they be who get it. Wanderers and brawlers, and keepers of comers and goers early and late night and day, or any who are seized with any sin witfully and willingly, or who have delight in any earthly thing, they are also farther therefrom than heaven is from earth. In the first degree, are many: in the second degree are full few; but in the third degree are scarcely any: for aye the greater is the perfection the fewer followers it has. In the first degree, men are likened to the stars, in the second to the moon, in the third to the sun. Therefore says S. Paul: "Others of the sun, others of the moon, others of the stars," so it is of the lovers of GOD. In this third degree, if thou mayst win thereto, thou shalt know of more joy than I have told thee yet. And among other affections and songs, thou mayst, in thy longing, sing this in thine heart to thy Lord JESUS, when thou dost covet His coming and thy going: "When wilt Thou come to comfort me: and bring me out of care, and give me Thee, Whom I may see, having evermore? My heart when shall it burst? for love then languished I no more. For love my thought has fast, and I am fain to fare away. I stand still mourning for the loveliest of lore; … is love-longing; it draws me to my day; The brand of sweet burning for it holds me aye: From place and from playing: till I may get sight of my sweet One, Who never wends away. In wealth be our waking, without hurt or night. My love is everlasting, and longs unto that sight."

CHAPTER IX

IF thou wilt be well with GOD, and have grace to rule thy life, and come to the joy of love: this name JESUS, fasten it so fast in thy heart that it come never out of thy thought. And when thou speakest to Him, and through custom sayst, JESUS, it shall be in thine ear, joy; in thy mouth, honey; and in thine heart, melody: for men shall think joy to hear that name be named, sweetness to speak it, mirth and song to think it. If thou thinkest (on) JESUS continually, and holdest it firmly, it purges thy sin, and kindles thine heart; it clarifies thy soul, it removes anger and does away slowness. It wounds in love and fulfils charity. It chases the devil, and puts out dread. It opens heaven, and makes a contemplative man. Have JESUS in mind, for that puts all vices and phantoms out from the lover. And often hail Mary, both day and night. Much love and joy shalt thou feel, if thou wilt do after this teaching. Thou need'st not covet greatly many books: hold love in thine heart and work, and thou hast all that we can say or write: for fulness of the law is charity: on that hangs everything.

CHAPTER X

BUT now, thou mayst ask me and say, "Thou speakest so much of love; tell me—What is love, and where is love. And how I shall love GOD verily. And how that I may know that I love Him. And in what state I may most love Him." These are hard questions to teach, to a feeble man and fleshly as I am. But nevertheless therefore, I shall not delay that I shall not shew my wit, and as I think it may be. For I hope in the help of JESUS, who is the well of love and peace and sweetness. Thy first asking is: What is love? And I answer: Love is a burning yearning after GOD, with a wonderful delight and certainty. GOD is light and burning. Light clarifies our reason; burning kindles our will, that we desire naught but Him. Love is a life, joining together the loving and the loved. For meekness makes us sweet to GOD. Purity joins us to GOD. Love makes us one with GOD. Love is the beauty of all virtues. Love is the thing through which GOD loves us, and we Him, and each one of us loves others. Love is the desire of the heart, aye thinking on that it loves; and when it has that it loves, then it joys and nothing can make it sorry. (Love is yearning between two, with lastingness of thoughts.) Love is a stirring of the soul for to love GOD for Himself, and all other things for GOD; the which love, when it is ordained in GOD, it does away all inordinate love in anything that is not good. But all deadly sin is inordinate love for a thing that is naught: then love puts out all deadly sin. Love is a virtue which is the rightest affection of man's soul. Truth may be without love: but it cannot help without it. Love is a perfection of learning, virtue of prophecy, fruit of truth, help of sacraments, establishing of wit and knowledge; riches of pure men; life of dying men. So, how good love is. If we suffer to be slain; if we give all that we have, (down) to a beggar's staff; if we know as much as men may know on earth, all this is naught but ordained sorrow and torment. If thou wilt ask how good is he or she, ask how much he or she loves; and that no man can tell. For I hold it folly to judge a man's heart; that none knows save GOD. Love is a righteous turning from all earthly things, and is joined to GOD, without departing, and kindled with the fire of the Holy Ghost: far from defiling, far from corruption, bound to no vice of this life. High above all fleshly lusts, aye ready and greedy for the contemplation of GOD. In all things not overcome. The sum of all good affections. Health of good manners; goal of the commandments of GOD; death of sins; life of virtues. Virtue whilst fighting lasts, crown of overcomers. Mirth to holy thoughts. Without that, no man may please GOD; with that, no man sins. For if we love GOD in all our heart, there is nothing in us through which we serve sin. Very love cleanses the soul, and delivers it from the pain of hell, and from the foul service of sin, and from the ugly fellowship of the devils; and (out) of the fiend's son, makes GOD'S son, and partner of the heritage of heaven. We shall force ourselves to clothe us in love, as iron or coal does in the fire, as the air does in the sun, as the wool does in the dye. The coal so clothes itself in fire that it is fire. The air so clothes itself in the sun that it is light. And the wool so substantially takes the dye that it is like it. In this manner shall a true lover of JESUS Christ do: his heart shall so burn in love, that it shall be turned into the fire of love, and be as it were all fire; and he shall so shine in virtues that no part of him shall be murky in vices.

The second asking is: Where is love? And the answer: love is in thine heart, and in the will of man; not in his hand, nor in his mouth: that is to say, not in his work, but in his soul, "For many speak good and do good, and love not GOD: as hypocrites, who suffer great penance, and seem holy in man's sight. But because they seek praise and honour of men, and favour, they have lost their meed: and in the sight of GOD, they are devil's sons, and ravishing wolves. But if a man give alms-deed, and take him to poverty and do penance, it is a sign that he loves GOD: but therefore loves he Him not, save when he forsakes the world only for GOD'S love, and sets all his thought on GOD, and loves all men as himself: and all the good deeds that he may do, he does them with intent to please JESUS Christ, and to come to the rest of heaven. Then he loves GOD: and that love is in his soul, and so his deeds shew without. If thou speakest good and doest good, men suppose that thou lovest good: therefore look well that thy thought be in GOD, or else thou deceivest thyself, and deceivest men. Nothing that I do without (outside) proves that I love GOD.

For a wicked man might do as much penance in body, as much waking and fasting as I do. How may I then ween that I love, or hold myself better, on account of that which any man may do? Certainly, my heart, whether it loves my GOD or not, wots no one but GOD, for nought that they may see me do. Wherefore, love is in will verily, not in work, but in a sign of love. For he that says he loves GOD, and will not do what is in him to shew love, tell him that he lies. Love will not be idle, it is working some good evermore. If it cease working, wit thou that it cools and goes away.

The third asking is: How shall I verily love GOD? I answer; Very love is to love Him with all thy might, stalwartly: in all thine heart, wisely: in all thy soul, devoutly and sweetly. Stalwartly can no man love Him save he be stalwart. He is stalwart, who is meek; for all ghostly strength comes of meekness;—on whom rests the Holy Ghost? in a meek soul. Meekness governs us and keeps us in all our temptations, so that they overcome us not. But the devil deceives many that are meek, through tribulations, and reproofs, and back-bitings. But if thou beest wroth for any anguish of this world, or for any word that men say of thee, or for aught that men say to thee, thou art not meek, nor mayst thou love GOD stalwartly. For love is stalwart as death, which slays every living thing on earth, and hard as hell that spares not them that are dead. And he who loves GOD perfectly grieves Him not, whatever shame or anguish he may suffer; but he has delight and covets that he might be worthy for to suffer torment and pain for Christ's love: and he has joy that men reprove him and speak ill of him. Like a dead man, what so men do or say, he answers not. Right-so, whoso loves GOD perfectly, they are not stirred for any word that man may say. For he or she cannot love, that cannot suffer pain or anger for their friend's love. For whoso loves, they have no pain. Proud men or women love not stalwartly, for they are so weak, and they fall at every stirring of the wind that is temptation. They seek a higher place than Christ; for they will have their will done, whether it be with right or with wrong: and Christ wills that nothing but well be done, and without harm to other men. But who is verily meek, they will not have their will in this world, but that they may have it in the other fully. In nothing may men sooner overcome the devil than in Meekness, which he much hates. For he may wake, and fast and suffer pain more than any other creature may: but meekness and love may he not have. Also, it behoves thee to love GOD wisely, and that thou canst not do save thou beest wise. Thou art wise, when thou art poor without desire of this world, and despisest thyself for love of Christ: and expendest all thy wit and all thy might in His service. For some who seem wise are most fools, for all their wisdom they spill in covetousness and care about the world. If thou sawest a man have precious stones wherewith he might buy a kingdom, if he gave them for an apple, as a child will do, rightly mightest thou say that he was not wise but a great fool. Just so, if we will, we have precious stones: Poverty and penance and ghostly travail, with the which we may buy the kingdom of heaven. For, if thou lovest poverty and despisest riches and delights of this world, and holdest thyself vile and poor, and thinkest thou hast naught of thyself save sin: for this poverty, thou shalt have riches without end. And if thou hast sorrow for thy sins, and because thou art so long in exile out of thy country, and forsakest the solace of this life: thou shalt have for this sorrow the joy of heaven. And if thou beest in travail, and punishest thy body reasonably and wisely, by wakings, fastings, and in prayers and meditations, and sufferest heat and cold, hunger and thirst, privation and anguish for the love of JESUS Christ; for this travail thou shalt come to rest that lasts aye, and sit on a settle of joy with angels. But some there are who love not wisely, like children who love an apple, more than a castle. So do many; they give the joy of heaven for a little delight of their flesh, that is not worth a plum. Now canst thou see, that whoso will love wisely, it behoves him to love lasting things, lastingly; and passing things, passingly; so that his heart be settled and fastened on nothing but GOD. And if thou wilt love JESUS verily, thou shalt not only love Him stalwartly and wisely, but also devoutly and sweetly. Sweet love is when thy body is chaste and thy thought clean. Devout love is; when thou offerest thy prayers and thy thoughts to GOD with ghostly joy, and burning heart in the heat of the Holy Ghost; so that men think that thy soul is as it were drunken for delight and solace of the sweetness of JESUS; and thy heart conceivest so much of GOD'S help that men think thou mayst never be departed from Him: and then thou comest into such rest and peace in soul, and quiet, without thoughts of vanity, (or) of vices, as if thou wert in silence and sleep, and set in Noe's ship, so that nothing may hinder thee from devotion and sweet love. For thou hast gotten His love: all thy life, until death come, in joy and comfort: and thou art verily Christ's lover: and he rests in peace whose place is made in peace.

The fourth asking was: how thou mightest know that thou wast in love and charity. I answer: that no man wots on earth that they are in charity; save it be through any privilege or special grace that GOD has given to any man or woman: that all others may not take example by. Holy men and women trow that they have truth and hope and charity: and in that do as well as they may, and hope certainly that they shall be safe; they wot it not so quickly; for if they wish, their merit were the less. And Solomon says it is so with righteous men and wise men, and that their works are in GOD'S hand. And nevertheless, a man wots not whether he be worthy hatred or love; but all is reserved uncertain for another world. Nevertheless, if any had grace that he might win to the third degree of love, which is called Singular, he should know that he was in love. But in such manner were the knowing, that he might never bear himself the higher, nor be in less care to love GOD; but so much the more that he is secure of love, will he be busy to love Him and dread Him, Who has made him so, and done that goodness to Him; and he that is so high, he will not hold himself worthier than the sin-fullest man that goes on earth. Also seven experiments are there, that a man be in charity. The first is; when all covetousness of earthly things is quenched in him. For whereso covetousness is, is no love of Christ. Then, if he have no covetousness, sign is that he has love. The second is, burning yearning for heaven. For when men have felt aught of that savour, the more they love, the more they covet: and he that has not felt, he desires not. Therefore, when anyone is given so much, till he love thereof (so) that he can find no joy in his life: token has he that he is in charity. The third is; if his tongue be changed, that was wont to speak of earth; now speaks of GOD, and of the life that lasts aye. The fourth is: exercise of ghostly profit. As if any man or woman give themselves entirely to GOD'S services, and meddle with no earthly business. The fifth is: when the thing that is hard of itself seems light for to do; the which love makes. For as Austin says: "Love it is which brings the far thing near-to-hand, and the impossible to the openly possible." The sixth is: hardness of thought to suffer all anguish and hurt that comes—without this, all the other suffices not. For whatso befalls him shall not make a righteous man sorry. For he who is righteous, hates naught but sin; he loves naught but GOD, before GOD: he dreads naught but to anger GOD. The seventh is: delectability in soul, when he is in tribulation, and makes praise to GOD in the anger that he suffers. And this shews well that he loves GOD, when no sorrow can bring him down. For many love GOD while they are at ease; and in adversity they grumble, and fall into so great sorriness, that scarcely may any man comfort them: and so slander they GOD, striving and fighting against His judgments. And that is caitiff praise that any wealth of the world makes: but that praise is of great price that no violence of sorrow can do away.

The fifth asking was: In what state men may most love GOD? I answer, in such state as it be that men are in most rest of body and soul, and least occupied with any needs or business of this world. For the thought of the love of JESUS Christ, and of the joy that lasts aye, seeks outward rest, so that it be not hindered by comers and goers, and occupation of worldly things; and it seeks within great silence from the annoyances of desires, and of vanities, and of earthly thoughts. And especially, all who love contemplative life they seek rest in body and soul. For a great Doctor says: "They are GOD'S throne who dwell still in one place, and are not running about, but in sweetness of Christ's love are fixed." And I have loved for to sit: for no penance, nor fantasy, nor that I wished men to talk of me, nor for no such thing: but only because I knew that I loved GOD more, and longer lasted within the comfort of love: than going, or standing, or kneeling. For sitting am I in most rest, and my heart most upward. But therefore, peradventure, it is not best that another should sit, as I did and will do to my death, save he were disposed in his soul, as I was.

CHAPTER XI

SEVEN gifts of the Holy Ghost are in men and women who are ordained to the joy of heaven and lead their life in this world righteously. These they are: Wisdom: Understanding: Counsel: Strength: Knowledge: Pity and the Fear of GOD. Begin we at Counsel, for thereof is most need at the beginning of our works, which we dislike not afterwards. With these seven gifts, the Holy Ghost touches separate men separately. Counsel is doing away with the world's riches, delights, and all things with which men may be ensnared in thought or deed: and therewith (i.e. Counsel) be drawn inwardly to contemplation of GOD. Understanding is, to know what is for to do, and what to leave (undone): and that which shall be given, to give it to them that have need, not to others that have no need. Wisdom is forgetting of earthly things, and thinking of heaven, with discretion in all men's deeds. In this gift, shines contemplation, that is, as S. Austen says "A ghostly death of fleshly affection through the joy of a raised thought." Strength is; enduring to fulfil good purpose, that it be not left, neither for weal nor for woe. Pity is: that a man be mild: and gainsay no holy Writ when it smites his sins, whether he understand it or not; but with all his might that he purge the vileness of sin, in himself and in others. Knowledge is that (which) makes a man in good hope, not making him quake for his righteousness, but sorrowing for his sin; and that a man gather earthly good only to the honour of GOD, and to other men's advantage more than to his own. The Fear of God is: that we turn not again to our sin for any egging on: and then is fear perfect in us and holy, when we dread to anger GOD in the least sin that we can know, and flee it as poison.

CHAPTER XII

TWO lives there are that Christian men live. One is called Active life, for it is more in bodily work. Another, contemplative life, for it is in more ghostly sweetness. Active life is greatly outward, and in more travail and in more peril, because of the temptations that are in the world. Contemplative life is largely inward, therefore it is more enduring and more certain, restfuller, more delectable, lovelier and more rewarding. For, it has joy in GOD'S love, and savour in the life that lasts aye, in this present time, if it be rightly led. And that feeling of joy in the love of JESUS passes all other merits in earth. For it is so hard to come to, because of the frailty of our flesh, and the many temptations that we are beset with, which hinder us night and day: all other things that come are light in regard thereof; for that may no man deserve, but only it is given of GOD'S goodness to them who verily give themselves to contemplation and to quiet for Christ's love. To men and women who betake themselves to active life, two things befall. One: to appoint their household in fear and in the love of GOD, and to find them in necessaries, and themselves keep GOD'S commandments entirely. Doing to their neighbours as they will that they do to them. Another is that they do, so far as they can, the seven works of mercy. The which are: to feed the hungry: to give the thirsty a drink; to clothe the naked: to harbour them that have no housing: to visit the sick, to comfort them that are in prison; to bury dead men.

All that can and who have property, they may not be quit with one or two of these; but it behoves them to do them all, if they will on Dooms-Day have the benison that JESUS shall give to all who do them. Or else they may dread the malison that all men have who will not do them, when they had goods to do them with.

Contemplative life has two parts: a lower and a higher. The lower part is meditation of holy writing, that is GOD'S word, and in other good thoughts and sweet that men have of the grace of GOD, about the love of JESUS Christ, and also in praising GOD in psalms and hymns and in prayers. The higher part of contemplation is beholding and yearning after the things of heaven, and joy in the Holy Ghost: that men have oft, although it be so that they be not praying with the mouth, but only thinking of GOD, and of the beauty of angels, and of holy souls. Then may I say that contemplation is a wonderful joy of GOD'S love; the which joy is praising GOD, that cannot be told; and that wonderful praising is in the soul: and for abundance of joy and sweetness, it ascends into the mouth; so that the heart and the tongue agree in one, and body and soul joy, living in GOD. A man or woman that is appointed to contemplative life, first GOD inspires them to forsake this world, and all the vanity and covetousness and vile lust thereof. Afterwards He leads them by their lone and speaks to their heart, and as the prophet says "He gives them to suck of the sweetness of the beginning of love": and then He sets them in the will to give themselves wholly to prayers and meditations and tears. Afterwards, when they have suffered many temptations, and when the foul annoyances of thoughts that are idle, and of vanities which will encumber those who cannot destroy them, are passing away, He makes them gather up their heart to them and fasten it only in Him, and opens to the eye of their souls the gates of heaven: and then the fire of love verily lies in their heart, and burns therein, and makes it clean from all earthly filth, and afterwards they are contemplative men, and ravished in love. For contemplation is a sight; and they see into Heaven with their ghostly eye. But thou shalt wit that no man has perfect sight of heaven, whilst they are living bodily here. But as soon as they die, they are brought before GOD, and see Him face to face, and eye to eye, and dwell with Him without end. For Him they sought, and Him they coveted, and Him they loved, with all their might.

Lo, Margaret, I have told thee shortly the Form of Living, and how thou mayst come to perfection, and to love Him whom thou hast taken thee to. If it do thee good and profit to thee, thank GOD, and pray for me. The grace of JESUS Christ be with thee, and keep thee. Amen.

OUR DAILY WORK

(A Mirror of Discipline)

THREE things are needful to every man; to increase his reward, through GOD'S grace helping, Who shall lead him. The first; that man be in honest work, without losing of his time. The second; that he do his work with a freedom of spirit, in place and in time, as work falls to each. The third; that his outward bearing, wheresoever he come, be so honest and fair, that praise is (given) to GOD, a stirring up of good to all who see him, as the Apostle bids: Omnia in vobis honesti et secundum ordinem fiant, that is "That ye do: be it done honestly and in order."

FIRST PART OF THE BOOK

AT the first: man shall look that he lose not his short time, nor spend it wrongly, nor in idleness let it pass away. GOD has lent man his time, to serve GOD in, and to gather grace with good works, to buy heaven with. Not only this short time flies from us, but also the time of our life, as the wise man says: "Our life-time passes away." And S. Gregory says:—"Our life is like a man in a ship; sit he, stand he, sleep he, wake he, ever he gets thitherward where the ship is driving with the force of the weather. So we, in this short time, whatsoever we do, we drive ever to our end." And our enemy, Death, follows us ever at our back, with a sharp spear to stick us through, therefore says Seneca, "life flies, death follows." And S. Augustine says "Life is nothing else but a swift running to death." Therefore, there is naught to tell by, how long man lives: save how well. Yet this short life is uncertain: wherefore says Job:—"I know not how long I may endure, and whether after a short space my Maker may take me away." And S. Gregory says: "I wot not the time I shall dwell, nor when I shall be taken hence and led to doom." And S. Jerome says:—"Nothing so much beguiles man, as that he knows not the time of his life, that to him is uncertain." And yet hopes he for long life for himself, as if he might, at his will, drive Death back. Thus was the rich man deceived of whom speaks the Gospel of S. Luke 16. Therefore saith the psalm: "if riches increase, set not your heart upon them." For riches fail and last not with man, but glide away like a phantom. But when men have got goods together, with right, or with wrong and poor men's curses, then suddenly, they go from their goods, or else their goods from them. And Holy Writ says "The world passeth away and the lust thereof." A man that is fallen in the water, and through the force of the water is borne forth and torn from the ground; if he may get anything that has good fastening like a root or a stake, he may hinder the water from carrying him away; but by anything that fleets as he does himself, he cannot fasten himself: and soothly, willy nilly, in this life, as if in water, we are ever passing with the goods of this world; and there is naught in this world to fasten by, so that we shall not pass: for the Wise Man saith, "We shall all die, and like water slip away into the Earth." And therefore Job speaks, as if he said "Riches and friends had I many, but they all could not hinder me from going forth and not coming again." And by what path, man shall go, the prophet shews: "All flesh is grass, and all the glory of it as the flower of the field." Man's flesh is as hay, and all his joy and splendour as the flower of the meadow. Hay is first green grass, and soon after brings forth flowers: and a while after, the flowers dry and fall; after it is mown down with the scythe, and dried and taken to a house to be beasts' food. Thus it befalls man: in his childhood he springs and grows as the grass does; after, he comes to manhood and flowers in fairness and strength and wit and having of goods; afterwards: he draws to age, and then his flowers fall, that are his virtue, fairness, strength, wit and other power; afterwards, he is stricken down with the scythe of Death, afterwards taken to a house to beasts' food, that is, dug into the earth to feed worms. Therefore says the holy man; "when a man dies, he shall dwell with serpents and beasts." A dead man is so disgusting to the world, that one cannot let him be in his house three days together; but bears him forth, that he harm none with the odour. Therefore, it is now time to work; for in the time to come there is no time to work, but to receive rewards for deeds done erewhile. And this the angel affirms with oath and says, "For the angel has sworn that there will be no further time." Do we then as the Apostle says: "While we have time, let us work good to all." And as the Apostle counsels us, he did himself: for from the first hour of the day until the fifth, he worked with his hands to win his food: and from the fifth to the tenth, he preached to the people: from the tenth to even he served the poor and pilgrims with such goods as he had; by night he was praying, and thus spent he his time.

In three ways, man loses his time: in idleness; or in works that no good comes of; or in good works, but not ordained as they should be. Against idleness, Solomon says—"Idleness teaches much evil"; and Holy Writ says "Whoso followeth idleness, is most foolish." A great fool he is who forbears not from the thing that harms him. More fool he is, because he wins himself no reward: most fool he is, because he wins himself pain. Therefore GOD blames the idle: and says "Why standest thou all the day idle?" Idleness wastes the goods that are prudently gotten, and entices the fiend to the house: for as by good works the fiend is hindered from entering man's heart, so idleness draws him thereto. And Seneca says: "he lives not to himself who lives for his stomach and the ease of his flesh whenever he can." For Job says "Man is born to labour." To work was man bound after he had sinned, through GOD'S bidding, Who said to him: "In the sweat of thy face shalt thou eat thy bread, till thou returnest unto the ground from whence thou wast taken; because from the ground thou art, and into the ground thou shalt go." Thou shalt work stalwartly and not faintly, for He bids thee work, "with sweat of thy face, even till thou returnest to the earth"; that is, all thy life time that thou losest no time in idleness. Idleness smites a man as if he were in a paralysis, and makes his limbs dry that he cannot work. Therefore says the Psalmist: "They have hands and handle not; feet have they but they walk not; mouths have they but they speak not; eyes have they and see not; ears have they and hear not"; for their limbs are so bound in sin, that to all good things, they are as dead; and to evil, they are easy. Idleness is nurse to all vices, and makes a man reckless about not doing what he is bound to do. And when the fiend finds a man idle, he puts in his heart foul thoughts of fleshly filth, and other follies that may bring him to sin; afterwards, he eggs him on to do them indeed, and thus he does against the Apostle's bidding: "Will not to give place to the devil." The idle man makes himself unworthy to dwell in any place but hell. In heaven he cannot dwell; for heaven is full reward to those who here spend their time in works that they hope are pleasing to Christ. In purgatory the idle may not dwell; for there only the good are purged in that cleansing fire, till they be as clean of sin as when they were christened: therefore saith the Psalm-wright:—In labore hominum non sunt et cum hominibus non flagellabuntur: that is thus for to say; "The idle work not with men; therefore in purgatory they shall not be pained with those men who are on the way to heaven."

Great shame it is to be idle in this time of grace, in the which we are hired to work; and if we work as we ought, great reward awaits us. GOD gives us an example of work, by Himself, as the Apostle says: "He emptied Himself, and took upon Him the form of a servant, and was made in the likeness of men; and being found in fashion as a man, he humbled Himself, and became obedient unto death, even the death of the cross: wherefore GOD hath also highly exalted Him, and given Him a name which is above every name, that at the name of JESUS, every knee should bow, of things in heaven, and things in earth, and things under the earth; and that every tongue should confess that JESUS Christ is Lord, to the glory of GOD the Father."

Over-proud then, and over-delicate is the servant, who rests in battle, and sees His Lord assailed and evil-wounded by His enemies. Also, we ought to work in this time of grace; for we are GOD'S bought thralls, with the price of His dear-worthy Blood, to work in His vine-yard: and yet He doth promise us reward, if we do with good-will that which, as a debt, we ought to do. To His private friends, before the time of grace, GOD promised only earthly goods, if they did well; to us the bliss of Heaven, if we do well. It was long after, before they might come thereto; for they went to hell and abode there, some a thousand years, some two, some three, before they came to heaven. But now may men in a little time win heaven, as, if any die soon after he is christened, or if he have done full penance for his misdeeds; or be martyred for GOD'S love. The time of supper that the gospel of S. Luke speaks of, to the which GOD bade His servants call all that were bidden, is the time of grace; which is now, in the which all is ready; so that there is naught else to do but wash and go to meat, that is cleanse them of all their sins that they have done since they were born. What losing of time it is to travail about things that no profit comes of. Man ought to travail only to the worship of GOD, and his soul-health. Thou shalt not deem the man has lived long though he go with a staff stooping, and be grey-haired; but deem him so old as he has lived well. Therefore answered Barlaham to Josaphath, his disciple, when he asked him how old he was: "I am," quoth he, "of 45 years." "Master," quoth Josaphath, "methinks thou art of 60 years and more." Then said Barlaham, "Since I was born has been 60 years; but those years that I spent in idleness and sin before I took me to this life, I hold as years of death. But all those I call years of life that I have served JESUS Christ my Lord in, through His dear-worthy grace." Whoso would bethink himself what time steals from him in long eating and drinking, in excess and useless works, idle speech, and idle and foul thoughts, useless jests and other vanities that men delight them in, he may soothly understand that though he be old in years, that he has lived little time in the manner that he ought to have lived; for he lived not to his profit, nor won him reward, but peradventure pain for losing time.

It were a wonderful thing if the man who gives himself to business of the world more than he need, had no hindrance in prayer, in rest of heart, in soothfastness of words, in perfection of good works, in love to GOD and all Christian men. Therefore, holy men, before now, who knew their hindrances, they fled the world with all its vanities, as if it had been accursed; for it seemed to them that they could not live a righteous life therein; and therefore went they into the wilderness, where they trowed to serve GOD in peace. Therefore says Seneca, "I have become more avaricious, and more cruel, and more inhuman because I was among men."

Three manners of occupations there are: as, various and much brawling; raking about; and much caring about earthly things. Against much brawling, Solomon says "The beginning of strife is as when one letteth out water." "Let the water out," that is, "let the tongue fleet out in quarrelling." But to the knowledge of GOD or of himself may no one come, who lets his heart fleet out with much useless speech: for he makes a way in himself for the fiend. Therefore Solomon likens such to a city without a wall: "He that hath no rule over his own spirit is like a city that is broken down and without walls." And because so much hindrance of good is in much speech, the philosopher binds his disciples with silence (during) their first five years. Also, Abbot Agathon bore a stone in his mouth for three years to teach him to hold still. Against those who are ever raking about to feed their wits with vanities and lusts is the teaching of the angel, who taught holy Abbot Arsenius and said:—"Arsenius, flee the world and its yearnings: keep thee in rest, bridle thy tongue," that it fleet not out in quarrelling nor idle speech. Where these three are is a way to GOD, and withdrawing from evil. It tells of an Abbot who (for) fully 20 years sat in his school, and never lifted up his head to see the school-roof. Against those who care over-much about worldly goods, Solomon says this:—"Vain is their hope, and their labour without fruit, because they can carry away nothing of all their labour." This is seen every day, by the dead, who, be they never so rich bear with them but a winding cloth.

The third manner of men are they that have a liking to do good, but because they do it not in the manner they should do it in, they lose their reward; for when good intent fails in any deed, the reward that should fall to the good work fails. And that may be in four ways; first, for the wickedness of the working; as the offering of Cain, that though he offered to GOD of the fruit that was new, GOD would not look thereon: but to the offering of Abel his brother, GOD looked. Therefore says S. Gregory:—"By the heart's will of him that offers is the gift received of GOD or rejected: and GOD was not pleased with Abel for the offering, but pleased with the offering for Abel, who in all his works was true and good; but to Cain and to his offering GOD would not look, for he who made the offering displeased GOD greatly." And why our offering, or what we do that is in its nature good, displeases GOD, the prophet says:—"When ye make many prayers, I will not hear: because your hands are full of blood." The second that reaves away a man's reward for his good deed, is vanity, which stirs man to do the good because he would be praised. For vain-glory makes evil of good: as if alms-deed that is good in nature be done for praising, it wins only sin. The third that snatches a reward from a good deed is boasting by him that does the good deed, as the Pharisee did, of whom GOD said to the folk that stood before Him, "Soothly, this man has lost his reward for all his good deed." Needful it is therefore that a man do what good he can, and do not pride himself thereof in thought or in word; for he has not the doing of a good deed of himself, nor of his own desiring. The fourth that snatches from a man his reward for a good deed (is) when he does it with the intent to be holden better than others, or to lessen the good deed of others, or to outdo it if he can. Of such, S. Gregory tells a tale in his dialogues: That once on a time the holy Bishop Fortunatus, chased the fiend out of a man in one evening; and the fiend, when he was chased out, put on the likeness of a pilgrim, and went through the city where the Bishop lived, weeping and yelling like a poor wretch, who was anxious for lodging that night, and thus he said; "Lo, what your Bishop, whom ye consider so good, has done to me: he came to the house where I had taken my lodging, and put me out by force: and now like a poor wretch, of lodging am I desirous; over all, I seek lodging, and none will have ruth on me." A man of that city who heard him, took him into his house, and set him by the fire and eased him, as he wished. When the man had inquired of him of far-off things, as men do to pilgrims, the fiend leaped at the child in the cradle, and wrung its neck in two, and cast it into the fire, and vanished away. Of this S. Gregory speaks and says, "Many deeds seem good, and are not good, because they are not done with a good will. And this man harboured the pilgrim for no pity of him, but because he spake evil of the Bishop, and in order that he" (the man) "should be held better and of more pity than the Bishop." Yet a good deed is lost, if a man covet by it to have of man, riches, or position, or honours or any worldly good. Yet through sin defiling, the good deed is lost; and here-unto accords Holy Writ that says, "who sinneth in one thing, loses many good things," which is, "he that in a deadly thing sins, he loses many goods," save he amend him with shrift, and do penance therefor.

SECOND PART OF THE BOOK

THE second part of this book teaches man to do his good work with freedom of spirit, in place and in time, as falls to each work: not compelled thereto, nor to do it with anger, nor with a dead heart. For Holy Writ says: "GOD loves a cheerful giver," or GOD loves him who gives Him aught with a glad heart: and certainly the works that turn out to the praise of God, and the health of man's soul, like prayers and holy thoughts, and a clear mind about GOD, and GOD'S deeds; these and others like them will allow of little rest, if they be well (done). Prayer is a sacrifice that greatly pleases GOD, if it be made in the manner it ought to be: therefore GOD asks it of us as a debt, when He says this:—"GOD created the peoples for His praise and His glory"; and "the Sacrifice of praise shall honour Me." And the Apostle, "we ought always to pray and not to faint." Therefore, it behoves man ever to pray and never to fail. He is ever praying, who is doing good. And certainly men of religion are bound to worship GOD with prayer, and men of Holy Church; for they live by alms and tenths: for all the world labours to bring them what they need close at hand, so that they may serve GOD in rest, and with their holy prayers make reconciliation between GOD and man. And also maidens and widows who have taken the oath of chastity, all these, more than others, are bound to pray. He that will please GOD with prayer will offer it to GOD with a free will and loving heart, and will prepare himself before, as Solomon counsels: "Before prayer, prepare thy soul, and be not as one that tempteth GOD." He tempts GOD who yearns not to win that for which he prays: or despairs to speed well therein; and who makes sin and evil life: such a man thinks not he loves. Of such S. Gregory speaks:—"What wonder if tardily our prayers are heard by the Lord, when we tardily or not at all hear the Lord when He commands?" And Isidore:—"He cannot have assured confidence in his prayers who even thus far in the commands of GOD is slothful, and whom the remembrance of sinful doing delights." Whoever will speed of his prayer, let him do what good he can; flee sin, call his heart from the world, and keep it at home as the Gospel teaches; "When thou prayest, enter into thy closet, and shut thy door, and pray to thy Father." "Enter," he says, "thy bed," that is, "call thine heart home," and "then fasten thy door"; i.e., "hold thy wits in thee, that none go out." For it is but folly to pray to GOD to come to us, poor needy wretches, to give us alms of His dear-worthy grace, and not abide His coming, but turn our back on Him. S. Isidore says that the soul must be cleansed from the stain of sin, and the heart be withdrawn from the provocations of the world, in order that prayer may rise without hindrance to GOD. For far is that man from GOD, pray he never so much, whose prayers are mixed with worldly thoughts: therefore says the Psalm "Be still, and see that I am GOD." This ought to stir us up to pray with great dread and consideration for we speak with Almighty-GOD, when we are naught but unworthy wretches. For so did Abraham, GOD'S private friend, who said:—"I speak to my Lord which am but dust and ashes." And Isidore says:—"we ought to pray with sighings and tears, and remembrance of our grimly sins, and of the many pains and bitter we shall endure for them, unless we amend us, and He have pity on us." Also, he who prays shall hope to speed well in that for which he prays; for Christ Himself said, "All things are possible to the believing": therefore we shall pray to GOD as to our Father in that for which we pray, if we love Him as our Father, and be His children. For He says to all His.... He says "Whatsoever ye shall ask the Father in My Name, He shall give it to you." There are six things to know in prayer: first, how a man shall prepare himself before. The second, to whom he shall pray: the third, for whom he shall pray: the fourth, what he shall ask in prayer: the fifth, what hinders prayer: the sixth, what might and virtue prayer is of. The first is written already, and begins at, "Before prayer, prepare thy soul," and lasts as far as here. The second, to whom shalt thou pray? Soothly, before all others, to GOD Almighty, as the prophet bids, "Be subject to GOD and pray to Him." And in the Gospel, GOD says, "Thou shalt adore the Lord thy GOD." Saints we honour and pray to, not as givers of goodness, but as GOD'S friends to help us to win from Him that we pray after. Therefore, let us believe in GOD with all our heart, and certain hope, and perfect charity: our Lord GOD is to be loved. The third, for whom shall men pray? A great clerk says, "Every Christian man is a living member of Holy Church, therefore is he bound to pray for all, but specially for men of Holy Church, as the Pope, Cardinals, Bishops, all who have cure of men's souls: also for our foes and our friends; and all who are in deadly sin, that they, through grace, may rise: for all who are in Purgatory, whom GOD'S mercy awaits; and after, all who have occupations, both quick and dead. And S. Gregory says that he who prays for all, the sooner shall be heard and sped of his prayer: and S. Ambrose; "If thou prayest for all, all will pray for thee." And S. Jerome; "Necessity binds a man to pray for himself, but charity of brotherhood stirs him to pray for all: and charity, more than necessity, stirs GOD to hear." The fourth, what shall men ask in prayer? Certainly, grace in this life, and endless joy in the other; for so GOD teaches us and says: "Seek first the kingdom of GOD and His justice, and all these things shall be added unto you." GOD is debtor to those who are righteous, to find them what they need of earthly goods: for righteousness makes men GOD'S children, and a father by his nature is bound to find for his children. Earthly goods are not to be asked in prayer, for they have done harm to many, therefore Solomon says "How long, ye fools, will ye desire those things which are hurtful to you?" Therefore, every man should ask of GOD with fear, that he ask and pray his Lord that if He see that his prayer be necessary and reasonable, that He will fulfil it: and if it be not necessary and reasonable, that He will withdraw it; for what may help and what may harm, the Leech knows better than the sick man. But one of these two shall we trust to have through prayer; either, that we pray for, or that which is better for us. The fifth, what hinders our prayer from being heard by God? Six things: the first is the sin of him who prays; as GOD says through the prophet, "when ye make many prayers, I will not hear; because your hands are full of blood." And David: "If I have looked upon iniquity with my heart, the Lord will not hear." And the prophet; "Our sins have hid His face from us." And the Gospel: "Because we know GOD does not hear Sinners." The second is the unworthiness of that for which men pray, and that GOD, through the prophet, forbids them to pray for: "Pray not for this people, neither lift up (praise) nor prayer for them; for I will not hear." It tells in the life of the holy Fathers that one who was bound in sin came to the holy Abbot, S. Anthony, and said, "holy Father, have mercy on me and pray for me:" to whom the holy Abbot said; "I will have no mercy on thee, unless thou helpest thyself and leavest thy sin." The third is foul and idle thoughts, that hinder us from thinking on our prayers. Of such false prayers, Gods says through His prophet. "This people honour ME with their lips, but their heart is far from ME." It is great wickedness of us unworthy wretches that when we speak with prayer to Almighty GOD, we also unwittingly hearken not to what we say. Soothly, great displeasure we do to GOD when we pray Him to hear our prayer, and we will not hear it ourselves: but it is worse to waste our time in foul and idle thoughts. Abraham, when he made a sacrifice to GOD, fowls of the air lighted thereon, and would have defiled it; and he cleared those birds away, so that none durst come nigh it, till all the time were passed, and the sacrifice made. Let us do so with these flying thoughts, which defile the sacrifice of our prayer. This sacrifice is agreeable to GOD, when it comes from a clean and loving heart. GOD bids: "send prayer to ME, and I shall send grace to thee; and whatso thou dost for ME, I forget it not." The fourth, that hinders our prayer from being heard, is hardness of heart; and that is in two manners; first hardness of heart against the poor; and thereof the prophet says "who shuts his ear to the cry of the poor, he may call and I will not hear him." The other is the hardness of those who will not forgive to those who have misdone them: to such, Solomon says:—"Forgive thy neighbour who has injured thee while he prays to thee, and thy sins shall be forgiven." And the Gospel says: "As thou standest praying, forgive if thou hast aught against any, and your Father which is in heaven will forgive your sins." The fifth, that hinders our prayer from being heard, is little yearning after the things that men pray for: and S. Augustine says: "GOD stores this up for thee, that with thy whole heart it may be desired; "for He will not to give to Thee hastily, that so thou mayst learn great things greatly to desire." And S. Gregory says: "if with our mouth we pray after the bliss of heaven, and do not yearn for it in our heart, we are crying still." The sixth, that hinders our prayer; is foul and idle speech, that we fill our lips with; for if thou givest a great lord drink in a slutty cup, were the drink never so good, he would feel disgust therewith, and bid throw it away, were his thirst never so sore: so GOD does with a prayer that comes from a foul mouth; He esteems it not, but turns therefrom. Therefore says S. Gregory: "The more our lips are defiled with foolish talking, so much the less are they heard by GOD in prayer." The sixth, what might and virtue prayer is of. Men who were before this age, who kept themselves in soothfastness, and spoke nothing idle, won from GOD what they prayed for: and that was shewn to a holy hermit Florentius, who dwelt in a wilderness unknown of men. So much vermin was there about this hermitage, that none durst come thither by a long way. A deacon was in that land, who heard of this hermit, and he came at the last to the place where this hermit was dwelling; but he saw so much vermin about that he durst not come near: but cried out for help in fear. The holy man came out to know who it was that cried; and he saw a man standing there, and inquired what he would have. And the deacon said; "holy Father, I have sought thee from far, and now I have found thee, I should have joy enough if I might come to thee, but I cannot for these venomous beasts that are here so many." When the holy man heard this, he fell down on his knees, and prayed GOD that He would destroy those worms: and all soon a grisly storm arose with a thunder, and slew all the worms. Then said the hermit to our Lord; "Lord, these beasts lie here so thickly, that I cannot come to him nor he to me, save we be poisoned by them. Lo, Lord, they lie here dead, but who shall lift them away?" At his word, many birds came, and carried them all clean away. Hereof speaks S. Gregory:—"Because GOD'S servants withdraw themselves from the world and its works, uselessly they cannot speak: so they bind them to silence that they dare say no word save it be teaching others or praising GOD: and therefore, when they ask GOD aught, He grants it at once." But we, woful wretches, who deal with the world, that chatter all the day like magpies; now lie, now twist, now speak evil, now quarrel, now backbite, now swear great oaths, these defile our prayer and hinder it, that it is not heard; for our mouth is as far from praying GOD, as it is near the world with idle speech." Prayer is so mightful if it have its right, that it masters the fiend, and hinders him from doing his will. For so it did the fiend whom Julian the Emperor commanded to go to the other side of the world to bring him tidings how it was there. When he had flown ten days' journey thitherward, he came over the place that Publius the hermit dwelled in, who was praying at that time. And his prayer overtook the fiend, and held him there fast fully ten days—for all that time, the hermit was in prayer: and when he ceased, the fiend turned back, for he could no further go, since prayer hindered him.

When thou hast gathered home thine heart and its wits, and hast destroyed the things that might hinder thee from praying, and won to that devotion which GOD sends to thee through His dear-worthy grace, quickly rise from thy bed at the bell-ringing: and if no bell be there, let the cock be thy bell: if there be neither cock nor bell, let GOD'S love wake thee, for that most pleases GOD. And zeal, rooted in love, wakens before both cock and bell, and has washed her face with sweet love-tears; and her soul within has joy in GOD with devotion, and liking, and bidding Him good-morning, and with other heavenly gladness which GOD sends to His lovers. Blessed are they above others whom GOD wakens, for they have many joys while others sleep, for they find that gladness before them, rise they never so soon; for GOD Himself thus says: "he that early wakens to ME, he shall find ME to speak with him, and shall rejoice himself in ME, and have ME at his will." Be then a waker, and rise quickly, and thank heartily thy Lord GOD, for the rest thou hast had, and for the care of angels. Since a knight has great liking to be called to come and speak with the king, when he knows it is for his great profit: with greater reason, ought GOD'S knight, that is every Christian man, to be ready at the calling of his Lord, Who calls him for his great profit, and for nothing else. Soberly, rise thou with a good cheer, and think that thou hearest GOD call thee with these words: "Arise My love, My fair one, and come and shew Me thy face: I yearn that the voice of thy prayer may ring in Mine ears." Think in thy rising, how that night many men perished in life, and some in soul, and some in body and soul: some burned, some drowned, some suddenly dead without repentance or shrift, and their souls drawn by fiends to hell; some fallen into deadly sin, as lust, gluttony, theft, envy, manslaughter, and other several sins. And from all these perils, thy good GOD hath delivered thee, of His goodness not of thy desert. What hast thou done to GOD that He should care for thee so, and suffer so many others to be lost? and peradventure thou hast done worse than they have done. If thou lookest well at what GOD has done for thee though thou hast not served Him, thou mayst find that GOD is as busy to do thee profit as if He had naught else to do, and as if He had forgotten this whole world, and thought only on thee. When thou hast this thought, lift up thine heart to GOD and say:—"I thank Thee, dear-worthy Lord, with all my heart, Who hast thus cared this night for me, a so unworthy wretch, and hast suffered me that with life and health I thus abide this day. I thank Thee, Lord, for this great good, and many others that Thou hast done to me, a so unkind and unworthy wretch, more than all others: that Thou shewest me such kindness against my evil deeds." And put thyself and all thy friends in GOD'S hands, and say thus: "Into Thy dear-worthy hands, my Lord, I yield my soul and body, and all my friends, kindred and stranger: and all who have done me good bodily or ghostly, and all who have received Christianity: that Thou, for the love of Thy Mother, that dear-worthy Maiden, and the beseeching of Thy Saints defend us this day or this night from all perils of body and soul, and from all deadly sins, from temptation of the devil, and sudden death, and from the pains of hell, and make us dread them. Do Thou hallow our hearts with grace of Thy Holy Ghost, and make us, whatsoever we do here, do Thy will, that we never separate from Thee, dear Lord. Amen." When thou hast done, go to the Church or Oratory: and if thou canst win to none, make thy chamber thy Church. In the church is most devotion to pray, for then is GOD on the altar to hear those that to Him pray, and grant them what they ask or what is better: and in presence of Saints, and in worship of churches that are hallowed, protection of angels who are there to serve their Lord and thee—for their office is to receive thy prayer, and bear it to GOD, and bring thee grace from Him, as S. Bernard says: "Rise then quickly, at GOD'S call, and put all heaviness from thee, and answer thy Lord with the words which Samuel said to GOD Who called him in the night: 'Speak Lord, for Thy servant heareth.' "

For eight things we ought to wake and ever be doing good: this short life: the strait way we have to go: our good deeds that are so few: our sins that are so many: death that we are sure of and wot not when: the strait and so hard doom of Doom's-day, for every idle thought shall be shewed there, then shall every foul word and sinful work be greatly pressed, for GOD says "For every careless word," etc.: and S. Anselm, "what wilt thou do in that day when all the time expended is required of thee; how it has been laid out by thee, even to the minutest thought." The seventh thing is the strong pain of hell: the eighth, is the joy of heaven. After thine uprising, pray for the souls that are in pain of Purgatory, and think that thou hearest them cry on thee the words of Job: "Have mercy on me, have mercy on me, my friends, for the hand of GOD is laid upon me," and help them with De Profundis, and Absolve. After, greet our Lady, with Salve Regina, on thy knees. Go then to the Church, and bid thy vain thoughts and business of the world keep outside thereof: and at thine incoming, say to thy soul, "Enter thou into the joy of thy Lord, and thou shalt hear His Voice, and behold His temple." Holy Church is the entrance and gate of Heaven. After, fall down before the Cross, and honour Him because He was slain on the Cross, and say "We adore Thee, O Christ, and bless Thee, because by Thy holy Cross Thou didst redeem the world." And then before thou uprisest, have in thy mind how hotly His love burned, That died for thee on the Cross. After, begin thy matins, but first cross thy lips and say "O Lord, open my lips": i.e., "Lord, open my lips that all night have been shut from praising Thee, and I cannot open them, except Thou help me." And then say, DEUS in adjutorium, with these words, pour out thine heart before GOD and say; "Lord, as my Doom's-Man, before Thee I stand: do Thou avenge me of my foes, which hinder me from serving Thee, and they assail me keenly so that I be soon overcome unless Thou dost help me." And at Gloria Patri, bow down and say with thine heart, "Lord, of Thy blessing, I beseech Thee." Turn thee to the angels who stand about to thy comfort and help, and as thy wardens to keep thee from thy foes, and thus say to them Venite exultemus, Domino. Afterwards, cast thine eye on somewhat, and keep it there while thou makest thy prayers, for this helps much to the stabling of thine heart; and paint there, thy Lord, as He was on the cross; think on His feet and hands that were nailed to the tree; and on the wide wound in His side, through the which way is made to thee, to win His heart; thank thy Lord thereof, and love Him therefor: for these, they who thither may win, find treasure of love. Think thou seest His wounds streaming of blood, and falling down on the earth; and fall thou down and lick up that blood sweetly, with tears kissing the earth, with remembrance for that rich treasure, which for thy sins was shed, and say thus with thine heart:—"Why lieth this blood here as if lost, and I perish for thirst? Why drink I not of this rich payment that my Lord gives me to drink and cool my tongue, and hear what GOD says to me: He who is thirsty, let him come and drink. Thou shalt taste and see how pleasant the Lord is; how sweet, how mild, how merciful. With such meditations, angels come to thy soul, and GOD is there, and says to His lover:—"What wouldest thou that I should do for thee?" and thou dost answer; "Lord it is enough for me, a sinful wretch and outcast of Thy people, to praise Thee and love Thee, if I could, for so I well ought." If thou canst win to such thinkings in thy prayers, thou shalt have such joys that it shall be a pain to thee to think of aught else. S. Bernard, for the liking that he had for such stirrings desired that matins-time might last till Dooms-day. Think, when thou standest or kneelest in prayer, that thou seest JESUS Christ come with angels and holy Saints on each side, and angels carrying before Him basketsfull of help which is left from the feasts of Saints who dwell with GOD in heaven: that GOD bade them gather up to help the poor with, that naught might be lost. This help is meat to us poor wretches, who would perish in default of it, unless GOD had pity on us. Think thou hearest GOD cry: "Whoso has need of meat, put forth thine hand, and have." And bow thou with thine head to GOD, and lament thy poverty to Him and say "There is no bread in mine house"; and also say, "Lord, so long meatless have I been, that I die of hunger save Thou takest pity on me; and naught can hold my life in me, save meat that Thou givest." Stir thyself up with such recollections, and by others that may kindle thy devotion and raise it to Him, even until thou thinkest thou hearest Him say to thee, "Open thy mouth wide, and I will fill it." And then, through GOD'S grace, shalt thou feel something of that heavenly food that feeds all Hallows, that thou mayest with liking sing the Maiden's Song, that is GOD'S Mother's, Magnificat anima mea dominum et exultavit spiritus mens in DEO salutari meo. When GOD, through His grace, sends thee such likings, turn thou kindly to the angels who stand before thee, and to them say: "I pray you as my keepers whom GOD has sent to me, that ye thank your good Lord for me." And turn thou then to the altar, where GOD truly is, and say, "Truly, O GOD, great is Thy mercy towards me," that is, "Soothly Lord, great is Thy mercy that Thou shewest to me." With such love-stirrings, GOD comes to His lovers: and waits not till the prayer be made, but presses in to the midst, and softens the languishing soul, with a bedewing of heavenly sweetness: and tears and sighings are messengers of GOD'S coming. Blessed are they who thus mourn and languish to GOD, for they shall never separate from GOD, but have Him ever at their will.

How GOD comes to His lovers; and how sometimes He departs from them. GOD, when He comes to His lovers gives them to taste how sweet He is; and before they can fully feel, He goes from them, and, as an Eagle, spreads His wings, and rises above them, as if He said: "Some part mayst thou feel how sweet I am: but if ye will feel this sweetness to the full, fly up after Me, and lift your hearts up to Me, where I am sitting on My Father's right hand, and there ye shall be fulfilled in joy of Me." GOD comes to His lovers to comfort them; he departs from them so that they should humble themselves, and that they should not over-much pride themselves for the joy that they have of His coming: for if thy spouse were aye with thee, thou wouldest esteem thyself over well and despise others: and if He were aye with thee thou wouldest impute it to nature and not to Grace. Therefore, through His grace, He comes when He will, and to whom He will, and departs when He will: so that His long dwelling makes one not more unworthy; but that after His departing, He be more yearned for and sought with zealous love and sighings and tears. But beware thou, GOD'S lover, though thy Spouse withdraw Himself from thee for a while, He sees all thy deeds, and thou canst hide nothing from Him: and if He wit thou lovest any but Him, unless it be for love of Him, or if thou makest any love-semblance to other than Him, so soon He departs from thee. Jealous is thy Spouse, delicate, noble and rich; seven times brighter than the sun; in fairness and might all others He surpasses, and what so He wills is done in heaven and earth and hell. If He sees any stain of filth in one who should be His dear, He turns from him soon, for uncleanness can He see none. Therefore, be thou chaste, shame-full, and mild of heart, and with love-longing yearn for Him above all things. And when GOD withdraws this heavenly likeness and sweetness from thee, as sometimes need be in this deadly life, give not thyself to fleshly lusts and likings of the world; but to prayer and meditation, reading of Holy Writ, or honest work. And ever mourn thou after thy love, as a young child who misses his Mother. For he that, after such knowing of GOD and tasting of His sweetness, turns him back and gives him to sin, he has no defence for his sin against GOD. An unhappy chance it is and full of care to love the fellowship of GOD and of His angels and Saints and to serve the fiend and follow his counsel with lusts and likings and works of sin: that heart which was hallowed through the Holy Ghost to be GOD'S temple, that was raised here above his nature to have heavenly likings and joy with GOD, all soon makes itself loathly and foul with foul thoughts: those ears that heard the words that it is allowable to speak to none, open themselves to hear back-bitings and lyings and other idle speech; those eyes that just now were baptized with tears, open themselves to see vanities: that tongue that just now spake to GOD in prayer, all soon with that dirty tongue, forswears, backbites, and speaks foul words. Pray we to GOD that of His goodness He keep us from these vices. Of GOD'S coming men may know by this that S. Bernard says: "When thou art stirred of man in outer or inner spirit to care for righteousness and stand up for it, to be meek and patient, to love thy brothers in GOD, to be buxom to thy superiors, to love chastity and cleanness in body and soul, token is it that Almighty GOD comes to visit thy soul." If thou takest godly chastening from thy friend for thy sin, or words that stir thee to virtues and good ways, this makes way for and token of GOD'S coming. Then if thou puttest from thee slowness and heaviness, and with a love-yearning likest such words; then dear-worthy GOD thy Lord hastes Him to thee, for the desire that GOD has to thee; kindles thy desires to have likings for such words, and makes thee bitterly repent thy sin and amend thy life. For, at His incoming, He wakens the soul, stirs it and softens it, and washes its wounds with wine, and softens them with oil; that is, stirs it to repent bitterly what it has misdone, and softens it with hope of mercy and forgiveness of sins. He rives sin up by the roots, as a gardener does evil weeds, and grafts good trees, and sows good seed, where the weeds grew. So does GOD, who is called a gardener while He is in man's soul: He rives up sins by the roots, and grafts in that soul virtues and good ways: what was dry He bedews it with grace: what was black and mirk, He makes it white: what was bound, He looses: what was cold, He makes warm with love. By these stirrings, mayst thou know thy Lord is come; by stirring of thy heart, destroying of vices, withdrawing from lusts, amending of life, repenting misdeeds, beginning of a new man in GOD, every day more and more. And by this mayst thou wit, when He goes from thee; the gladness wanes, slow thou waxest dry and heavy, as a stone; love cools in thee like a pot that had been welded, and the fire was withdrawn therefrom. But then needs the soul to mourn sorely until He come again. If foul thoughts egg thee on to leave the Lord thy GOD, say this "Whose is this image and superscription?" if he says "Caesar's," that is the prince of this world, that is the fiend of hell, say to him, "Go again thou foul fiend with thy false money: bear it again with thee to hell; for my gates are shut, and my Lord dwells herein, therefore have I no time to deal with thee." Think on that holy greeting that Gabriel made to that maiden, Mary in Nazareth, how joyful she was in body and soul in that time; through that quieting, with her assent, she was fulfilled of grace, so that she won might and power, in heaven, and earth, and hell; and on her hangs all the world's health and restoring of those that fell. Think on the birth of her Child, how she bare Him without sorrow and grief that all other women have naturally in time of birth; and she clean maiden after. Think when He was born, they laid Him in a crib before an ox and an ass, other cradle had He none. There was none to serve Him with the light of torches as men do before great lords: therefore there came a fire from heaven that lighted the house He was in, and Bethlehem; and angels came from heaven to sing the child asleep with a merry voice. Think how Three Kings came from far lands through knowing of a star, and offered Him gold, incense and myrrh: think how sweetly the child smiled on them, and with His lovely eyes sweetly looked on them. Think how poorly His Mother was clad when the Kings kneeled before her: for on her she had but a white smock as the clerks say, more to cover herself with than for shewing of pride. Think how His Mother came with Him to the Temple to make her offering of cleansing, and bowed to fulfil the Law as if they were sinful. Think how the old priest Symeon took the Child in his arms, and blessed GOD: for there, through the stirring of the Holy Ghost, he saw the Saviour of all this world between His hands, and prayed that he might pass out of this world, "for mine eyes have seen Him Who saves the folk." Think of that sorrow His Mother had when she missed Him and sought Him three days, and then found Him among the Masters, hearing and inquiring of points of the Law. Think how He came to be christened of S. John: how the Holy Ghost lighted then on Him in the likeness of a Dove, the Father there with voice recorded that He was His Son. Think how He hallowed wedlock in the house of the Ruler of the Feast, and there, to show that He was Almighty GOD changed water into wine. In the wilderness, how he fasted 40 days without meat; how He overcame the fiend that tempted Him with three: with gluttony, and covetousness, and vainglory, and of the wonder men had of His preaching, for all the words He spake to them were full of grace. How He healed the sick, raised the dead, gave sight to the blind, speech to the dumb, health to the leper, with touching of His hands: and many other sicknesses that were in their nature incurable, He healed through the might of His words, for

He could do more than Nature. How He was weary of much going; rested Him at the well; and then He bade give Him water to drink for He thirsted sore. Then, open thine heart with sore sighings, and think on the passion and pains that JESUS Christ suffered, as they are written before on the xviii leaf.

He may ask grace of GOD, and certainly trust to speed, who here stirs himself up with good works, and with devotion and likings: flavours them so that they may be savoury to his dear Lord. Works of penance, as fasting, waking, hard fighting, forbearing of fleshly lusts, prayers, almsdeed, and other things that we do with devotion and likings in GOD, it behoves that so they be done with a glad heart, and with a freedom of spirit. Devotion is a worthy affection that GOD sends to the heart to gladden it with: but unworthy is he to have this gift, that will make no dwelling-place in his heart for it. We seek with our belief what is above us, but it savours us not, for we are so full of earth that we have lost our taste. Why do so many men feel the stirrings that the fiend forges, and suffer his enemy so often to overthrow him? I see nothing that does this, save lack of grace. Among all other (things) I trow we grieve GOD most, because we will not labour to win this grace of GOD: and GOD promises His grace to all that will to receive, if that their vessel be clean and empty to receive it in. But S. Bernard says: "The heart that is loaded with covetousness of the world, it can have neither devotion nor liking in GOD; for soothfastness and vanity, a lasting and a failing thing, a ghostly thing and a bodily cannot be brought together at any time." So worthy a thing is the comfort of GOD that it will not rest in a breast where other comfort is. So delicious is the liking in Him, that with no other liking can it accord. Whoso yearns after other comfort to glad himself with, witnesses against himself that he withstands GOD'S grace: unless it be honest comfort betimes that he may thereby glad his nature with, and better serve GOD. After thou hast spent thy time in prayers, and holy thoughts and good works, in GOD'S holy dread, prepare thyself for food to strengthen thy nature which would else fail. And to this intent shall every Christian man clothe and feed his body; that it may the better serve his Lord, in whatsoever he does. In the morning, thou shalt go to thy meat, with soberness and measure; care for thy self in thy meat-time; and after meat, make thou praising to thy Lord that He has fed thee, and also before meat, and for all the good deeds that He has done to thee. First, or ever thou goest to meat, thou shalt mourn as holy Job did, who thus says, "Before I eat I sigh," because my nature is made weak and feeble for Adam's sin; and every day needs bodily meat to uphold the nature that else would fail in a little time. And, as it tells in the life of the holy Fathers; Isidore that holy man, when he ate, he wept sore and said, "I am ashamed of myself for I live by beastly meat as other beasts do that have no reason by nature; and I, GOD'S reasonable creature, made like to Himself, that should have dwelt in Paradise, and there have been fed with heavenly food." When thou findest delight or savour in meat and drink, think on the heavenly Saints whom all likings pass by, and we be never satisfied till we feel thereof. Men of religion hear lessons of holy men's lives at their meat, so that as the body is fed with bodily food, so the soul be fed with holy words. Man's body is as a burning furnace, and specially in the young; and delicious and hot meats and drinks make that fire to burn hotter: therefore says S. John:—"Plenty in time of youth is double fire." Therefore all that kindles sin in the flesh is to be fled from. The wise man says, "If thou wilt abate the flame, abate the brands." And S. John; "Flesh-meat and wine are kindling of fleshly stirrings." And S. Austin; "the flesh is as a wild colt, which is to be tamed with bridle and hunger." And Solomon; "Rod and burden fall to the ass," that betokens our flesh. Wisely should a man consider the meat that comes before him, and take of them in such measure that they grieve him not, but that through them, he may serve GOD better. Therefore S. John bids:—"Ever when thou eatest, ever hunger thou, that after meat thou mayst read and pray and serve GOD better.

Holy men who have been before us enjoyed strong sharp meat, more to abate hunger than for pleasure. Some lived by grass, some by roots, some by spices and herbs and fruit that the earth bore; and in whatso they ate they destroyed all taste that might stir them to pleasure. Also, S. Germanus mixed ashes with his bread, that he should feel no pleasure in his meat-time. Other sauce than hunger, they took none. S. Gregory says: "bread made of bran and water, with cold or other simple pottage is good food to the well-taught stomach, with sauce of GOD'S love if he have it therewith: without this sauce, no sustenance has savour that man enjoys." Some eat no meat before the night; some only every other day; some fast three days together. Machari fasted all the Lenten-tide, save Sundays, and ate naught but raw leaves. Some take no heed when they eat, nor what they eat, flesh or fish: all tasted alike to them, so that afterwards, they wist not what they ate. Some, when they were set down to meat, and meat was brought before them, they forgot to eat, for so they spent the day and the night in holy speech, that they thought of naught else, till the undern-tide of the second day, so that the brethren came to them and asked why they could not eat: and then, for the first time, thought they of meat, and they ate then as they thought good, in GOD'S holy fear. When thou art set to thy meat, make before thee a cross on the board with five crumbs to stir thee up to think on Him who died for thee on the Cross; and think, here lies His head that was crowned with thorns, there His hands, there His feet that were nailed full fast; there was His sweet side that was opened with the spear, from which came both blood and water to heal my dirty wounds. When thou hast so done if thou canst, take part of thy bread and of thy fish, and lay it by itself, and say thus quietly in thine heart, "Lord, what wilt Thou give me for this pittance I make to Thee? how many tears, how many love-yearnings and longings after Thee? how many comforts of the Holy Ghost, how many stir-rings to good things, how many lookings towards me with Thy lovely eyes? Lord, wilt Thou for this meat that the poor hungry man shall have for Thy sake, give me the love of Thee?" When thou hast eaten what thou thinkest good, thank thy Lord that He hath fed thee. After meat, be thou worthy, and keep thee from much speech and idle games, and hold thy wits inward in fear of GOD. Seemly it is to man, and pleasing to GOD, that his bearing be more honourable and temperate after meat than before: that no taking of excess be seen in him, that the flesh may serve the soul better in reading, praying and other ghostly works, that may help to good things. Then Even-song say, with the devotion that GOD sends thee, in Church or Oratory, or wheresoever thou mayst say it best, away from the noise and throng of the world. After, if thou needest, go sup: and short be thy supper time: so in measure take thou meat and drink that it be no burden nor grievance to thy nature, nor hin-drance to serve thy Lord; or in time of rest reave from thee thy sleep; or the fiend defile thee with foul temptations in thy sleep, as he often does him who goes to bed with a full stomach. Every man eat, as S. John says, "according as he is strong or old, or according as his body is greater or less, or whole or sick; take what is needful for sustenance of nature, and not as pleasure asks." After supper, go to the Church or other place, where thou mayst be most at rest, and say thy Compline, for in this time as S. Ambrose saith, "birds in their language praise their Lord, and thank Him after their kind, for the goods He has sent them." Call thou then on thy GOD and say Converte nos DEUS salutaris noster, as if he said, "Lord, I have been this day hindered by the world, that has greatly hindered me from serving Thee; through temptation of the fiend and of my flesh oft this day have I done amiss; therefore, my Lord, turn me now from the world, and from all that may hinder me from praising Thee with a pure heart and with all my wits, so that they be intent on Thee to work Thy will." And then, say forth thy Compline, and after, other prayers with the devotion that GOD sends thee. And after, before thou goest to bed, hold a chapter with thine heart, and ask it in what things it is better than it was. Hast thou shriven thee of that sin that thou didst then and there? of the words that thou spakest there? of that evil will that was in thee then? of that wrong that thou didst and saidst there to him? of that handling? of that blame? of that foul thought? of that thing left undone that thou should'st have done? art thou willing to leave off such vices? What temptations withstood'st thou this day? in what art thou meeker than thou wast? in what more chaste, more sober, more patient, more temperate, more loving thy GOD in thy brother, or more liking in GOD hast thou than thou hadst? Hast left that sin that thou, through habit, fallest into so oft? and other many vices that thou hast done and pleased the fiend with: and grieved thy good GOD, and hast barred thyself against the grace that should help thee. And then, with a repenting of those sins that bite thy conscience, knock on thy breast and say a Pater noster with Ave Maria, on thy knees, and soon in the morning shrive thee of those sins. And if thou doest thus, I hope the fiend shall be afeared to tempt thee, for thou art under GOD'S ward, whilst thou bearest thee thus. After this reckoning, where-through thy soul is raised to a blessed hope to the Father of mercy, and thy flesh waxes heavy, go to thy rest: for if thou hinderest thy flesh of its necessity, and work it beyond its might, faintly will it help thee, or hinder thee withal. And or ever thou goest to rest commit thyself and thy friends into GOD'S hands, who for us was nailed to the tree, and beseech Him, for His mercy, that He guard thee from all perils of body and soul, and arm thee with the token of the cross; for where the fiend sees this mark soon he flies. Of this mark, it is written in the life of S. Edmund: that as he went one time alone, a child appeared to him who was wonderfully fair, and said, "Hail, my friend, whom I love in GOD." S. Edmund was surprised at this greeting, and the child said to him, "knowest thou me not?" And S. Edmund said to the child, "How should I know thee? I never saw thee before." And the child said to him, "When thou didst learn in school, I sat ever by thy side; and ever since I have been with thee, wheresoever thou hast dwelt; for so my Lord has fastened me to thee, that I might never part from thee, such is my Lord's will. But behold on my fore-head, and read what thou seest there." He looked as he told him, and with heavenly letters, these four words, he saw there written, JESUS Nazarenus Rex iudeorum. Then said the child, "This is my Lord's name, thou seest thus written. This name I will that thou have in mind, and print it in thy soul, and cross thy front with this name; before thou goest to sleep; and from harassings of the fiend, it shall protect thee that night, and from sudden death, and all who thus by night cross themselves therewith." And when he had spoken these words, he vanished away. Carry some holy thoughts to bed with thee, and say thy prayers, till sleep fall on thee. To have soft sleep and sweet, a sovereign help is measure and soberness in meat and drink: with recollection of GOD'S law and Holy Writ; as GOD says through the prophet, "Keep My law and My counsel, and if thou sleepest thou shalt not be afraid; if thou dost rest thy sleep shall be sweet." And ever, as thou wakenest, lift thine heart to GOD, with some holy thought, and rise and pray to thy Lord that He grant release from pains to the dead, and grace to the living, and life without end. If temptation of lust stir thee in bed, think that thy good Lord hung on the Rood for thee; think on His five wounds that streamed down of blood: think that His bed was the hard knotty tree, and instead of a pillow He had a crown of thorns. And say then, with sore sighing, till thy desire cool, "My dear-worthy Lord hanged on the Rood for me; and I lie in this soft bed, and welter me in sin, like a foul swine that, loves but filth." Rise then quickly, and hold thee with prayers, love-sighings and tears. Of three points beware. The first, that the devotions thou hast through grace stirring, be not known of others: hide them, so far as thou mayest with will and deed for fear of vain glory. The second, that thou thinkest not it is in thy power to have such devotions and stirrings when thou wilt: but only through GOD'S grace when He will send them. The third, that thou thinkest not over-well of thyself for such stirrings; nor thinkest thou art therefore dear to GOD; nor deem another more unworthy who does not as thou dost; but when thou hast done all well, think soothly by thyself, and grant it in words; "It is nothing worth I do, Lord: for I am but a useless thrall." If thou wilt lose no reward, deem none other, but hold thyself most unworthy; for if thou fastest or prayest more than another, perchance another surpasses thee in meekness, and patience and loving. Therefore think of what thou lackest, and not only of what thou hast. Nevertheless, GOD wills that thou should'st think on those graces and goods He has done for thee, to stir thee up to know thyself indebted to Him for them, and serve Him and love Him the more; or if thou beest in grief to glad thee with. Sometimes, it falls out that in GOD'S doom, one is better whom men deem evil than some that men deem good. Many are worthy without and unclean within. Some worldly and disso-lute, and GOD'S private friends within. And some, in man's sight bear them-selves like angels; and in GOD'S sight, they stink as sinful wretches. And some seem sinful to men's doom, and are full dear to GOD Almighty, for their inward bearing is heavenly in GOD'S bright sight. Therefore, judge we none other save ourselves. And pray we for ourselves and all others to JESUS Christ, Mary's Son, Who for us was nailed on the Rood, that whoso is bound in deadly sin, He loose them; and they who are in good life, that He grant them end therein.

Two messengers are come to thee to bring thee tidings. The one is called Fear, who comes from hell to warn thee of thy danger: the other is called Hope that comes from Heaven to tell thee of bliss thou shalt have if thou doest well. Fear says he saw so many betortured in hell, that if all the wits of men were in one, he could not tell them: of gluttons, unchaste, robbers, thieves, rich men with their servants who harmed the poor: judges who would not give judgment except for reward: treasurers who by subtilty maintained injustice: deemsters who condemned loyal men and delivered stark thieves; workmen who worked dishonestly and took full hire; tillers of the soil who tilled badly; prelates, with the care of men's souls, who neither punished nor taught them; of all sorts of men who have wrongly wrought; then I saw that every one bought it bitterly. For there I saw want of all good, and plenty of pain and sorrow; as hot fire burning ever, brimstone stinking: grisly devils like dragons gaping ever; hunger and thirst for ever lasting, adders and toads gnawing on the sinful. Such sorrow and yelling and gnashing of teeth, I heard there, that nearly, for fear, I lost my wits. Such mirkness there was, that I could grip it; and so bitter was the smoke that it made the woe-ful wretches shed glowing tears; and bitterly I heard them ban the day when they were born. Now, they long to die, and cannot. Death, which, sometime they hated, were liefer to them now than all the good of this world. And therefore I warn thee that thou amend thee of thy sins with shrift and penance, and have a steadfast will to leave them for ever: a seat I saw made for thee in hell of burning fire, where devils should pain thee ever unendingly.

That other messenger, who is called Hope says he is come from Heaven to tell thee of that untellable great joy that rules GOD'S friends; "to tell thereof as it is may no earthly man speak though his tongue were of steel. For there is a gracious fellowship of all GOD'S friends, orders of angels, and of holy saints, and Almighty GOD above, Who gladdens them all. Of all goodness, I saw plenty; beauty and riches that last for ever; honour and power that never shall fail; wisdom and love and everlasting joy. Then I heard melody and song of bright angels. So worthy is that joy and so great withal, that whoso might taste of it a blessed drop, he should be so ravished in liking of GOD, and such yearning he should have to win thither, that all joys of the world were pain to him. With so great a love he should be overtaken in yearning to win to that bliss, that by a hundred times it should more stir him to love virtue and flee sin than any fear he might have of the pain of hell. And I tell thee for sooth, if thou wilt leave sin, and do GOD'S bidding, and love Him as thou oughtest, a rich and a fair seat GOD has made for thee wherein thou shalt dwell with Him unendingly.

THIRD PART OF THE BOOK

THE third and the last part of this book teaches a man to bear himself, wheresoever he comes, and whatsoever he does: that it be to the praise of GOD, and an example of good to all who see him: for thus the Apostle counsels: "Let everything be done honestly and in order"; that is "all that ye do, look ye do it honestly and orderly." Then at the first, let every lover of GOD see that ye yearn not to mingle with the world, that hinders and deceives all who deal with it, and hinders them from the many good deeds they might do. And the man who will nowhere rest but aye rake about; their eyes see many things, that the eye sends to the heart, and such come not out easily when they are once imprinted. S. Bernard complains of the harms that he felt in the world whilst he was therein, and says "the world surrounded me and weighed me down": that is "The world has besieged me on every side; and through the gates of my five wits it shot at me and wounded me full sore; and through the wounds, death presses in, to slay my sorry soul. Mine eyes look, and my thought changes and kindles me in sin. Mine ears hear and my heart bows me thereto. I smell with my nose, and it pleases my thoughts. With my mouth I speak, and in my speech I please or beguile others: and with a little over-soft feeling, lust kindles in my flesh; and the fiend, my foe, whom I cannot see, stands ever against me with his bow bent." Therefore, if necessity make man to go into this world, where are so many stirrings to sin, with great fear shall he go, as into a battle to fight his foes. It needs he be well armed against the arrows of his foe, that severely shoots at him; and the more may he dread him because he cannot see him: with foot-traps and snares is the way set full. Therefore, let him who shall go forth, arm him with GOD'S holy fear. GOD warned His disciples to be wary in the world when He said thus: "Soothly the world shall withstand you with temptations." Therefore, if thou must go out, for thine own profit or that of others, colour not thy going with any false hue, to feign for thyself an occasion to dally with the world, for pleasure or command, or to be known with praise before others....

And therefore they make a show with words and feign as they can, to be holden holy of all who see them, that give themselves to dalliance with the world, more than needs, as to buying, selling or quarrelling about earthly things. And all their outward bearing so accords with the world that David says: "They have mixed themselves with the peoples; they partake of their works": that is, they mingle them with the folk of the world, who have no knowledge of GOD, and such works as they see them do, such works they do. Therefore, when thou needest to go forth, cross thyself with the holy name of JESUS, Mary's Son, who died on the Rood for thee, for then thou art more secure, whithersoever thou goest, as S. Austin said to his brother, when they went forth. And S. John says: "Whitherso thou goest, and whatsoever thou doest, thy forehead and thy breast mark thou with the cross; for there is no other mark the fiend so greatly dreads." See that thine outer-clothing be not over-loathsome, nor over-curious, in shape nor in hue. Keep thy limbs to their business, to which they were made, and do not cast thine eyes about like a child; flourish not thine hands, and leap not with thy feet. When the heart of man is out of ward, the limbs sometimes fail in their office. And, as thou orderest thine outward bearing when thou goest forth, also look thou that thou beest devout within, and specially in praying to and praising the Lord. If in going out, thou canst not rest in saying thy prayers, go the softlier. Many things hinder thee in toiling to pray; weariness of limbs; men thou meetest who speak to thee; then thy five wits fleet out of ward, and then the devotion of him who prays, cools. When walking thou hast said thy prayers that thou art bound to say, lift up thy heart to GOD, and pray to Him in thy thoughts in a blessed recollection: think on the good things GOD has done for thee, and shall do if thou truly servest Him: think on His biddings and do them indeed according to thy might, for so GOD bids thee when He thus says:— "The words which I command thee shall be in thine heart, and thou shalt relate them to thy sons: and thou shall meditate on them, sitting in thine house, and walking on thy journey, sleeping and arising." Or in working, tell fair tales to thy fellows, or something from Holy Writ that may soften your way, or glad you in GOD. And sometimes say the Seven Psalms for the quick and the dead, that GOD give grace to the quick and rest to the dead. When thou comest to the town to ease thy body, seek where thou mayst most worthily dwell for thy condition and in most peace: and where thou mayst most profit to thyself and others. Let flesh-lust and vanity entice thee to no place: but inquire where any is who most loves GOD, and thither draw thou. Seek not where thou mayst be fed best, for there peradventure are many stirrings to sin. Harbour thee with no woman unless thou knowest good of them for a long time. When thou art come to the house thou shalt rest in, hold thy wits inward in GOD'S holy fear; so that thine outer bearing be so ruled with grace that thou mayst stir to good all whom thou seest, and through GOD'S grace destroy mirkness of sin, and so fulfil GOD'S teaching, who says thus, "So let your light shine before men, that they seeing your good works may glorify your Father Who is in heaven." And S. Gregory says: "Neither is it greatly praiseworthy to be good with the good, but to be good with the evil; for even as it is of more heinous guilt not to be good among the good, so is it of unwearied honour to have stood for the good among the evil."

Keep well thine eyes when thou art come to harbour, from all things that may kindle sin and make thine eyes forward, as Job did, who said "I make a covenant with mine eyes lest I should think upon a maid." After sight, comes thought, and thereafter deed, and therefore said the prophet Jeremiah, "Mine eye hath laid waste my soul." When so holy a prophet lamented him of his eyesight, sorely may another complain who oft sins therewith. Augustine: "Shameless eye is the messenger of shameless heart." Gregory: "It is not lawful to look after that which it is not lawful to desire." David: "Turn away mine eyes that they may not see vanity." Look also that thou hearest nothing that may stir thee to sin, as unclean words, backbiting, false judgments, great oaths, controversy, striving and other such vices. Also at thy meat, bear thyself orderly, and hold thee in measure, and seek after no dainties, but be pleased with common meats. Consider in speaking, to whom, what, when, how, of whom, and where: and have thyself so orderly that thou beest not like other worldly men, but fulfil the Apostle's words; "Be not conformed to this world, because your conversation is in heaven."

Though our body be in this world as a clot of earth, it is needful that our spirit which was bought with the dear-worthy blood of GOD Almighty be with mind and will in heaven, not soil itself here with sin, as swine do in a ditch. And whatsoever thou doest, and wheresoever thou comest, do as the Apostle teaches: "Shew thyself to all men as an example of good works," for through a good example GOD is worshipped and praised, men are helped and taught and strengthened in their belief. Bear thee so that men who dwell with you may say of you as was said of the Apostles Paul and Barnabas, "The gods are made like men, and have come down to us." DEO gracias.

OTHER WORKS

ON GRACE

THREE degrees of grace there are. The first GOD gives to all creatures, to uphold them with; and this is called GOD'S help freely given to all creatures; and without this gift of grace, creatures cannot do, nor last in their kind; for as water is made hot through fire and becomes cold again if the fire be withdrawn, so, as S. Austin says, "All creatures that are made of naught, so are they worth naught in a little time, unless GOD upholds them with His grace." Therefore says the Apostle "Through the grace of GOD, I am what I am." As if he said, "That I live, that I feel, that I speak or hear or see, and all that I am: all this I have only through GOD'S grace." The second degree of grace is more special: that GOD gives freely to every man who is a good and reasonable creature: and this grace stands ever at the gates of our hearts, and knocks on our freewill, and bids it let it in. This, GOD says that He does: "Behold, I stand at the door knocking," that is, "I stand at the door of thine heart and knock; let Me in." And this grace is given freely to man before he deserves it. Then let every man make himself worthy and ready to receive His gift of the Holy Ghost, Who ever stirs man's freewill to good, and calls it from evil. Two things are needful to the health of man's soul. The first is this grace that I speak of: the second, is man's free-will according thereto. And without these two, no man can do thoroughly what he ought, that should help him to health of his soul; for neither free-will, without this grace stirring, nor this grace without free-will assenting, can do aught that pleases GOD. Therefore, says S. Austin, "He Who made thee without thee, will not justify thee without thee"; that is, "He Who made thee without thee, will not make thee righteous, save thou helpest thereunto." And though the free-will of man cannot make the grace of GOD in man, nevertheless, let man do what is in him, and prepare himself, that he may be ready and able to receive the grace, when it comes. If thou wert in a mirk house one day, and doors and windows shut: if thou wouldest not let the sun come in, who was to blame if the house were mirk. Also blame none save thyself, if thy grace be less. For S. Anselm says, "Man lacks not this grace, for GOD gives it to him; but he has it not, because he does not make himself ready to receive this grace as he should." GOD is not stingy of His grace, for He has enough thereof; for though He deal it out never so far, and to so many, He never has the less; for He only wants clean vessels, to put His grace in. Therefore says S. Austin; "GOD by vast freedom and abundance fills all creatures according to their capacity": that is, "GOD through His great freedom of His great grace fulfils all creatures according as they are able to receive His grace." If man opened his heart to this grace when GOD sends it to him, he would shew it in works; for the Apostle, when he had won it, said, "His grace in me was not in vain," that is "the grace that GOD has given me, is not useless in me"; for he enjoyed it ever in work. We unite with GOD in His grace, as merchants do together: for GOD sets His grace against our work; but for His grace and His death, He wills (to have) naught but our praising and thanking, and He wills that man should have all the profit that may arise thereof. But they try to reave from GOD, His part, who would be praised of men for good deeds. Against them, GOD says, "I will not give My glory to another"; that is, "Praising and worship that belong to Me, I will give to no other." Thou shalt understand, that freewill of man is to turn freely to good or ill. Three states there are of man; before sin, after man's sin, and after man is confirmed, that is, after man is departed out of this deadly life, and come to that joy that shall never end. In the first place, before man sinned, was man's will so free, that he could sin or not sin: in his free-will it was, to do good or ill. In the last state, that is confirmed, shall man sin no more. In the second state, in which he may sin, and may not but sin, man's will is free to ill, till it be strengthened with grace: and when grace leads the will, then it is free to work the good. Before man sinned, no hindering had he from doing good, nor no need to do ill: but now has sin joined with our flesh, and bred what S. Paul calls the "law of the flesh," so that it is master of the flesh, and withstands GOD'S law in all that it can. This hinders our will from assenting to good; and stirs it to ill so that it may not work good, unless grace helps and accustoms him away from sin. Every man before he sins, has a free will to do good or ill, but when he is bound to the fiend, through works of sin, he may through no power of himself come out of his bonds: and then he fares like a ship that in a tempest has lost all that could help it, and is cast from wave to wave whither the tempest drives it. Right so, a man who lacks GOD'S grace, because he be fallen into deadly sin, he does not what he would, but aye wavers from hand to hand, at the fiend's will, and unless GOD give him grace to rise out of his sin, he shall be in sin to his life's end, and after, be lost body and soul, and damned to endless pain. If the folk or the common people choose them a king, and he be confirmed in his kingdom, he be never so ill to them, they can do naught to him, unless it be through some other, who has more power than he: and so, it behoves them suffer, do he them never so much ill. Right so, man before he sins, has a free will to choose whether he will be under GOD or the fiend; and when, with his will, he chooses to serve the fiend, he cannot after, when he would, come out of his bonds. And therefore, worldly men who are bound in sin say to them who counsel them to amend their lives, "fain would we rise, but we cannot." No, they cannot through might of themselves, but through GOD'S grace helping them they can. The third grace is most special; for it is given only to those who receive the second grace; and with their freewill fulfil it in deed, and can say as S. Paul said, "The grace of GOD was not in vain in me." And S. Austin says; "GOD, working with us, fulfils that which He, through grace stirring, began in us." For neither without His helping can we do good to ourselves, nor please Him: as GOD says Himself "without Me, thou canst no nothing." GOD'S grace stirring, goes before good will, and stirs it to do the good and leave the ill.

Grace, when it comes first to visit man's soul, wakens him as out of a slumbering and inquires of him with those sharp words: "Where art thou? Whence comest thou? Whither shalt thou? "First he says, "Where art thou?" as if he said, "Bethink thee, unhappy wretch, how foul thou art cast down, and what peril thou art in. For, for thy sin thou art fallen into the enemy's hands, who above all things dost covet to work thy woe; and naught may deliver thee out of the foe's hands, but Almighty GOD, thy good Lord, Whom thou hast forsaken." After he says: "Whence comest thou?" as if he said, "thou wretch, behold how thou hast wasted thy life in sin; thou comest from the fiend's tavern—Where are all the goods that GOD has given thee to help thee with, and to worship Him? Sorrily hast thou lost them. Thy Lord made thee rich, and thou art become a poor wretch.' After, he inquires, "Whither wendest thou?" "Woeful wretch thou wendest to the woeful doom, that GOD dooms men to; for as thou hast served so shalt thou be judged. So awful shalt thou see GOD there, that thou shalt for fear be out of thy wits; and to the mountains and hills thou shalt cry with a grisly noise, and pray them to fall on thee and hide thee, that thou see Him not. Woeful wretch, thou wendest to hell, if thou dost forth as thou hast begun, where thou shalt find fire so hot and so raging, that all the water in the sea, though it ran through it, should not slake a spark thereof. And because thou stinkest here to GOD, for thy foul sin, there thou shalt feel everlasting stink: and because thou lovedst mirkness here, for aye to be in sin, there shalt thou feel such thick mirkness that thou canst grip it; and because here thou didst rest thyself in sin against GOD'S will, there shalt thou shed more tears than there are motes in a sunbeam. Thou shalt suffer pain ever after pain, ever to renew thy woe."

When GOD'S grace has stirred man and wakened him with these three, and has made him to know the peril he is in, then he conceives a terror of GOD'S awful doom: and therethrough, he begins to repent whatever he did ill, and covets to amend himself through GOD'S grace, that stirs him to flee ill and give himself to good: and then comes grace following, to help the goodwill of man to fulfil it in deed. For though man have a good will to do the good, through grace before stirring the good will, yet can he not do indeed without GOD'S grace following and helping: and this the Apostle affirms of himself when he says; "But not I, but the grace of GOD in me"; that is, "the good which I do is naught, but GOD'S grace does it with me"; as if he had said, "I can do no good, unless GOD'S grace help me." GOD'S will is also a hand-maiden to grace, to work all her will. GOD'S grace, wherever it be, will not be useless, but ever working and growing more and more, to increase thy reward. Therefore do we as the Apostle counsels us, "We exhort you, brethren, that ye receive not the grace of GOD in vain"; that is, "I pray you and bid you, my brothers in GOD, that ye receive not GOD'S grace in vain." He receives GOD'S grace in vain, that enjoys it not in good, when GOD sends it to him; and therefore perhaps, he shall never after win thereto. Isidore tells of a little fly that is called Saura, and this fly betokens grace stirring beforehand. This kind of fly is said to be the enemy of all venomous worms, so that when he sees any worm (going) toward man to sting him when he sleeps in the wilderness; he flies before to the man, and lights upon his face, and bites him a little; and therethrough he wakes before the beast comes to sting him. By this Saura is understood grace that GOD sends to man against the temptations of the fiend, who often stings venomously: it cries unto thee, as the Apostle says; "Awake, thou that sleepest, and rise from the dead, and Christ shall give thee light." But the unthankful act against this grace, and ruin it: as Virgil did with this little fly that saved him from death. He lay asleep, and an adder came toward him: but this fly Saura flew before, and lighted on his forehead, and pricked him a little, and therewith he wakened; also the adder came; but this Virgil, in his waking, felt his forehead smart, and smote himself on the face; and so he slew the fly, and so repaid him for his service, who saved his life. Therefore do thou not ruin GOD'S grace when it comes to thee, to warn thee of harm and stir thee to good. Glad ought man to be of GOD'S grace, when GOD sends it to him, and to take care full warily of so rich a gift: for grace is earnest-money of that lasting joy which is to come, as the Apostle says: "the grace of GOD is eternal life"; that is, "GOD'S grace is like a help and way to everlasting life." Therefore, He sets grace before us as the way that leads to everlasting joy: and also a pledge, if we keep it well, to make in us certainty of endless joy; as the

Apostle says, "Who gave us His Spirit as a pledge in our bodies," that is "GOD has given us the Holy Ghost as pledge of endless joy." Hold we then this heavenly pledge; and enjoy we it well in work; for it is well for us in this life, if GOD'S grace lead us; and when grace leaves us, we fail of that welfare. Therefore, through help of grace let us destroy in ourselves everything that is against grace, be it less or more, that our reason says is against GOD'S will, that is, all that is sin, or may stir to sin: and let us have repentance in our heart, shrift in mouth, and withstanding, with will never to turn again.

AN EPISTLE ON CHARITY

By what tokens thou shalt know if thou lovest thine enemy: and what example thou shalt take from Christ to love him.

AND if thou beest not stirred against the person by anger or fell outward cheer, and have no privy hate in thine heart for to despise him, or judge him, or for to set him at naught: and the more shame and villany he does to thee in word or in deed, the more pity and compassion thou hast of him as thou wouldest have of a man who was out of his mind, and thou thinkest thou canst not find in thine heart to hate him, for love is so good in itself, but prayest for him, and helpest him, and desirest his amending, not only with thy mouth as hypocrites do, but with thy affection of love in thine heart, then hast thou perfect charity to thy fellow-Christian. This charity had S. Stephen, perfectly, when he prayed for them who stoned him to death. This charity, Christ counselled to all who would be His perfect followers, when He said thus: "Love your enemies, do good to them that hate you, pray for those who persecute and calumniate you." And therefore, if thou wilt follow Christ, be like Him in power. Learn to love thine enemies, and sinful men, for all those are thy fellow-Christians. Look and bethink thee how Christ loved Judas, who was both His bodily enemy and a sinful caitiff: how goodly Christ was to him; how benign; how courteous; how humble to him whom He knew to be damnable; and nevertheless, He chose him for His Apostle, and sent him to preach with the other Apostles; He gave him power to work miracles: He shewed to him the same good cheer in word and deed; also with His precious Body; and preached to him as He did to the other Apostles: He condemned him not openly, nor abused, nor despised him, nor ever spake evil of him: and yet even though He had done all that, He would but have said the truth! And above all, when Judas took Him, He kissed him and called him His friend. All this charity, Christ shewed to Judas whom He knew to be damnable. In no manner of feigning or flattering, but in soothfastness of good love and clean charity. For though it were truth that Judas was unworthy to have any gift of GOD, or any sign of love, because of his wickedness; nevertheless, it was worthy and reasonable that our Lord should appear as He is.

He is love and goodness, and therefore it belongs to Him to shew love and goodness to all His creatures, as He did to Judas. Follow after, somewhat if thou canst; for though thou beest shut in a house with thy body, nevertheless in thine heart, where the place of love is, thou shalt be able to have part of such a love to thy fellow Christians as I speak of. Whoso deems himself to be a perfect follower of JESUS Christ's teaching and living, as some men deem that they be, inasmuch as one teaches and preaches, and is poor in worldly goods as Christ was, and cannot follow Christ in His love and charity, to love his fellow-Christians, every man, good and ill, friends and foes, without feigning, flattering, despising in heart, angriness and melancholious reproving, soothly, he beguiles himself: the dearer he deems himself to be, the further he is. For Christ said to those who would be His followers, thus: "This is My commandment, that ye love mutually as I have loved you."

"This is My bidding, that ye love together as I love you, for if ye love as I loved, then are ye My disciples." He that is meek soothfastly, or would be meek, can love his fellow-Christians: and none save he.

CONTRITION

RICHARD HERMIT rehearses a … tale of perfect contrition that the same clerk Cesarius tells. He tells that a scholar at Paris had done full many sins of which he was ashamed to shrive him. At the last, great sorrow of heart overcame his shame, and when he was ready to shrive him to the Prior of the Abbey of S. Victor, so great contrition was in his heart, sighing in his breast, sobbing in his throat that he could not bring one word forth. Then the Prior said to him, "Go and write thy sins." He did so and came again to the Prior, and gave him what he had written, for still he could not shrive himself with his mouth. The Prior saw the sins were so great, that with the scholar's leave, he shewed them to the Abbot to have his counsel. The Abbot took the writing wherein they were written, and looked thereon. He found nothing written, and said to the Prior, "What can here be read where naught is written?" Then saw the Prior and wondered greatly, and said "Wit ye that his sins were here written, and I read them: but now I see that GOD has seen his contrition and has forgiven him all his sins." This the Abbot and the Prior told the scholar, and he, with great Joy, thanked GOD.

SCRAPS FROM THE ARUNDEL MS

SINFUL man look up and see, how ruefully I hung on rood;
    And of my penance have pity with sorrowful heart and dreary mood:
    All this, man, I suffered for thee: My flesh was riven, all spilt My blood;
    Lift up thine heart, call thou on Me, forsake thy sin: have mercy, GOD.
    Think oft with sore heart of thy foul sins,
    Think oft of hell-woe, of heaven-kingdom's wins;
    Think of thine own death, of GOD'S death on rood,
    The grim doom of Doom's-day have thou oft in mood:
    Think how false is this world, and what its reward,
    Think what, for His good death, thou owest thy Lord.
    RICHARD ROLLE.

Made in the USA
Middletown, DE
29 July 2019